THE HUNGRY GENERATION

The
Hungry Generation

Religious Attitudes and Needs
in a State University

BY JOHN A. HARDON, S.J.

Western Michigan University and
Bellarmine School of Theology

THE NEWMAN PRESS, WESTMINSTER, MARYLAND

1967

Imprimi potest: John R. Connery, S.J.
Provincial of Chicago Province
February 25, 1966

Nihil Obstat: Francis J. Zipple, S.T.D.
Censor Deputatus

Imprimatur: ✠ Alexander M. Zaleski, D.D.
Bishop of Lansing
October 10, 1966

The *Nihil Obstat* and the *Imprimatur* are official declarations that a book or pamphlet is free of doctrinal and moral error. No implication is contained therein that those who have granted the *Nihil Obstat* and the *Imprimatur* agree with the contents or with the opinions expressed.

CONTENTS

THE HUNGRY GENERATION

INTRODUCTIONS are supposed to inform the reader why an author wrote the book and what he expects to say.

On both counts, I can introduce the present volume in a few words. My purpose in writing *The Hungry Generation* is to open the eyes of pedagogues and administrators of higher education, especially in tax-supported institutions, to the need for teaching more than skills and information, at the risk of undermining the foundations of American culture, which I take to be Judaeo-Christianity.

To this end, I have called on my students at a state university to tell those who are seldom talked to, least of all by undergraduates, in the hope that someone somewhere among the policy makers of education will listen and be willing to learn.

In some ways my experience has been unique: a priest teaching theology, and not just the philosophy of religion, at a state university; hired and paid by the state, and feeling all the tensions that might be expected in this anomalous situation.

It seemed too rich an experience not to share with others, or only with college faculties. Teachers in elementary and secondary schools should know how to prepare their pupils for the challenges of university life; parents ought to be told how deeply home-life and example affect the future of their children; the clergy must learn something of the problems, moral and intellectual, that young people are facing and not solving; legislators have to see that tax money for education is spent to build, and not to tear down, the moral edifice of society; and millions of college students of the next generation look for guidance in their youthful dreams. They want to do great things, and they have the talent and ambition, but their sheer numbers—a sea of humanity—prevents anything like personal counsel and direction.

"The modern world has lost God, and is seeking Him" was Whitehead's estimate of present-day man, who knows all about everything except why he exists and whether life is even worth living. If these pages bring a single college man or woman closer to the ideals of his faith, and make him stronger to meet the doubts of an atomic age of insecurity, they will have been more than worth writing.

PART ONE

A Personal History

THIS book has a personal history that must be told before the experiences it describes can be understood. For ten years before coming to Western Michigan State University, I had been cooperating with such agencies as the American Council on Education to help teachers communicate moral and spiritual values in the public schools. In 1962 I was invited by Western Michigan to join its department of Philosophy and Religion and since that time have been a member of the university faculty, under salary from the State of Michigan.

The background of my appointment goes back to 1958, when I served as consultant to the American Association of Colleges for Teacher Education, which sets the standard for about four hundred teachers, colleges, and departments of education. My work with the AACTE was to cooperate with the Protestant and Jewish consultants in evaluating a five-year research program of study to raise the religious literacy of the teaching profession. Western Michigan was one of the pilot institutions for the project, and a member of its School of Education was national coordinator. One result of the study was that Western Michigan founded a new Department of Philosophy and Religion.

From the beginning, the department included both philosophy and religion among its course offerings, and this is still the catalogue arrangement. But members of the department consider themselves really distinct academically, although the hyphenated name is retained in official university publications and there is one head for both sides of the department. Separate departments are planned for the near future.

Early in 1962 the Society of Jesus was approached by a representative of Western Michigan about the prospects of having a priest teach on their faculty: "The professor hired would be asked to set up a program of Catholic studies. It is hoped that a four-year program might eventually result." Officials at Western were conscious of the pioneering nature of the project:

The idea of a state-supported university hiring a Catholic theologian is a revolutionary one, and the opportunity offered to advance the cause of the Church and true religion would be enormous. Obviously the man to fill such a position would have to be a scientific theologian who was able to resist the temptation to proselytize, and in no sense would he be under the authority of the Newman Club chaplain or have any pastoral obligation at the Newman Club.

He would be, of course, as free as any other professor to carry on any activities, pastoral or otherwise, which he might wish when he was not at the university. It is essential in the hiring of this professor that he be in no sense presented by the Church or any of its agencies as an official candidate for the position.

Dr. Loew (head of the department) wishes simply to hire the best individual he can find, and the fact that he might be a priest or a member of a religious order must remain coincidental so that there would be no danger of difficulty on the church-state question.

As a result of this invitation, I visited the university to

confer with members of the faculty, the dean, and the vice-president. One problem seemed insurmountable, the dilemma between sectarian teaching (which university officials feared was inevitable for a Catholic theologian), and academic freedom (to which I appealed in my conferences with the administration). One paragraph in the university's official policy on academic freedom was crucial:

The teacher is entitled to freedom in the classroom in discussing his subject, but he should be careful not to introduce into his teaching controversial matter which has no relation to his subject. Limitations of academic freedom because of religious or other aims of the institution should be clearly stated in writing at the time of the appointment.

The dilemma was resolved by the university's offering me a contract, subject to renewal, and without any written statement of limitations of academic freedom.

During my four years at Western I made some remarkable discoveries. Not the least was to find how the students migrate towards the courses in religion. From 1956 to 1962 enrollment in the department quadrupled, and then again more than doubled in my first two years of teaching. Full credit towards graduation, with the option of a religion major or minor, elective or (within limits) basic studies fulfillment, attracted up to ten percent of the total university student body.

My own course offerings included the Fundamentals of Catholic Theology and Catholic Moral Theology, along with classes in comparative religious culture, notably The Shaping of American Religion. Depending on the section my students were either mainly Catholic or mainly Protestant, and I never made an effort to identify their religious affiliation. Those who identified themselves usually waited until the final term paper to do so, as the quotations in the chapters that follow will show.

9

If I were to describe the student response, regardless of their affiliation, I would call it enthusiastic with obvious differences of reaction in the different classes. Treating of contraception in a class of moral theology arouses more interest than talking about *maya* in a course on Hinduism!

Students ask questions with a freedom that shows interest in the subject and an inquisitive mind that is looking for answers to some of life's most fundamental problems. I could write a book about these *quaesita* to illustrate the kind of thinking going on among students at state universities.

Catholics are often critical of their early training. "Haven't we been brainwashed into believing what we do? . . . How could we think otherwise than as Catholics if from childhood we were given only one side of the question? . . . Are the Sisters in parochial schools equipped to prepare people for life in the real world, when they have little or no contact with that world? . . . Why were we never told about the population explosion until we came to a secular university?"

Response varies, with a general pattern that suggests a more negative attitude in proportion to less previous Catholic schooling. Students with no Catholic high school and especially those with little or no formal Catholic training are most critical of their heritage and (perhaps unexpectedly) very receptive of the religious studies at Western Michigan.

I try to relate the courses to students' attitudes and needs, and consequently evoke reactions that reveal the tension under which many of them labor. More often these tensions are not expressed publicly, but jotted down on the homework assignment or mentioned in conversation. "Every time religion is even mentioned, it bothers me," one student confessed in an afterthought scribbled on his test paper. Yet this same student, with no previous religious education, lately admitted that he is finding "something to hold on to" in life because of the challenges raised in class outside reading.

Even in classes that are mainly theological and only accidentally connected with morals, many students feel that morality is not based on objective standards but varies according to relative circumstances. Catholics and the more traditional Protestants toy with the idea and are tempted to question the whole body of moral principles which Christianity has "imposed" upon them.

Time and again they told me the rudest shock they received on coming to Western was the discovery that so many people do not consider wrong what they had previously been told was sinful. "How do I know it's a sin," they wonder, "if respectable men and women think otherwise?" This opinion is confirmed by the textbooks, teachers, and classroom discussions that create the atmosphere of the university.

When lecturing on marriage, the Church's position on divorce and birth control was challenged—and not only by Protestants. "Are not Catholic countries so backward because they are forbidden to practice birth control? . . . Is it not better to allow young couples to divorce and remarry than have them suffer until death for the mistake of choosing a wrong partner? . . . Where does the Church get the right to tell the people what to do in their married life?" At the same time the Catholic stand on marital morality is respected, and the students want to learn it.

Among the heartening aspects of class is the evidence that students are often hearing for the first time truths which they instinctively recognize will be of great value in later life. Sensing the topic is important, I spend some time on concupiscence when taking the fall of man in the Judaeo-Christian tradition. I explain that concupiscence is natural to man, and therefore the irrational desires we ex-

11

perience are not in themselves sinful; they become wrong only when deliberately indulged, and much of man's merit consists in not yielding to passion. The response among students, in and out of class, shows they appreciate this clarification on a crucial area of moral behavior.

About midsemester all the classes receive a set of directives for the term paper which I consider the most important student participation in a course. Ten pages are the minimum, and a carbon is turned in along with the ribbon copy, the latter returned with comments, and the former retained by the teacher. Many of the suggested topics are consciously evocative: "Why Pray? . . . What Does Religion Mean to Me? . . . The Eucharist is Christ . . . The Causes of the Reformation . . . Faith and Science, in Conflict or Cooperation?" Several asked permission to canvass their fellow-students on one of the general topics, like prayer or the meaning of religion in their lives. For canvassing of opinions on prayer, students were asked to tape-record their statements; these were then typed out and became matter for analytic study. One student drafted a list of thirty questions on religious background and attitude, and knowledge of the Bible. His survey would be a revealing document on what happens to the Christian faith on a university campus, either smothered under an avalanche of agnosticism or inspired to new life by the daily challenge of a secular atmosphere.

These term papers are the main source material for *The Hungry Generation*. Without apology, they are quoted at length and were not retouched for publication. Out of more than fifteen hundred contributions, about one hundred were used for inclusion in the book, with a conscious effort to give a balanced insight into the student mind and attitude and without prejudice to any theological position.

Private conferences with the students became another

staple of my work at the university. Circumstantial needs and the school's official policy combined to encourage my giving whatever time could be spared for counseling. As stated in the university's directives to the faculty, "Ability as a teacher includes proficiency in classroom instruction, initiative and skill in the development and administration of the teaching program. It includes also interest and success in student guidance. The function of the teacher as a guide and counselor extends beyond the classroom into every phase of the life of the student as a member of the college community."

Without betraying confidences, I can say that student problems are kaleidoscopic in variety and often breathtaking in their intensity. Most of them are occasioned by the contradiction set up in the mind between ideals and religious commitment inherited from home and previous education, and the strong neutralism of studies and atmosphere at the university. Some are easily solvable, by just a word of direction, the right book to read, or a bit of prudent advice. Others are more complex and, when they impinge heavily on the moral side, I put the student into contact with the respective chaplains for further action.

At times the problems are critical, and my only regret is lack of time and facilities for working along with the people the way I should like. One young man bolted up to me at the student center and began pouring out his mental confusion: a chaos of half truths, cliches, and generalities that erased the Catholic faith he once enjoyed. In a later conference he admitted being on the verge of despair; yet he is now "coming out of the woods," partly because he was able to talk himself through and get the advice he needed.

Sex activity is so widespread and deep rooted that this one problem would be enough to keep a dozen counselors busy all year long. In a survey that one of my students

13

made, he questioned and interviewed a thousand students (personally and through others) and concluded that the majority of students, or at least of the men, indulged in full sexual experience during their four years in college. It is impossible to describe the tension this creates in a believing person whose moral standards are shaken to the foundations within a month of enrollment in school.

Teaching at the university is only a fraction of faculty involvement. Administration-sponsored programs and service on college committees are an integral part of campus life. A gratifying experience in this respect was my participation on the task force committee which spent almost two semesters in studying student discipline, its problems, and possible solution.

The committee set itself to examining what should be the philosophy, organization, and function of student personnel services. It was asked to prepare detailed statements in this area and to define the role of faculty, administration, security officers, and agencies external to the university in their bearing on the conduct of the student body.

Meeting every week with the three deans and a small delegation, I was encouraged to help draft the philosophical norms for the committee. The principles I worked out were accepted with only minor changes and have since been submitted for incorporation into the university's statement of policy. The preamble to these norms illustrates a state institution's concern for maintaining moral and spiritual values in higher education:

The philosophy of discipline at Western Michigan University should first of all recognize the distinction between discipline as an external means of keeping good order, and discipline as an integrated method of educating the students for responsible personal and social living not only in school but in their later lives.

14

Yet both forms of discipline require that the university express its "ideal of the institution," referred to in the annual catalogue, namely some basic philosophy which identifies the values that support this school's educational policy. It is suggested that these values include at least three principles: acknowledgment of the nature of man's moral and ethical responsibility, recognition of the difference of right and wrong in human conduct, and the responsibility of the university to help educate the student for responsible personal and community living.

In addition to accepting these theoretical norms, the committee favorably voted on a set of recommendations which the writer offered, that reflect the inner workings of a secular university better than any amount of factual information. Under subtitle of "Discipline as Education," the following means were suggested by which disciplinary problems can be anticipated and through which the students may become more ethically sensitive and responsible:

The university should study ways in which students can learn what is expected of mature, educated citizens. Available means like classes in psychology, the social sciences, philosophy and religion should be developed in this direction. Other means, like lectureships, seminars, workshops and discussion may be added.

In its present setup the university provides minimal facilities for interstudent or faculty-student discussions outside of formal class. Yet unless such provisions are made on a broad scale, it seems we are indoctrinating students without giving them corresponding opportunities for self-expression, which is the root of self-responsibility.

A studied effort should be made to encourage all students to participate in some form of social activity currently provided by the university. Too often, those who have most need to cultivate their social virtues are the last to enter or participate in a society, whose main purpose is to foster cooperativeness and outgoing generosity.

Here is a fruitful area for development, if the university officially studied and promoted student participation in such organizations as the Red Cross, Social Services, civic and art societies, and welfare groups. At present the city goes its way and university people go their way, with only occasional thought to the great benefits both to city and university if the latter would enter more effectively into the volunteer and welfare work of the community.

What most students need is to have someone of mature judgment interested in them. Faculty and administration should be tapped for availability to have private conferences, and to be called upon for assistance, not only when a critical problem of discipline arises, but all along the line.

Reports indicate that only a small fraction of students presently avail themselves of the facilities offered by the various religious agencies on campus. First a study might be made to make an objective appraisal, and then steps taken to more closely integrate the student's life with a religious organization of his preference. One recommendation is to find ways of having campus chaplains more directly responsible to the university.

The same might be said of the existing parishes and church societies in the city. They should be alerted to the university's interest in the students' religious and moral welfare, and positive measures taken to involve students in a parochial and church-orientated situation to which they may otherwise be strangers.

With the present arrangement students in residence halls are at the mercy of their dorm-mates and others as regards private study for any length of time. Facilities should be provided in greater abundance and with more encouragement to enable students to study or read quietly, without having to travel half a mile to the library.

This seems to be crucial because the main reason for people entering college is, presumably, to apply themselves to serious study and intellectual pursuits. Yet if the university does not do everything possible to encourage and promote this, it is little wonder that the scholarly atmosphere is replaced by the social, and disciplinary problems are multiplied.

A delicate phase of student discipline which the committee handled was the need for some way of getting the faculty to cooperate. No single area of secular university life is more crucial and, at the risk of excessive detail, I should like to outline the main point of the problem to which the committee addressed itself.

Basing our reflections on professional studies made by faculty members of state universities, we discussed the fact that so far from cooperating with the advancement of ethical development, some teachers hinder the process by their cavalier treatment of moral norms which are the mainstay of responsible ethical living.

Among the private notes circulated with the committee was a study by the chairman of an eastern state university. He charged that in college teaching there is a good deal of academic irresponsibility hiding behind the mask of academic freedom. The moral predicament of the typical, American university, he said, could be illustrated by a hypothetical Professor Jones who informs his sociology classes that mind is a function of matter, that sound mental hygiene holds that "free will" and "responsibility" are fictions of the philosophers, that beliefs are really determined by social environment, that we should never blame, but only praise, individuals, that churches are helpful only if they enable us to fulfill natural desires and free us from fear, and that premarital relations may be helpful in relieving frustration. If someone protests that such teaching is a violation of academic responsibility, to what can one appeal that is recognized by both faculty and administration?

Without pretending to solve the problem of academic responsibility at a state university, we did everything possible to alert the administration to a critical need. Some thirty meetings on the discipline committee convinced me how indispensable is the right kind of faculty to communicate the values on which our Judaeo-Christian culture depends.

The Western Michigan experience has given me a new understanding of higher education and a new concern for the progress in teaching religious values.

Even philosophers like Whitehead recognize that "the essence of education is that it be religious," and they define religious education as "an education which inculcates duty and reverence." Duty is said to arise from our potential control over the course of events, implying freedom and obligation based on the knowledge of the Infinite, and the foundation of reverence is admittedly a perception that the present holds within itself the secret of the future.

Every stage of the educational process is coming to be seen as filled with religious values, and no school worthy of the name may deprive students of what they need in the development of their faculties. Universities are no exception to this law of mental growth, and state support does not change an institution's intrinsic nature.

Christian educators who are not Catholic have been the prime movers in restoring religion to its rightful position in the university curriculum. Dr. George W. Forell, Professor of Protestant Theology at the State University of Iowa, is perfectly clear:

The scientific investigation of religious faith and its various expressions is one of the oldest academic enterprises. For many centuries, since their inception, universities have been the centers of theological learning. The Sorbonne, the University of Vienna, Oxford and Cambridge, Heidelberg and Wittenberg were publicly supported universities whose reputation was largely derived from first-rate courses of instruction in religion. When Shakespeare had Hamlet go somewhat unhistorically to the University of Wittenberg (founded in the sixteenth century), it was because the great English dramatist was familiar with the fame of its theological faculty.

To deny a university the right to deal in a scholarly and scientific manner with religion is to deny it the right to be a complete university. This means that any American university, regardless of the source of its support, should have a faculty which could deal competently and sympathetically with the phenomenon of religion in general and the Western religious heritage dominated by the Judaeo-Christian tradition in particular. In other cultures the emphasis might be appropriately different.

Whatever view may be taken of teaching moral values in public schools below the college level, there is no serious legal objection to teaching religion in state universities. The most intransigent neutralists do not claim that this contradicts the American concept of separation of church and state. Leo Pfeffer, the constitutional lawyer who would allow no teaching of religion in the lower grades, holds that the situation is quite otherwise in public higher education. "It would seem," he admits, "that tax-supported colleges may constitutionally provide for the objective study of religious institutions, practices and principles. Such study must obviously be multisectarian and nondevotional; and since the doctrine of some religions prohibits examination into the content of other religions without special ecclesiastical authorization, it must be noncompulsory."

I could not do justice to the depth of spiritual hunger among the students, which is not being satisfied in the present system of public university education. Each contact with the undergraduates gives further evidence that

19

they want to learn desperately about man's relations with God.

There are several reasons for this. Most college people had only a smattering of formal religious education before they finished high school. Some had a few years in childhood, which they have come to associate with preadolescent immaturity. Those who had a full complement of church-affiliated schooling often feel unprepared to meet the challenges of intellectual criticism that envelopes them like an atmosphere the moment they enter the college precincts.

I would stress the students' desire for knowledge of why they believe what they do or why anyone should believe at all. Two kinds of students come to college: those who enter with a definite religious commitment, and the minority who have only the vaguest notion of what commitment means. Perhaps there are more Catholics in the first class and more Protestants in the second. But this is not universal. The number of uncommitted Catholics would shock any census taker and surprise the experts who write so easily about the strong faith of our American Catholic youth.

Every type in either class, however, is looking for the intellectual integrity which they have not been able to secure (with rare exception) before entering college. This is partly explained by the fact that the mind does not generally mature to a critical peak until the late teens. It should also be accounted for by the relative absence of a philosophical approach to religion in church-affiliated secondary schools.

The students, therefore, need and generally want to have their faith grounded in the rich soil of conviction, and brought to maturity through a sharp scrutiny into the meaning and purpose of life. The four years in college are perfectly suited for this kind of maturation: psychologically to keep pace with the native development of the mind, socially because of the recognized conflict with a solvent naturalism, and spiritually because after college one's happiness is seen to depend on a sound religious philosophy.

Catholic educators are taking a long and hard look at the statistic that only thirty percent of Catholic college students are in institutions conducted by the Church. No doubt this figure would level off if more students were financially free to attend the college of their choice. Yet the Catholic Church needs its colleges and universities and needs them badly. In the words of Pius XI, where else can dynamic apostolic leadership be better produced than in the atmosphere of institutions whose goal is to graduate supernatural men and women of character who will model their lives on the person of Christ?

Protestant leaders are asking the same questions. They see their own denominational colleges catering to a tiny fraction of church membership and wonder what the future may be. Conservative Protestants have a special concern as they watch in dismay the scrambling effort of some church-related colleges to win over the student body by adaptation to the times.

"It would be wise," Calvin Seerfeld recommends, "for would-be Christian colleges everywhere to examine themselves whether they be in the spirit of God. There is one unholy spirit which has captivated higher Christian education again and again, beginning with the Christian university of Alexandria in the second century: the appealing, respectable, vitiating spirit of Christian accommodation to the traditions of men. It is the driving concern to combine Christianity with the best that has been said and thought in the world, the moving attempt to fuse into one grand product the Christian faith and centuries of general human culture. This catholic, synthesizing spirit has a devastating influence upon a Christian education."

More liberal Protestants have less trouble adjusting to modern times and, in fact, this adjustment is almost normative for such major bodies as the Methodists and Presbyterians. Schools like Harvard, Yale, and Princeton have become practically non-denominational, and even smaller institutions with strong church support (like Emory or Kalamazoo) are acclimatized to the secular culture of the age.

This adjustment is partly the reason why a growing number of graduates of interdenominational seminaries, e.g., Chicago and Union Theological, are going into higher education instead of the ministry. Many of their doctorates are teaching in state universities. At Western Michigan, for example, the Dean of Liberal Arts and the Chairman of the Department of Religion are both ordained ministers in their respective denominations.

Catholic as well as Protestant leaders, therefore, recognize it is futile to suppose that a trend which is thirty years in the making will suddenly be reversed. The number and percentage of Christians in secular colleges continue to increase. It would be a mistake either to bewail the situation or simply tolerate it because nothing better can be had.

Many Christians come to a secular school because they believe it will better equip them for the problems and opportunities of a pluralistic society. They choose a secular college because they think the faculty and student contact it offers will give them a balance in dealing with the world, which another four years in a church-related institution would not afford.

Behind this reasoning stands a century of religious higher education that has grown in numbers and equipment but not always in adaptation to the times. Both secular and church-related schools can profit from reappraisal. Denominational colleges are beginning to see their duty to prepare graduates for an integrated life among people who are not Christian and not believers. Tax-supported universities are more slowly admitting their duty to prepare young Americans for religious maturity without sacrificing academic integrity.

The more difficult reassessment will be on the part of state universities, who enjoy tax support and are currently riding the waves. In the fall of 1965, I was invited to speak to the delegates of some thirty state institutions of higher learning, on the subject of "The Crucial Need of Religious Studies in State Universities." Symbolic of the changing times was both the topic and the invited speaker.

I will take the liberty of repeating what I said at the University of Southern Illinois, that the teaching of religion in state universities is crucial for the students attending these institutions, crucial for the future of tax-supported higher education, and crucial for the welfare of the nation.

Out of more than a dozen years' involvement in public education has come one dominant impression: the young people of America are hungry for religious maturity. Each contact with undergraduates gives further evidence that they want to learn something more than facts or computation; their deepest need is to make sense of human existence and how to resolve the dilemma of preparing for a career and of becoming themselves.

These young people want nothing more (even when they cannot vocalize their needs) than some value-centrality to their studies, to keep them from becoming schizophrenic personalities—the one half trying to understand money, marriage, entertainment and politics—and the other half concerned with the soul-searching questions of life and the mystery of death.

They want direction and purpose to their studies, without which all the classes and courses would be useless. Why exert myself—what for? Unless I have a goal in life, why prod my mind to intellectual effort or train my emotions to self control?

As psychologists explain it, the whole period from infancy to manhood forms one grand cycle. Its stage of romance stretches across the first dozen years of life, its stage of precision comprises the whole school period of secondary education, and its stage of generalization is the period of entrance into adulthood.

For those whose formal education continues beyond school age, the university course or its equivalent is the great period of generalization. The spirit of generalization should dominate a university, where the mind is developed not merely to think but to think philosophically and constructively.

Part of this process of philosophizing is to challenge existing beliefs—to ask and come to grips with questions like: is there a God, or a life after death? Is faith itself only a subjective projection of the Ego—as Feuerbach would have it—or the acceptance on God's word of His objective communication to man?

The student desire to ask and answer these and like questions is beyond doubt. This desire reflects a dire need. And the need should be met as effectively and comprehensively as possible—with benefit to the intellectual life of the next generation that I wish no one in public education would deny.

Another crucial area of religious studies is their role of fulfillment of community needs in a democratic society.

Our philosophy of democracy may be summarized in Lincoln's description as belief in a government of the people, by the people, and for the people.

Public education, including higher education, comes under the same democratic concept. Its function in American society is to respond to the people's wants and answer to their needs—as expressed through their qualified representatives in the executive, legislative, and judiciary arms of the government.

The crux here makes the teaching of religious studies not only crucial but critical if we read aright the signs of the times.

In one state after another, state universities, supported by public taxation, are growing to a point unprecedented in American history. In California 83 per cent of college students are in tax supported institutions; in Michigan 79 per cent; and in Wisconsin 69 per cent.

At least three different classes of Americans are showing concern over this trend, and any realistic appraisal of religion in state universities cannot ignore their concern.

The first are those who fear the state's expanding control in education. With John Stuart Mill, they feel that "a general state education is a mere contrivance for moulding people to be exactly like one another." In a word, they dread the prospect of a nation molded by a government to think what the government wants, without the protection that religion gives from within man's soul against the coercive forces of political expediency.

Second are those who see private colleges and universities, mostly religion-oriented, dwindling out of existence for sheer lack of funds—now being deviated to tax-supported institutions. They point out, for example, that in Wisconsin the state university and colleges had a recent freshman class increase of 17.7 per cent. All the independent colleges of the state, on the other hand, suffered a freshman class *decrease* of 1.6 per cent. When state universities can skim off the best talent from private colleges by simply doubling a man's salary, this is past the stage of normal competition and, some would say, beyond the law of institutional survival.

The third class of people concerned are religious bodies and agencies, who are not looking to the state universities to do their work, but who believe that if higher education is to train the mind in every form of human knowledge—religion belongs by right and not by sufferance or apology as an important phenomenon deserving scholarly study and explanation in colleges supported by people who belong to these religious bodies and institutions.

All three groups are becoming more vocal, and the standing tribute to state university administrations is the hope that they will to meet these concerns equitably and honestly.

The final area of crucial significance for religion and theology in state universities affects the welfare of the nation.

The issue can be simply stated: If the principles on which our nation is founded are those of Judaeo-Christianity; and if these principles are to remain vital in the lives of our people, can the universities which educate most of America's leaders ignore the responsibility to a country which makes their very existence possible?

I believe, with Harvey Cox, that we have seen the last of elite education. The kind of society we will live in during the next twenty years will make a college diploma as important as a high school diploma was to our fathers.

A cybernetic culture requires a larger percentage of highly educated and technically adept people. Making it possible for all qualified young people to go to college is not just a handout by the welfare state. It is a grave necessity. Ignoramuses cannot manage an automated society.

We are gradually accepting the fact that as the percentage of students in college increases, those taking advanced degrees will increase proportionately, and we will see a colossal growth in graduate education.

These are the salient facts about the *body* of a university as it faces the future, its statistical development in numbers, its equipment, and the size of its budget. But what about its *soul?*

I do not hesitate to say we are at the crossroads in American higher education, which is becoming more dominantly state university education.

For years a variety of factors conspired to produce a cleavage between the sacred and secular, between God and man. One result has been the tragic bifurcation between theology and humanism, of which the very term "secular university" is a pathetic symptom.

But the nation, no less than individuals, cannot long subsist on this double standard. It needs, as much as individuals, a sense of unity in its thinking—to be communicated by the potentially most unitive force in America, the state university.

The country was understandably shocked by the announcement that a group of college students was circulating a well written petition for the assassination of President Johnson. They argued that since the President was forcing young men to die, unwillingly, in Viet Nam, he should be removed from office by an assassin's bullet.

I do not think this episode, or student protest demonstrations, or draft card burnings and pacifist agitations are signs of college student rebellion against authority. They are symptomatic of a spreading malaise that needs serious study and courageous attention.

The student riots at Berkeley symbolized more than meets the eye. All the books analyzing what happened in

27

California intimate that the basis of this protest was general discontent with students getting spoon-fed computer data, and not being treated as responsive human beings, with human desires and fears, and above all with human ideals and destiny. They see a nation weakened by family disintegration and torn apart by racial conflict, the East and West sparring for what may be a nuclear war; they are being inducted into the armed forces and told to risk their lives to save the free world from Communism. But what have the universities given them to explain the struggle they are forced to enter, or to solve the problems of which their inner anxieties are a constant witness?

No society is stronger than the bonds which unite its members. And the indispensable bond that unifies a nation is the love of its citizens for their country—which at heart is the love of one's fellowman even at great cost and sacrifice of self.

It would be naive to suppose that such love of one's fellowman is possible without the moorings of religion—where these moorings are not based on emotion or credulous piety, but founded on the solid rock of intellectual conviction that arises from faith, indeed, but is deepened and strengthened by hardheaded intellectuality through an equally hardheaded religion curriculum of a university.

As we look to the future of teaching religion (or theology) we are faced with two main problems: one is semantic and the other historical.

On the semantic side religion has come to mean for many people emotional states or devotional practices with little or no reflective mental ground for their being. This is not to disparage the psychic value of a sermon or the uplift given by congregational singing. But it is to remove religion so understood from its valid inclusion in a college curriculum, whether church-affiliated or tax-supported.

On the historical side, religion as such or as theology

has been so closely associated with institutional belief that state universities have objected to religion being sectarian.

Both problems are real. Religion when taught on a university level should not be proselytizing evangelism that seeks to recruit new members to the church. It should respect that faith while challenging it; but the challenge is of the essence of what a university stands for, intellectual inquiry and studious analysis before the bar of reason.

Correspondingly, theology in a university should not be so narrowly sectarian that its position is not compared with rival systems or its claims never demanded to give an account of themselves. At the same time no theology should be refused a hearing just because it represents a school of thought that others do not accept. On that premise the university could scarcely teach anything. There are divergent theories of art, different opinions in history, conflicting ideas in political science; and the essence of literature is to see the variety and contrariety of human genius revealed in such disparate writings as *Hamlet* and *The Death of a Salesman,* or in such writers as Camus and T. S. Eliot.

There is no easy solution to the teaching of religion in state universities. If there were no problems, we should not have so many qualified persons spending so much time and effort studying means of doing it.

Yet the difficulties are secondary once the will to do what needs doing is decided upon. The latest figures show that ninety per cent of tax-supported institutions of higher learning, from junior colleges to graduate schools, offer some courses in religion or theology. But, as we know, this datum is deceptive.

Until the last decade religion had been the exception in state universities. It has not yet received anything of the deliberate attention which is given to other disciplines. Attention has been marginal and apologetic. Moreover, the issue is charged with emotion. People feel strongly about it because they sense that deeper values are involved than just another department or a new set of courses.

What too few understand is that secularism has entrenched itself in American public education not as an accident of history but, as one writer put it, as the finest product of five centuries of thoughtful statesmanship. Secular institutions, including tax-supported universities, emerged out of the necessity to create harmony among diverse economic, social, and religious classes. Freedom in each of these areas was thought possible only because a secular, i.e., irreligious, world makes an equilibrium of complementary forces. Where the secular ethic asks how conflict can be solved through compromise, the ethic of religious institutions inquires who is right according to their various forms of absolutes. Thus an uneven contest developed between the apparently humane attitude of secularism and the intransigent impasse of different religions.

Secularism has consequently posed as protector of the freedom of the human spirit and of the liberty of divergent groups and faiths. Many consider the secular state, with its independence of religious principles, one of the most precious realities of modern times.

But such a view is changing. While the realization is hard in coming, historians of American culture are suggesting that the development of public, secular schools and universities has thrown the whole matter into a new and dangerous focus. They believe that the elimination of public schools as channels of our religious heritage will gradually lead to the destruction of our society. They fear that there will come a time when the sovereign State will have nothing left to protect except the vacuum produced by its own self-imposed neutralism.

They are right. What is at stake is nothing less than the future of Western, certainly American society, whether it sinks still deeper into the morass of pragmatism; with graduates looking to a welfare state to provide not only their food and lodging, but the comfort of a regimented mind; or whether the products of our universities will have learned the meaning of facts, which is wisdom; and the purpose of life, which is religion; and the freedom of action, which alone makes education worthwhile.

This book was already in galley form when I decided to add the paragraphs that follow, and that are among the most painful I hope I shall ever have to write. For reasons that by now have been widely publicized, the university administration decided that I should not return to Western as a member of the faculty.

Two basic reasons have been offered by the administration for its action, one personal and the other a matter of principle:

On the personal side, it was officially stated that "he seems to feel that doctrine can be taught in a state university in the same way as in a Catholic or other religious school where indoctrination is taken for granted."

On reading this, I promptly conferred with its alleged author and asked if this meant "proselytizing," which I would have considered libelous. I was assured that no charge of proselytism was intended.

Among the unsolicited letters written to the university protesting my dismissal was one by a former student, not a Roman Catholic, currently in graduate studies for the doctorate: "I can testify that Father Hardon taught intelligibly and objectively, always taking care to be fair to all points of view on a given point. Few teachers in my opinion have given so much of their time and energy to teach and help students overcome their intellectual difficulties. Western Michigan has been fortunate indeed to have him on its faculty. To dismiss him for the reasons given (indoctrination) would not only be a grave injustice to him but a tragedy for the university."

The matter of principle was summarized in a statement by the president of the university, that release was inevitable because "the differences that presently exist between Dr. Hardon and his colleagues are of a very fundamental nature concerning the teaching of religion."

Regretfully I agree that these differences are fundamental. It is argued that "the academic discipline of religion has as its basic methodological principles and presuppositions those of the community of scholars and not those of the church," whether Catholic, Protestant, or Jewish. As I have learned from experience, this means the exclusion of concern for the religious faith with which the student enters college. Maturing this faith intellectually is excluded from the legitimate aims of a teacher of religion; and where he presumes to respect this faith and tries to deepen its rational understanding, he is excluded from "the community of scholars."

In view of these developments, *The Hungry Generation* takes on a new significance. Its message is directed to those who share my concern for the students in higher education, wherever religion is taught in the college curriculum, that educators ask themselves the hard questions: What is religious education? Is it only an academic exercise, or also a training of the personality? If it is also a training for life, who determines the premises on which the discipline is taught? May the teacher exclude from these premises the beliefs of the student (commonly received from an established religious group), and substitute his own, with the facile excuse that his are from "the community of scholars" but those of the church are "sectarian"?

A few days ago, one of my students who comes from a Protestant background, but has since lapsed into agnosticism, came to tell me about his mental confusion. I asked him to write a few words describing the situation. I quote his letter to me verbatim:

We arrive at college as naive freshmen with our moral and philosophical codes being challenged on all fronts. For many of us, our bubbles of "Truth" burst, and our rug of convictions is yanked from under us. We're confronted and confounded and usually have more questions than we can answer. But whom can we turn to? Practically none of our professors are willing—or able—to help us wade through this muddy confusion. Our profs fill our brains with equations, formulas, names, and dates, but most of them miss the boat in helping us understand the really important things—ourselves and the people around us.

Granted, as college students we're here to learn to think, and to increase our knowledge. But believe me we need much more than intellectual stimulation. Most of us are groping for firm principles to guide our lives.

Though I've been an agnostic for several years, I've thought a great deal about religion and the existence of a Higher Being. Many students have similar feelings. We refuse to accept religion on faith alone or through blind indoctrination. The voices of atheism and agnosticism ring loud on the campus, but where are the reasoning words of the intellectual believer?

For one man or woman who faces the crisis of faith so frankly, a dozen are unable even to formulate their problem. Less still are they able to find "the reasoning words of the intellectual," who believes and whose faith has not stultified but satisfied the hardest demands of an intellect searching for a meaning in life.

33

PART TWO

The Hungry Generation Speaks for Itself

I T WAS not easy to decide on a format and structure for the personal testimonies that follow. For a long time I debated with the idea of assimilating what the students told me and passing on to the reader a summary of their thoughts. But this seemed unfair and risked my intruding into the privacy of their own life-story accounts. It would also have lacked the authenticity of direct citation and the savor of intimate contact with their struggles and aspirations.

As a result, I have not hesitated to quote pages in sequence from the autobiographies I received. I have mentioned it before and will repeat several times, that these accounts have not been retouched. They remain intact, with only necessary alterations in time, place, and names as might protect the writers' anonymity and that of any persons whom they describe. In all cases I have been given permission to use the material quoted, and I hereby thank my students for sharing with me their own experiences, which I told them I would share with others so that thousands could profit from these communications.

Many told me it was the first time in their life they were asked to talk about themselves, unhindered; and their readiness to do so was in large measure encouraged by the unusual circumstance that I was both a priest and an educator. They felt at ease in unburdening themselves of their inner trials to a priest, and they were confident that, as an educator, I would know how to teach others from what they had taught me.

I make no pretence of having chosen always wisely among the statements given to me. By actual count, I used less than five per cent of otherwise quotable material. Nor do I claim to have commented accurately on these testimonies. My only hope is that the choice was sufficiently representative, and that, in spite of their teacher and counselor, the students will impress the reader (as they impressed me) with their sincerity and idealism, sometimes their anguish, and always their desire to learn how to live for something more than many educators are giving them.

ONE

CREDO

Faith and Unbelief

Any attempt to describe the beliefs of college people is doomed to failure if we follow traditional patterns. Undergraduates defy neat classifications, and the worst blunder, in their eyes, would be to reduce them to a few simple categories. They are not believers or non-believers, churchgoers and the unchurched, but span the whole spectrum of religious intensity whose single most dominant feature is search for commitment.

They are desperately searching for someone or something to which they can give themselves unreservedly. With some, the search is more academic, with others more deeply personal. Those with a strong religious background from home and previous schooling make the inquiry cautiously, for fear of losing established values. Those with little or no formal religious training sometimes belie what they are doing, and may give the impression of being fixed in their unbelief or even belligerent towards God and the churches; but once you come to know them you discover this is only a "front" that hides the same basic hunger underneath.

No group or religious affiliation is exempt from this process, which is partly the result of intellectual development in the post-adolescent and partly the effect of mental stimulation that a university is expected to provide. Not the least mistake that educators make is to assume that college students are already set in their philosophy of life and treat them accordingly. They are highly impressionable and easily moved in whatever direction their teachers or surroundings may lead, precisely because they are looking for direction in the most elementary notion of that term—a goal and purpose of their own choosing. They want to know what life is all about and where, if anywhere, their own lives are going.

It was not a beatnik but a highly sensitive intellectual who asked himself, "Must I decide whether to be a Buddhist, a Hindu, Moslem, a follower of Judaism, or a Christian?" He admitted being worried over "the possibility of accepting a belief that others call Buddhist or Confucian lest you become a kind of outcast in your church or community. It's a comfortable feeling to believe that one's own culturally given religion is the best of all religions." In his judgment, few people have the courage to make a radical decision to break with their upbringing, even when such choice is being urged by everything they meet in college:

Most of us have a deeper need in addition to our readiness to follow the past or to be like the people around us. Beneath our apparent activities and interests lies the seed of desire to discover for ourselves who we really are and what in life is important. No matter how many millions have asked these questions before us, and no matter how sure they have been of their answers, each one has a private yearning to go exploring for himself.

It is important that we keep within us this desire of search and wonder. There is more faith in honest doubt than in all the unexamined creeds of past and present. In this sense each of us must articulate his own religion, that is, his own concept of what is of supreme worth in living, his own mode of expressing that concept, his own commitment in daily life to the values he believes to be basic.

The tragedy is that too many of us remain content even in our adult years with answers or descriptions offered by some one else. We limit ourselves to what others say instead of re-exploring the basic questions for ourselves. Many of us cling to the values emphasized by some past leader without exploring their meanings in the present. Almost all of us have closed off certain areas of thought somewhere along the line.

What are these doors that the mind instinctively closes against inquiry? They are beliefs that build walls around oneself or around one's community, shutting out an honest concern about why other people believe what they do; beliefs that persist because our underlying guilt feelings or anxieties are stirred thereby; beliefs that stretch one's shortcomings at the expense of one's virtues; beliefs that cramp the spirit and stifle courage or morale. These attitudes of a closed mind cannot be legislated or forced out of existence. "They must be outgrown." And the greatest benefit of a college education is to be helped to outgrow these blind spots and reach a religious maturity that sees the goodness in other religions than one's own and is willing to change accordingly.

In their search for values college men and women begin with the premise that leaving home to enter higher education is symbolic of a new venture. Speaking for thousands, one of them says, "When I was young I went to the church of my parents, for it is impossible for any child to choose a religion other than that of his parents. When I grew up to high school age, there was still only one way for me to go in religion, the way of my parents. But when I left home to go to college, I settled into a new way of life, new ideas were expressed and new ways of life were observed, new codes and patterns of other religions were seen." For the first time in his life he started to think for

41

himself, to compare and to wonder. "I was free to do this wondering as there were no parents to tell me what to do and what to think. It was somewhat frightening to me because all my life I had been brought up to believe one certain viewpoint, one way of life that was supposed to be the best." Contact with others who also thought their religion was best soon punctured this complacency, and then started that inward quest which typifies the collegiate mind.

The first discovery students make is that religious beliefs are unlike other forms of knowledge. They ask themselves what it is that allows people to believe in things "for which there are no concrete proofs," in the ordinary sense of the term. What causes people to live by these principles and never waver, to model their conduct according to norms which another person cannot conceive? It is faith. "You have faith when there can be no human way to prove something that you know to be true. Faith is what keeps people in line with their religion, telling them to do things week after week, year after year, although they have no earthly reason for doing them." Above all, it is faith that urges a man to continue professing his religion "after a son is separated from the father who can no longer direct his religious life."

But this creates a dilemma that strikes at the heart of religious conviction. On the one hand, the student sees all around him the deepest kind of commitment, often so strong it resists the least touch of criticism. On the other hand, a bit of experience reveals that these commitments are not only different but in many ways contradictory. One man believes that Christ is divine and worthy of homage due to God alone, another may respect the person of Jesus but frankly considers him no better than Socrates, Plato, or Gandhi. One man holds that sexual intercourse outside of marriage is forbidden by the divine law and that fornication, in the words of St. Paul, debars a person from the kingdom of God. Another sees nothing wrong with extra-marital relations and smiles at this credulity even when he respects those who act on such faith.

Mild Agnosticism. A familiar reaction is that of slight scepticism. It allows a person to keep certain positions in his (generally Christian) faith, but with broad reservations that cut into its inner meaning.

Take the matter of life after death. Christians are told to look forward to a better life after this one. When they are oppressed and see no prospect of human assistance, they are bidden to hope for deliverance from their misery in the heavenly possession of God. When they are poor and forced to watch others gorge themselves in wealth, they are consoled with the Gospel parable of Dives and Lazarus, where Lazarus was taken into Abraham's bosom and Dives was buried in hell.

"I have mixed emotions on this subject," the believer-sceptic decides. "This 'pie in the sky' belief is good in that it keeps order here," and keeps people from open rebellion against their lot in life:

But I think it stops people from trying to get ahead because it makes it easy for them to say, 'Well, I am poor and suffering now. But no need to worry because in the afterlife I will be rewarded for my suffering.' This attitude helps people remain in their suffering and ignorance, but without trying to do something to relieve their condition. This almost stops them from doing anything to help themselves by changing things.

If only people would devote some of their time to helping themselves here and now, and less time rationalizing their unproductiveness with thoughts of an afterlife, the world would be a better place for everyone.

What bothers the sceptic, however, is not so much that

hopes of heaven may stultify effort on earth, but that the Christian faith demands belief in both heaven and hell. The option is not between receiving a reward if you are good and nothing if you are bad. "You don't actually have a choice. It is not up to you to decide if you want to go to heaven or not. You must go to heaven or else you will go to hell. And of course you don't want to go to hell. So once again this is a way to keep people in line." The only trouble is that it postulates a deity in whom many young people no longer believe:

I don't believe God is a vengeful or hateful God who would condemn a person to hell. I believe God is a merciful and loving God. How could a spiteful and revenge-seeking God have made all the beautiful things of nature—the birds and trees, hills, and fields and water? No, I do not believe you should have to fear God. Anything you do for him should be out of love and respect, and not out of fear of what will happen to you if you disobey. I don't think there is any place for fear in religion—only love. If a person cannot do something out of love for God, he should not do it at all.

Coming from a Protestant background in the Congregational church, this student saw himself in the second of three stages through which every human being must pass on the road to religious maturity: infancy, inquiry and inner conviction. "I am in flux, as it were, my ideas are being re-evaluated and my beliefs re-examined. I am trying to take stock of my earlier beliefs and mode of conduct to adjust wherever necessary and bring up to date this standard as a basis for my adult life." He concludes with a Credo to which many students would subscribe:

I believe there is a Supreme Power at the head of the universe, but what his shape, powers, or scope are I do not know. How much of our life he really controls and how much

44

he leaves to us I don't know. I believe he has a plan for the world in his mind, if it is called a mind. I also believe he has caused the world to be different and caused us to have many religions. He has not made any single human being exactly like the next. He made the world different for a reason. I think his plan is to have us use our minds by way of comparison and contrast, and come up with what we will.

If we all came up with the same conclusion or the same answer, what a boring world it would be! I think it is out of controversy that a lot of good thoughts are born. It is on this that I base my belief that we were made to have different lives, different countries, different thoughts, and different religions.

Not everyone is so easily satisfied with religious pluralism, accepting it as part of the divine plan to keep people from getting bored with their uniformity. Encouraged by some of their teachers, students may explain religious differences as the growing pains of society trying to find its true meaning. In this theory religion is the conglomeration of tentative opinions that may take centuries to resolve.

Answering the question, "What is religion?", one man defined it as a complex of arbitrary ideals by which people sanction daily existence, "an institution created by man to put value and rule into his life." Immediately he pointed out that religion and theology are related as spontaneous instinct and mental construct, where the former arises unbidden in the human heart but the latter is developed by the mind to rationalize its desires:

What we do not contend is that gods, God, or these other ideals either have or have not existence. What we are trying to establish is that at best theology is only a part of religion; that religion and theology are independent and can be dealt with apart without losing or destroying anything.

Theology is created by man as a foundation for his reli-

gion, but this foundation is arbitrary. Therefore we must refrain from explaining religion in terms of theology for its
nature is sociological. We divorce the two, theology and religion, not to attack one by the other.

In the spirit of Bertrand Russell, who is quoted exten-
sively, the campus agnostic admits that segregating theology from religion is only a description of reality. People
are naturally prone to defend their positions, and religious
people are no exception. But this should not blind us to
the inherent value of religious ideals. "Man needs his religion. All of mankind are not supermen, nor as intelligent
and courageous as Bertrand Russell." Evolution is a slow
process and mankind is still in its infancy:

To take religion from man now would be to cast him into
the obscurity of the sea of time and he would become lost in
the chaos of his own waves. It is easy to scorn and condemn an
institution with its many manifest defects; it is harder to understand that with all its defects religion is essential and functions vitally for man. Here we must see the whole picture:
man needs his religion; and we must see it in this way, not as
an end in itself but as a means sustaining him until an age
when he grows stronger and wiser. We must strive to do this so
as not to blindly grope in the darkness and obscurity of the
present but to see the dynamics of man's evolution through
the spaces of time.

No doubt religion will eventually become archaic for
some people in the present generation and for mankind in
the distant future. Meanwhile it allows man to live an
orderly life until he reaches true mastery. "Man now becomes the object of his religion, a god. Or in Plato's dream,
more fully than he believed possible, all men will have become Philosophers. No longer will, blasphemously speak-

ing, man need God even if he so exists." All of this is inevitable. All that we need is time.

Moral Functionalism. American universities now cater to a growing number of adult students, men and women who are married and have families but who want to finish their education. They set a new tone to college life and bring into the classroom a degree of serious thinking that must be counted one of the major developments in higher education.

Yet here, too, the general pattern is much the same: a hungry quest for meaning and a thirst for understanding the purpose of life. Only the clarity and depth of insight are greater.

A senior who was getting her certificate in education would reduce religion to a form of emotion that has grown and matured down the ages. "We can mark out love," she wrote, "by saying it is a certain type of emotion felt toward a fellow human. Patriotism is a similar emotion felt toward one's homeland. But when love widens its horizons, it becomes religious; when patriotism passes from a mere animal attachment to a certain piece of ground into a loyalty for which one's country stands, it too merges into a religion."

But we must not think of religion chiefly in terms of subjective exhilaration or personal consolation. Religion is needed to affect conduct and character. Refugees from life, mystics, hermits, dream-world personalities are not solving our human problems. They suffer from 'ingrown religion.'

The admirable forms of religion tap moral energies and widen social vision. The emotional aspects of religion should not be wasted, but their potentialities must be used for moralizing human life. Jesus said, 'By their fruits you shall know them.'

Unfortunately the religious emotions of dependence and humility are not always used in altruism. Pious acquiescence in things as they are, as the will of God that may not be tampered with, can be irritating. The smug righteousness of the well-dressed rich and their prayers "from comfortable pews" can be offensive to sensitive spirits.

Historic religion claims to be more that strong emotion, even emotion that follows the example of Christ in doing good. The real scandal of established religions is their claim to having special access to the Deity, and obtaining graces that are closed to non-believers who do not use the sacraments and rites:

Certainly if believers are justified in assuming that their rites have direct efficacy to secure desired blessings, they are right in considering them of central importance. If the petitions for blessings we crave are really answered, then we should be fools not to utilize these shortcuts to our heart's desire.

But modern man finds himself unable to retain these consoling beliefs. He is beset by doubts and fears, torn between trying to know if his actions are from spiritual guidance and therefore in obedience to the will of God, or if what he does is simply an expression of his own willfullness in rebellion against the divine will.

Without denying that ritual and ceremony have their place in religion, this student has misgivings about their supposed efficacy beyond the aesthetic one of nurturing pious emotions. Too many believers have the comfortable sense of having done their duty for the week when they have gone to church. Where religious rites are elaborate they can become a meaningless burden and a poor substitute for the devotion to concretely useful ideas "such as charity, justice, and brotherliness."

This critique of ritual was only a prelude to expressing

her real feelings. There must be more to religion than ceremonial, and not all believers are hypocrites. But where do you find the secret of believing with perfect security, or is that only a mirage?

To the writer the attempt to attain faith and have it grow so that a person can reach his highest nature, is a process of constant, never ending introspection. It is a cumulative process of self-examination that more times than not results only in showing how far one must yet strive and how miserably little has been attained. If undertaken in true humility, this process would not permit one the solace of those self-righteous people who are so prone to speak of their 'faith that is without doubt' in the face of any of life's ordeals.

The problem with Christianity is not that it places too much burden on the mind to believe, but too much weight on human nature to bear. It asks its followers to accept the cross and love it, without understanding the reason why. "Christianity is simple to understand, but it is desperately hard to put into practice. It is much easier for people to believe an elaborate theological creed than to live a simple Christian life. Religion in this sense begs no question, rests upon no dubious postulates. It has verifiable values. It does not antagonize science or corrupt education. It may unite men of every fold, instead of dividing them into a hundred sects."

On a prophetic note religion is to be redefined in something more than creeds and cults, at the risk of disintegration "as in Russia today." Religion must be conceived as "that good which can reach man and transform him with the power to see and act for the highest good of mankind. It must give him the devotion of heart and mind to love God, indeed, but to prove this love in charity towards his fellowman."

Viewing religion in this light reveals new problems. If

49

doing good to others is essentially religious, when do I practice charity and what is morally good? "Can we define morality as the technique of securing the greatest attainable happiness for all? Then what behavior codes do we follow to be moral. Again the writer must plague herself and the reader with questions."

Perhaps Christians have been too ready to describe the morally good life in terms of divine sanction, and to say, without much clarification, that conduct is right or wrong because God commands it:

If we obey, He will save us; if we disobey, He will damn us! This unhappy idea has been taught by parents and teachers, the clergy and self-appointed prophets—without the sensitivity to understand the fears it can produce in man and child; without the education to explain God's commandments logically, and the results of our disobedience compassionately.

The terrible misuse of this divine revelation has produced more mental and emotional illness than any other aspect of man's nature. Credit for this abomination must be laid in the laps of ignorant and overzealous parents, teachers, and clergy who, this writer suspects, engage in the ghastly trade because of their own terror of God.

The surest way of getting into harmony with the will of a loving God, who wishes for us what is really best, is not to accept some tradition blindly. Rather study patiently the needs of human nature and find by careful empirical research what kinds of conduct observably have the best results. In this way we should discover the best reason to call upon God's will and respond in obedience to His commands.

One of the most crucial features of college life is the pressure put upon students to conform to accepted norms. For all the lip-service paid to independence, they are under constant duress to follow the conduct and thought patterns of their environment. No one is exempt from this constraint, although women perhaps feel it more than

men and, unexpectedly, upperclassmen (especially sophomores) can be more impressionable than many freshmen.

The urge to conformity is strengthened by a widespread theory in the social sciences which defines morality
in terms of the prevalent customs of a community. What a
community judges to be acceptable thus becomes morally
good, and what is socially taboo automatically becomes
bad.

"Is our behavior moral because it is approved by the
community?" is a question asked implicitly by thousands
of young people, although voiced only by the more dis-
cerning, like the senior I am quoting. We usually approve
such conduct as the community approves and condemn
what it condemns, is her frank reply. Then she launches
into a denunciation which too few undergraduates have
the courage (or the intelligence) to make:

This makes morals mores, variable and too complex to
define universally. Morals are relativistic, predicated on this
view. To be moral is simply to be true to the code of the group
to which you belong. Morality is conformity to the group instead of to God. And conduct is so conformed that it dare not
deviate, be there a need to improve or reform (and there
usually is) the group—no matter how stupid and non-
progressive, how immoral or intolerant the group may be.
Conformity goes much deeper than sameness of possession
and behavior. Conformity is the pathetic attempt to deny
our uniqueness and the uniqueness of our fellows, because this
uniqueness is so terrifying in its alienation. Conformity is the
salve of simplification to the complexities of life. It is the
desperate banding together to find communion that lacks
communication. Conformity is the lifetime masquerade ball
with all the costumes alike, so we don't have to think about
what is in the costume. We see it, we recognize the outerness,
and assume or more than hope we recognize what is inside.
This is our spider web security.

51

Apparently opposed to the doctrine of conformity, but really its complement, is the campus (and classroom) idea of self-realization. Students are led to believe that the acme of human existence is to develop all their latent capacities, to make the most of themselves and of life. Growth is the ideal, no conformity here; we must expand, strive to enrich our experiences, bring out what the real "us" is. "But the big question is what potentialities should be realized. What should man develop, which are worth developing? A man can develop himself into a successful criminal or racketeer—to which our nation can attest for more than its share." These are all potentialities. Does this mean that to develop oneself a man must feed all of his appetites, on the assumption that to deprive an appetite would be detrimental to full self-realization? But, then, "some appetites can only be fed by the exploitation of other people. Do we build ourselves by creating a pyramid of exploitation?"

There are hidden dangers in this kind of egocentricty, from which the college person should be spared. "At this point a suggestion might be made, to the effect that more self-denial would induce morality. The concept of self-realization as it is being endorsed by many today only compounds the problem. There is too much concern for one's own needs and too little willingness to sacrifice what we individually might do for the general good."

Once again a complaint about traditional religion. Reflecting on her own experience, the student critic confesses that "some people raised in some environments of Christianity" have been taught practically to equate pleasure with sinfulness, and any suggestion that virtue might be enjoyed was tantamount to blasphemy. This cannot be true. "The really virtuous act must bring happiness, and the greater part of building a structure of morality is to get rid of unhappiness," in the deepest sense of frustration that immorality always brings in its wake.

Paradoxically, however, virtue cannot be enjoyed without reference to pain, and one of the deepest lessons she learned is to ignore the easy formulas advertized in the newspapers that collegians read. She quotes one of them recommending a heroic panacea: "The world is full of good and evil. If you pasture your mind on the good, then for you there is no evil. A mind so full of the fine things in life has no room for trouble to enter. The spiritually aware have perceived this throughout the ages to their own profit and advantage." She reacts with impatience. "The spiritually aware are tormented by evil in the world and realize that pasturing the mind on the good means physical and spiritual effort to relieve suffering. Having one's mind so full of the fine things of life there is no room for trouble to enter is not only idiotic but unrealistic and disgracefully selfish."

Along with these profound insights into religion and morality, there is great uncertainty in the student's mind. In her own words, she is confused and looking for answers to life's problems. "Am I unique in my ignorance," she wonders, "or just truthfully searching my mind and heart." Anyone who knows American universities would say this is not unique, and from many conferences with this student I know that her search is honest.

Devotion to Christ. It is impossible to estimate, but a sizeable minority in college are dedicated persons whose early training or religious temperament shields them from the need (or opportunity) of discovering a philosophy of life. They seem always to have had one, or at least they developed a set of values before they came to college.

Their mental range is generally higher than average, contrary to a popular myth that intelligence begets scepti-

cism and that only the more naive are strong believers.
They cut across every religious tradition and, when analyzing themselves, are surprisingly unanimous in their approach to reality.

The most common form of this dedication is to the
person of Jesus Christ. "I am a member of a Christian
faith," a junior declared, "because I believe in Christ and
His teachings. I have found Christ personally and have
accepted Him as my own. Certainly my parents' guidance
has influenced my choice of religion (Methodist), but my
faith would be meaningless if I had not taken this step of
acceptance by myself on the strength of my own convictions." Then follows a series of eleven cameo essays, each
briefly telling how "Jesus is many things to me. He is life,
pardon, peace, power, provision, companionship, hope,
truth, assurance, joy, and heaven." They are a picture of
what goes on in the interior lives of sophisticated university students:

In Christ I have found the final answer to my greatest
needs, the abiding satisfaction of my deepest longings, the
complete dispelling of my darkest fears, and the rich fulfillment of my highest aspirations. And having found these, I
have found life—life full and free. For I have learned that 'if
any man be in Christ, he is a new creature.'

Of all the things that Jesus means to me, He is above all
else my Savior. By His suffering and death in my place upon
the Cross, He has paid the penalty of all my sins.

In our passage through this world, says Jesus, we shall have
tribulation. But . . . 'in Me, peace!' That has been my great
discovery. In Christ I have found peace in the midst of all
adversity, peace in the midst of conflict, peace in the face of
opposition.

I receive power from Christ by believing. I accept the helping hand of Christ by simply trusting Him. I seek daily reas-

surance of His power through prayer. More than once, when the burden seemed too heavy, I have called upon Him, and always He either has lightened the burden to match my strength, or has increased my strength to match the burden.

There come moments into the life of every one of us, when the world seems to pass us by, and we are forced to eat the bread of loneliness. The human heart cries out against the aching pain of loneliness. And its cries can never be completely silenced until it has found the solace and strength which comes from true companionship. I have found that true companionship . . . in Christ.

Commitment of this kind may reach back to the earliest days of childhood, but more often it comes with adolescence, as in the case of a young woman who first discovered the "companionship" of Christ in her early teens. She used to walk a half mile to the store after dark, and along the way were two large and empty fields to be passed. "Having been warned about kidnappers and other such dangers, I could not possibly have made the trip alone. Foolish as it seems now, I conquered my fears with an imaginary companion who, I decided, was Jesus." Although his presence offered her no physical protection, she was content with the peace of mind received from the "spirit of the idea," and this became the basis for a more mature relationship with Christ later on.

The remarkable thing about this student is that nothing in her home training would have encouraged it. Only twice in her life could she recall religion being mentioned by her parents for something other than the sake of argument. One of these was when her father came home after an office Christmas party and told her how wonderful Jesus was. That was also one of the few times he expressed regret over not giving his children a religious education. The other intrusion of religion into the family occurred when her father lost his job for the first time in twenty years, and everyone went to church until he found employment in about four or five weeks.

She began attending church regularly only after starting college. The first sermon she heard in a downtown (Lutheran) church touched her deeply. Overwhelmed by the sacrifice of Christ on the cross, she came to realize "the true and full power of Love that a spotless being like Jesus has for the mass of humanity." Her life is no longer the same. "I love Jesus Christ," she admitted freely, "and if there were not such a strong urge in me holding me to mortal men, I would spend what small life I can offer Him for Him alone. As it is, I love a few men in the way I love Jesus, but not so strongly and with a few other elements mixed in, for obviously no one else can deserve what is meant for the Lord."

Interestingly she had gone through a period of "ostentatious atheism" during high school, followed by a desire to convert to Catholicism because the Catholic Church "has something to hold on to." After some inquiry she decided against the Church because of its practice of confession and what, in her judgment, was the overlay of interpretation on the simple gospel message of salvation. "There is such a thing as going too deep and making too much from decisions made by men on the words and meanings of God." Christ alone is enough for her, without "the symbolism and ritual of the church" and without interference from man.

One effect of a secular atmosphere on campus is to stimulate the zeal of a number of students to neutralize this secularism by work and religious example. Most of them are satisfied to influence their classmates in a quiet, unpretentious way: a remark here, an invitation there, yet all the while conscious of what they are doing. A few are more obtrusive, but unless they are careful they are soon put down as "queers," and their influence practically disappears. In any case, the inner motivation of every type of zealot is part of the atmosphere of a university. It offers a counterpart to the campus atheist who is never subtle and whose evangelism-in-reverse is nothing if not obtrusive.

Starting with the premise that everyone who is serious about a specialty is committed to his field, a Protestant student in American Religion argued that a Christian should be the most committed of individuals. Not only is his faith important enough to demand a whole-souled dedication, but the example of his Master should urge a believer to give himself completely to the cause of Jesus Christ. In practice this meant the winning of souls to follow the Christian life. "Many times I ask myself this blunt question: How long has it been since I have led someone to Jesus Christ?" and then he expanded on what this commitment involves:

I consider myself an evangelist in spite of myself. For some reason Christ chose me to be an evangelist, and I am. I call for commitment. I'm not ashamed, but every time I do it I perspire, and it is torture. Why should it be so hard to say to someone, 'Now, why don't you accept Jesus Christ?' I want to avoid it, and to escape it. Is this obedience to God's will? Am I going to be obedient? One can organize wonderful programs, but I realize that here or wherever I am, the most crucial thing is speaking to one person and leading that person to Jesus Christ. An organization can be just an escape, because face to face contact is the crucial area, the place where Satan fights the hardest.

I told a girl the other day that often I feel like a little boy on the edge of a great crowd and Jesus Christ is way over there where I can barely see Him. Here I am, but that's all right with me. That's where I want to be, where I can see Him. This girl asked me, 'Does He know you're there?' I thought for a moment and then replied, 'Yes, He looks at me once in a while.' He has, I know the times when He has really looked at me. I could mention the instances.

This man understood the need of being committed himself, before he could effectively influence others. "To make a commitment for evangelism," he admitted, "I need a deep attachment to Jesus Christ, like a boy with his father." He compared himself to the father of a child whose attachment to his parent has been cultivated through years of kindness, mutually shared. "I know that Jesus loves me in this way. He delights in me. I can commit myself to Him without fear. I'll fail, but He will still love me and that is what really counts." That is also what a Christian needs to experience if he expects to communicate to others a personal love for Christ.

As a rule Catholics do not stress personal relationship with Christ as much as Protestants. Their religion tends to be more institutionalized, or so it seems to most students. But there are notable exceptions, like the girl who was a cradle Catholic but insisted that about five years ago she started seriously to evaluate her religion and ask how strongly she believed it. "Today I can firmly state that this is my chosen religion." Most of her reasons for being a Catholic were catechism answers, until she came to the climax. " I want to honor God and show my love for Him in the best way I humanly can." She discovered this was possible through union with Christ, whom she described interchangeably as God or the Lord:

I do not believe you can feel a unity with Christ unless it first comes from within. These inner feelings towards God are usually formed when you are a child, and should develop as you grow older. I feel a definite union with God at certain times in my life: right after confession, when I feel as though I lost a heavy weight; during and after Mass, especially if I

58

received Holy Communion; after an extra visit to church, even if it's just for a few minutes; and when I look around me and see all that God has created to make me happy and more loving, not only towards Him but also towards my fellow-man.

I learned this unity with God through my upbringing in the Catholic faith. Since questioning this faith and still being satisfied, it is even stronger in me. I could not trade this union with our Lord for all the treasures on earth. These originally came to me through my religion, so how could I possibly exchange it for something less?

The defensive tone is not characteristic. It was occasioned by the context in which the student wrote, to show why she was a Catholic. This will appear more evident when we examine the grounds on which young people hold traditional faiths.

Commitment to God. One of the most common and least definable words in university circles is "commitment." We have seen some of its implications where it means devotion to the person of Christ. More elusive is the notion of being committed to God, and yet not many terms would come closer to describe the meaning of religion in American university life.

A fine piece of self-revelation on commitment came from a young man who was a great admirer of Peter Marshall, late chaplain to the United States Senate. He took one of his statements as a motto of the Christian faith. "The measure of a life," according to Marshall, "is not its duration, but its donation." For a long time this passage haunted him, because it exposed the basic weakness of his concept of religion. He had always wanted God to give to him and never thought of giving to God in return. Once it dawned on him that Christianity is reciprocal, a new era opened to the future. But more even than reciprocation, religion came to mean placing self-will into the hands of God to make Him a "partner" in one's life:

> Commitment to my understanding begins with a person dying to his own self-will. The word 'dying' leaves many people standing on the porch of indecision. They either fail to understand what dying to oneself means or fail to see whether such dying would be worthwhile. This is one reason why many people fail to comprehend commitment. Yet I repeat; its first step must be a willingness to die to one's own self-will in order to become a useful vessel in the hands of God.

Immediately this changes a fundamental attitude in one's relationship with God. Given the freedom of choice to respond to God's advances towards man, our concept of religion shifts from a stress on duty to the idea of opportunity. After all, we are free agents:

> It is my contention that commitment removes obligation and instills the attitude of privilege. Obligation is often understood as an act or thought that a person must effect, or else the consequences will be disastrous. In other words, obligation conveys the idea of being gripped by the fear of consequence.
> Privilege, on the other hand, conveys the idea of love and willingness without the dread of consequences as one's essential purpose. It means commitment to God, therefore, through the love He exemplified in His Son, Jesus Christ, who counted it a privilege to serve God. Thus it is through losing or giving that we gain, not for our advantage (for that is what we have sacrificed), but for God's purposes.

His family background had prepared him for self-sacrifice. "My home," he recalled, "had been such that God was always the center of attraction. He was not made obnoxious by demanding parents but introduced in love. Because of this ideal relationship, I grew early in life to

want to serve Him." Then began a series of disappoint-
ments. Eager to serve God in the person of others, he
found that people were not responsive. "I do not wish to
complain or paint a picture of despair, but it was not long
before I discovered that not everyone shared my enthusiasm. It seemed that people had no concern with the concept of God that I had been privileged to experience."
The result was a chastening enlightenment:

No one can appreciate apathy until he meets it. No one
can feel the pains of seeming defeat until he experiences it in
the light of his enthusiasm.

How can one express the burning desire to reach men's
hearts with God's love? What can one give, or do, or say that
will better convey life to those who are dead? These questions
burned my heart. I think that I am beginning to see the
answers to these questions though. My mistake lay in the idea
of selfism—the desire to push God aside, as it were, and take
over for Him. I was attempting to serve in the finite that
which is infinite and thus not only was I misleading people,
but I was missing the core of true commitment towards those I
was trying to serve.

Although still an undergraduate, he had found that his
failure was due to a weakness in himself. Quoting someone
to the effect that, "the world has yet to see what God can
do with a fully dedicated man," he concluded hopefully:
"I should like to say that with God's help I shall be that
man." Anything less, he felt, would be merely existing; it
would not be living.

Other students have also learned the hard way, but
their lesson was more elementary: why they need God and
why, without Him, there would be no sane purpose in
life.

A coed who was fond of asking her dorm-mates about
their religion found that most Protestants give a better

account of themselves than Catholics, who "take God so much for granted they seldom stop to probe why they believe unless some misfortune enters their lives." She knew because it took a tragedy to reveal Him to her.

She was a sophomore in high school the day it was announced that school was being let out early. The students thought there must be something wrong with the furnaces because Thanksgiving vacation was not to begin until the next day. When she came home, she found it had all been done for her sake. The principal was afraid somebody would hear the news and spread it around the school.

Her brother who was away at college had become mentally ill and while in that condition had committed a criminal offense. "I just couldn't believe it when I heard it. The only person I could turn to was God. I don't think I ever realized He was beside me always just waiting for me to take His outstretched hand. The other members of my family had their own problems so that I just couldn't pour my thoughts out to them. To this day I don't know what would have happened if I didn't have God to talk to."

Radio, television, and the newspapers followed the whole story and trial in close detail. She remembered reading articles on her family that she had never heard of before but that was news and the readers were hungry for more. "We received hundreds of cards and consoling notes, and many Masses were offered for our intention. This was all very nice, but my real peace had to come from within. I believe God finally became known to me or at least I got to know God." She did not know how to explain it, but felt that she received the strength and grace to face people and help her parents and younger sister through the crisis:

God was always there to push me to see that good does come from evil. I could accept God allowing this to happen to my brother and family. 'Why?' was the hardest question for me to answer. I just knew for some unknown reason that God had a reason for this to take place. God became my real Light of the Way. He gave me reasons for living. It is true in every great trial of life that without God, real and alive beside you, you have nothing.

The test of my faith didn't stop just at the time of the incident. I'm always being tested: the time of my brother's trial, then his years of imprisonment for the criminally insane, and now his life of readjustment in society bring their constant challenge to my faith not to run away from it all.

During the years of her brother's imprisonment, her family visited him as often as they were permitted. Again deeper understanding of her need for God. She began to see how trivial her troubles were compared with those of people whose families throughout the state had similar or graver problems to face. "We weren't the only ones who had been sent their crosses to bear. Our family was even blessed because we stayed and grew closer together. My brother realized how much he needed us and we realized this need." There were men in confinement who had no families outside. If they had no faith, there was no reason for them to live. "Many did and will continue to take their own lives. I was exposed to a completely different life which showed me the importance of God."

She recognized that suffering was the means God used to make her sense her complete dependence on Him. Based on this fact, everything else takes on meaning, especially the value and dignity of other people. "If I didn't believe in God, the rest of mankind would mean nothing to me. I would step on them as one steps on a crack in the sidewalk without disturbing one's stride. There would be no respect for another's property, and the family would lose its value." Her own family had learned the indispensability of God.

TWO

GOD

Desire and Destiny

IF THE test of a man's religion is the prominence he gives to God, college students are religious-minded people. They are more preoccupied with God and their relations to Him than most educators (including college teachers) suspect, and they need only a chance to express themselves to show how deeply they feel on the subject.

One of the pathetic experiences in my contact with students is to see them struggling to tell you about the inner workings of their souls, searching for words to understand the meaning of God in their lives, how better to know His will, and give themselves to One whom they recognize as worthy of their love. Some are more communicative than others and some are more intelligent, but even the least cultivated are willing to talk about the Reality that the very neutralism of a university seems to encourage thinking about.

It is impossible to classify their approaches which vary as much as one personality differs from another. But each one offers a new insight into the minds of the silent generation whose only opportunity to speak is in class essays that never see the light of day.

A number of years ago, a leading psychologist conducted a survey on what his students thought about God. Their reported answers were startling. "I think of Him," they said, "as real, actual skin, blood, and bones, something we shall see with our eyes someday, no matter what lives we live on earth . . . I have always pictured Him according to a description in *Paradise Lost* as seated upon a throne, while around are angels playing on harps and singing hymns . . . I think of God as having bodily form and being much larger than the average man. He has a radiant countenance beaming with love and compassion. He is erect and upright, fearless and brave." Without questioning the investigator's accuracy, it could not be further removed from what I know the average college person thinks about God. His ideas may be vague and they are seldom metaphysical, but they are never bizarre.

Groping Intuition. Believing in God without a clear concept of who He is becomes a problem for maturing minds. As one of my students in the Introduction to Religion put it, "to have faith in God without knowing what you mean by Him seems to be impossible." Young men and women are not atheists nor even agnostics. They always supposed that they believed in God, but they are now facing a bewildering question: What does the word mean? What is God like? How can He be imagined? Somewhere near the center of their search for identity is the question: Who is God?

They try to apply the norms of modern science, and when these fail them they are disappointed. Those who cut through the ritual make a wonderful discovery. Instead of looking at God "from a purely materialistic point of view," they look instead to the workings of the spirit within:

I have formulated my own concept of God. This concept is probably much different from others. The difference lies in the fact that I view God from a more spiritual approach. I have not tried to view Him as to shape or form because I have nothing concrete to base my assumption on. Instead, He represents to me everything that was, is, and will be. I do not question His existence because I can see what He has done and what He can do. In no way has it been possible or, for that matter, necessary for me to prove the existence of God by reasoning from material things.

I have firmly established in my mind that the place where man virtually finds God, deals with God, discovers the qualities of God, and learns to think religiously about God is not primarily among the stars but within his own experience of goodness, truth, and beauty. The truest images of God, therefore, are to be found in man's spiritual life.

The man who "formulated" this concept used it to question his friends about religion and found they shared his opinions. "We were discussing the importance of religion related to faith," he recalled. He asked an upperclassman how he was sure that God existed and what would his feelings be if it could suddenly be proven that everything in the Bible was wrong. The answer was "one simple fact that justified his faith." No matter what could be proved or disproved from the Bible, "the spiritual richness and satisfaction received through following what his faith had built" was enough to withstand any objections about the existence of God.

Another junior appealed to intuition. "It is not unusual to find skeptics," as the first week in college revealed, "but it seems unthinkable that all I intuitively know of God has no basis in the reality of existence. Do I exist or do I not exist? The question is inconceivable. Does God exist or does God not exist? Again the question seems inconceivable. Knowing that I am and that I want to be justifies my existence. God's presence even more so justifies my existence," because without Him nothing else would be:

Regardless of how rational or reasonable a person must be when he speaks of God, this is not the basic consideration. I must know that God exists. There are those who would have me believe that there is something beyond the notion of God; that He can be explained in terms of logic which completely justifies His existence. While this is not meaningless to me, the really important thing is that I know God exists.

I think it is possible to have simple belief and to know I am right, almost intuitively. I suppose my brain movement toward God, other than to explain the order of the universe and to justify its existence, is in the love of God.

Such coupling of intuition and affection is not uncommon. It appears to come from the way people naturally interpret spiritual reality in human terms and draw analogies from personal experience. No one loves what does not exist. "It didn't take me long to realize that even thinking or feeling that you know God is followed by a love of God." Therefore He must be real. Moreover, there are many things we can understand "without knowing the exact logic" of them, as happens regularly in the friendships that we form. "How is it possible to love God without (fully) understanding and not be able to love God without understanding Him?" In both cases the secret of growing in knowledge is to love more. "Love must be nurtured with God as love must be nurtured for our fellow man," except that with God, "the longer you live with Him, the longer you live within Him—the more you understand and love Him. Not to give Him my greatest love is to deny Him."

The striking thing about these sentiments is that they come from a man who professedly is dissatisfied with institutional religion, which he found a restriction on his liberty. On his own terms, he is not aggressive. "I am timid and in need of assurance. Having a need of God is the way of my life and having God is my hope." Since boyhood days, "organized religion has told me to believe, but believe within the confines of its structure. I can have my God but within the confines of the church structure. I am then told that my God is personal. How can it be so?" How do you reconcile the intimacy of divine friendship with the institutionalism of the churches? They are irreconcilable:

Community religion removes the 'solitariness' from belief. Somehow I am not capable of understanding God. I repeat that the important decision is not how I believe but that I believe.

There is no way to undermine the importance of allowing people of common belief to come together. With greater organization of things to make sense of God, greater authority is given to some and less to others. The person with less authority, or no authority, is allowed to say nothing. If he wants to stay in the church he obeys the authority of that church. There is no room for conflict; either accept all the teachings or the teachers reject you.

I've been told that not being able to accept the whole of one teaching is somehow psychologically unsound. However, believing that a church cannot have all the answers is more in keeping with the nature of man who cannot understand anything completely. I admit it is threatening to be on the outside from that which is held by others. I look to God for reassurance and guidance. I can better understand by listening to *all* of God's interpreters.

It never occurred to him that the community of believers was itself part of the faith. Torn between the desire to reach God and the churches' claims to satisfy his needs, he found refuge in the sincerity of his faith. His feelings are an echo of those who are outside the pale of organized religion and yet inside the vast circle of believers:

As I grope for discovery of God, I find that I cannot be

68

wrong but only right in varying degrees. It would simplify things if God would reveal Himself completely to me and open the way for me to see. That would increase the simplicity of it all but in a way decrease His Godliness. The important thing is that I realize God. At times I have felt on the outside of other men's beliefs, but I have never felt apart from God.

I know He is present and he wants me, but, because I am influenced by other men I find myself in the apex of an inverted cone. There is no way I can escape my obligation. Yet as I look above me I can see everything I desire. I can see light, I can see understanding; I know that God wants me. At times I have the feeling that the greatest share of light is only reflected and does not approach me.

It is as if God has revealed certain things to me and certain things to others. Through some fault of my own I have not been able to relate to others what God means to me and what God means to others. It is a never ending struggle to know God and I cry out: Help me, God. I need your help to know you.

To read these lines is to read the soul of one of the millions of "unchurched" Americans that belong to no denomination and appear on no religious census. Somehow the churches have failed them.

Faith under Trial. Coming into college from a religious background may spare a student the trouble of discovering the meaning of life and his relation to God, but he is not spared the necessity of conflict which challenges his beliefs. The whole issue is wider than holding on to one's faith, and there is danger of losing perspective by citing isolated instances. Yet part of the maturation of university life is to re-examine even the foundations of religion, including the existence and relevance of God.

Men and women differ in their response to conflicting situations. As a rule the man's problem will be to find rational justification for his beliefs and satisfy his mind that the religion of his parents "makes sense." He may resort to subjective norms to strengthen his faith, just as he may appeal to intuition to discover the meaning of God as all. But validation is important for a man and the worst stigma he fears is to be unreasonable. Women are less concerned to prove their religion is true; they are more anxious to know it is good—good for them personally and good for others who profess the same affiliation.

A university woman told the story of her own confrontation. As a small child she found it easy to accept God. "Now that I am older I realize that accepting God does not mean you understand Him or know Him, perhaps not even that you have faith in Him." The odyssey she traveled is familiar:

Attending Sunday School was more a social function than a worshipping of God. It was a place to wear fancy clothes and visit with friends who didn't attend the same school. When I attended confirmation class I learned very little. It was an inconvenience to me; it took away the morning I could sleep in late and the one day I could have had all to myself. As I think back now I wonder what I thought justified my motives.

About the time I entered high school, I started attending church regularly. I had good intentions. I sat through the sermons really trying to pay attention to what was being said. I joined clubs associated with the church in my community. I knew religion should have meant more to me at this time than it did, and I decided to do something about it. At times it seemed futile for I felt no change or great revelation within me and this was disheartening.

Never losing her faith, yet struggling to make it meaningful, she found that college did not solve her problem. If anything, it compounded the difficulty. She still insists, "I do believe in God," and therefore "know there is a reason for living, a definite purpose for being alive." But all the while she confesses herself to be a poor Christian. Doubts assail her, and they cannot easily be brushed aside. They are not so much concerned with God's existence, as with His providence in her regard:

At times I feel so lost, as though there isn't a place in this world where I fit in. A good Christian would not question his purpose or place in life, for he would know that God would show him his place when He is ready.

When I was younger I never had these feelings of insecurity. My life was planned and I had no choice to make. However, in the past two and a half years since I graduated from high school my life has been filled with so many important decisions and they all seem to have such a strong and direct bearing on my future. I know that the importance of these decisions which have to be answered correctly has drawn me closer to God, but I am afraid at the same time they have caused me to doubt God.

The ambivalence this girl described is a curious thing. Under duress the religious emotions may be heightened, while at the same time the intellect may recede in its grasp of the faith. At that point one of two things happens: either the person takes refuge in more intense fervor or he tries to find more rational grounds for his belief. Most women, as here, intensify their devotional life, unless they give up their religion. Some consider the struggle too much and leave the university.

Another woman had almost the same kind of background. She was a Catholic who went to public school except for three years under parochial instruction. The nine years when she was not in a parish school she attended religious instructions. "I learned about God, His teachings, and how to be a good Catholic." In the meantime her faith has been confirmed in a variety of ways. "My belief is strengthened every time I go to Mass and receive Holy Communion. I also get my belief in God through prayer. I know that I do not always get what I want, but I realize that God has a reason." Certain events, in answer to prayer, added to the same conviction: like the time her brother escaped near death when his bicycle ran down a hill into a panel of glass, and when her grandmother's death was accepted with resignation to the divine will.

But college life produced a new situation. Exposed to the pressure of alien values, she decided to leave school "because I cannot find myself here, and I do not know where to start. The world today is based too much on materialistic gains. I have found this to be very true right here on campus." The conflict was not one of hostility but of estrangement. "I am sure if I am at home I will have a better chance to think and pray better," and solve the problems that contact with "materialism" had raised.

With a touch of hyperbole, a senior claimed that "in my first year of college, everything that I was taught and believed in was being challenged by associates and instructors." Because of his previous education he felt he could answer the challenges easily, but found that he was no match for the environment:

I read every book by disbelievers in God that I could get my hands on. Russell, Voltaire, Marx, Dewey became a living part of my battle against God and religion. These men convinced me that there was no God, Jesus Christ was not the Son of God, and there was no life after death. In general I believed that nothing could be explained that never was, heaven could be obtained on earth, and life was the end of existence. I felt, at that time, I could argue these points and make logical conclusions. Yet, I was not satisfied. It seemed I was avoiding reality completely instead of coming closer to it.

So again I began my journey through book after book. Finally after reading Marx and Engels three times, and

Hegel's dialectic theory, I thought I found the truth. Marx was my God and the *Manifesto* my Bible. A number of times I found myself defending Marxism as I once tried to defend Catholicism.

After three years of searching he found himself but only by making a strange distinction. "I still disbelieve in many existing religious practices, but this does not mean I am not a Catholic. On the contrary, I am a Catholic and, as one, I must have the right to criticize some of its teachings. I consider myself a very religious person even though I am not a frequent church goer. Religion is not practiced only at the foot of the altar or within the walls of a church." He survived the conflict by adjusting the faith of his childhood to what he considered adulthood standards of thought.

Unshaken Belief. Most students who enter college with religious convictions retain them, and some even develop and deepen their faith. The conflicts they meet serve to bring out latent resources that might otherwise never be brought into play. Above all, they are grateful for any chance to assess their beliefs. They know that every assessment frankly made under competent guidance will help them cope with the worst critic of religious commitment, a hungry intellect that cannot be satisfied with anything less than the truth.

Writing with no outline and trusting only to a free association of ideas, one man told me how pleased he was to express his beliefs on paper, "because religion means a lot to me." He began by stressing the fact that religion means many things to different people. Some have no religion at all. He did his best to say what "religion means to me." This accent on the personal pronoun is characteristic and explains more about college people than meets the eye:

I believe in God. I believe in the Holy Trinity. I have no

73

doubt whatsoever as to the existence of these beings. No person, no circumstance, or group of circumstances could ever lead me away from God. Only fools say there is no God.

Great minds of the world realize the existence of God. For example, Newton, whose scientific work has been called the most stupendous achievement of the human mind, argues that the order and harmony of the world prove that there is a living, almighty God. Einstein says, 'My religion consists of a humble admiration of the illimitable, superior spirit who reveals himself in the slight details we are able to perceive with our frail and feeble minds.' Robert Millikan, who was the first to isolate the electron, even writes, 'I have never known a thinking man who did not believe in God.'

God's rapture and beauty are reflected in nature. I think of the beautiful mountains I have seen in the western portion of the United States. I think of a majestic sunrise with a large lake in the foreground, or a thrilling sunset that reflects the blue sky. These are awe-inspiring to me; they make me think about God and His almighty power.

It is my belief that everything has a creator, except God. He has no beginning and no end. He is all knowing, all powerful, and present everywhere.

I am a Lutheran. If I were brought up a Catholic, I'd be a Catholic. If I were brought up a Jew—I don't know. I only wish that more people of this world could be led to the true faith and therefore be saved.

Something of a poet, he indulges in what he calls reverie, thinking about the smallness of man compared with the greatness of God. "Man knows very little. The more I learn the more I find that this is true." If he spent his whole lifetime reading and studying, he would still not know a great deal. He might master a few facts and memorize some platitudes, but "man's mind is not powerful enough to understand God." A moment's reflection on the vastness of space can bring this home:

I think of our universe which I define as a transparent sphere with an unknown diameter. There are many planets up there. I am wondering if God will let man reach these. I am also thinking if these planets hold any secrets. Will God limit man in his conquest of space?

In this world man realizes many great things at which he can only wonder. But they are beyond his limit of comprehension: matter itself, chemical reactions, stars, planets, and sun. The innermost portion of his thinking tells the intelligent man that behind all these great works is almighty God.

Looking inside himself, he asks a series of questions that "lie at the very core of every normal human being." How did this world in which I find myself ever come to be, and why is it such as it is? Does the world run itself, or is it under the control of some great unseen power? If so, what is my relation to that power? Is there any meaning and purpose to my life beyond what I see in it from day to day? When I have lived out my time on earth, is that the end of all so far as I am concerned? How does it happen that I feel uneasy and guilty when I have done something wrong or even hurt someone inadvertently? Could this possibly be a token that there is Someone who does know and to whom I am responsible? "These questions are the most far-reaching we can ask. And as they are answered one way or another, our whole view of ourselves and of the world itself will be deeply affected." Moreover they cannot be evaded.

The mystery is that some people are disappointed because they cannot find ready-made answers and then decide that no answers are possible. "The least that we can reasonably do is to acquaint ourselves with what claims to be reliable information and carefully consider it. I always say this when I am involved in a lively discussion of religion."

A standard objection to religion is the history of

superstition and bigotry to which it has given rise. "This, however, no more argues against the possible truth of a genuine religion than the freakish actions of African witch doctors call into question the achievements of modern medicine." Of course religion can be abused. But the very possibility of abuse suggests the existence of something good from which people can deviate. "In spite of the strange outgrowths that appear in some forms of religion, the world-wide conviction that there are superior powers of a personal kind remains a remarkable fact. It looks as if this conviction were natural to the human mind, so that it takes an effort to overcome it by means of argument or teaching." Left to himself, man is not irreligious.

Unbelief is too obvious to be denied. What to make of it? This man puts it down as prejudice. Anyone who refuses to hear the claims for theism convicts himself of bias. "His mind is closed. He refuses to see what is new to him and thinks that he, and only he, knows all." Then on a suasive note, "It is our duty as Christians to try to reach such people, whenever possible, and help them see the light. We could begin by asking them questions, through stimulating statements like those dealing with creation." He admits, however, that not all unbelievers can be convinced of God's existence.

A woman student professed faith in God as the indispensable element in any valid religion. "To me, religion means having a belief in God and showing this belief through prayer and sacrifice." Whatever else it is, though, religion is not something to which a person can be coerced. It is sovereignly free, and it is this very freedom to believe that explains why some people choose not to believe in God. "I know that I do not have to believe in a religion if I do not want to. I have the choice also to believe in any religion I want," or in no religion at all. Yet "it is difficult for me to see how some people do not believe in a Supreme

Being who made the earth and all of the people. It is hard
for me to know that some scientists see only evolution as
an explanation for the way we came into being and rule
out the existence of God. I am familiar with this idea,
having a brother who is questioning if God exists. He does
not know for sure, and I was shocked when I heard him
say this as we started off a discussion about God and evolution." Without speculating, she felt that one reason why
some people stop believing in God is because they had
stopped taking their religion seriously; gradually disinterested conduct led to disbelief.

The exact form that a religion takes, she thought, is
secondary. Acceptance of God is primary. In fact, "the only
thing, above all and upon Whom the Christian and Jewish
faiths are built is God." But once again the personal factor. "God is what makes religion important to me. I feel
that this is the only right answer for the question at hand.
This answer does not explain other peoples' 'religions'
who do not believe in God, but it does seem to be right for
me and what I believe."

Then "step by step, I will try to show why I believe it
is God who makes religion so important," and, indeed,
even possible. Her logic is typically Christian and typically
feminine:

First of all, God is love. Any believing Christian or Jew
knows this, as it is repeated many times in the book from
God, the Bible. I believe that because God wants us, the people on earth, to know about Himself and His love, He sent us
His word. Through the Bible we can see the guide that we
need for our lives. We have the story of how God created the
earth and the stars, the seas, darkness and light, and then man
and woman. Also in the Bible are the Ten Commandments
given by God to Moses. These are what God expects us to obey
so that we may know the right way to live.

Moreover, everything we receive from God reflects His love

for us. God did not have to make the earth or men and women, but He wanted to. God gave man the power to love. Through love and by marriage, a man and woman become one and, if they are able, have children. Thus life is the result of God's love given to people in marriage, who are showing their love for each other.

Giving us minds with the ability to choose is another way God shows His love for us. We can decide whether we wish to be good or evil. I believe God places evil before us to make us understand that we must be strong to be good. When we realize that we are doing the wrong thing, we can ask God to help us find the right way.

Through the Bible, therefore, through life, and through the power of choice, we see how God shows man His love.

Consequently the evidence for God's existence is the outpouring of His love. Reflection on this manifestation of divine goodness, she would say, is a guarantee of belief in God, even as ignoring these proofs of His bounty will lead to unbelief.

But not only women are impressed by the biblical definition that God is love. Among the exceptional students I have taught at the university was a young man whose life story will never be told because he hardly knows it himself. He was born and reared under National Socialism in Germany, as a product of one of the Nazi fertilization farms whose purpose was to crossbreed the best specimens of Aryan culture with a view to developing the master race of Hitler's *Mein Kampf*. This person's intelligence I would rate among the highest that I have met in more than a dozen years of college teaching.

His approach to God was through the human instinct of survival, the deeply spiritual appetite to continue even endless existence. "The one wholly inescapable fact for every human being," he wrote, "is that he must die. In this fact man shares the lot of every living creature—but life

with a difference." Animals, like human beings, have a
biological urge to live; they fight tenaciously for life themselves, and, in higher forms, for their young. But to the
best of our knowledge, animals below man have no vision
of the future which would lead either to long for death, or
to create a philosophy of resistance to it. Animals do not
commit suicide, nor do they yearn for immortality.

It is man's glory that death for him is far more than a
biological event. Try as he may to make it a purely physical
fact, his higher spiritual impulses refuse to accept it as such. It
means the cutting off, or the continuance, of all that is most
precious to him, and he must have an answer. Hence, the
necessity of a faith, and the appearance of belief in immortality in all the great religions of mankind.

Transmitting the significance of immortality in other
religious systems, this Paper Technology major felt that
life after death occupies a central place in the Christian
faith. For one thing, Christianity was born in the Resurrection experience of the early disciples. "Death, where is
thy sting?" became the rallying cry of the fellowship that
formed the Christian Church:

But this is not our only witness. Even without the record of
Christ's resurrection, Christianity would in all probability
have made personal immortality a central tenet of its faith.
It belongs with the kind of God and the understanding of
man which Jesus not only taught but demonstrated.
It is the Christian faith that God is our Father. It is irrational to suppose that a God of fatherly love and sustaining
power, who has made man in His own image and who loves all
men as His children, could let men's lives be abruptly cut off
without hope. A God who would let millions of helpless victims of war, and others dying of starvation in time of peace, be
snuffed out utterly would not be the God of Jesus. Nor would

79

He be the God even of our own best human insights. A God
able to make us is able to preserve us. A God good enough to
give us this present life, mixed as it is, can be trusted to complete it in a better one. Without immortality there is no real
answer to the brevity of human existence or the unmerited
pain that ranges throughout the life we know.

Because man is God's supreme creation, a creature of infinite worth and dignity, it is irrational to suppose God shatters
ruthlessly His handiwork. And because with all our faults and
frailties we are still God's children, we can know our destinies
are safe within His enduring care. Were there no other reason
for believing in immortality, the goodness of God is reason
enough.

If trust in God's goodness is at the heart of man's hope
of immortality, confidence in His daily assistance is almost
a description of man's practice of religion. Running as a
theme on what students talk and write about is the idea
that reliance on God is absolutely necessary to weather the
storms of human life. Nothing is too trivial for bringing
God into the picture. When a man fails an exam, he can
say to himself, "God must have had a reason for wanting
me to fail this test." Every angle is considered. "If the
student had not studied, perhaps this was God's way of
persuading him to study for the next test and learn something. If he had studied, maybe God had the motive of
persuading him to study better or differently. Still another
reason could be that God wanted him to be humble because he was not as smart as he thought. If a student stops
to consider these reasons, he can attain peace of mind."
Call it pragmatism, but the principle is meant to apply to
every contingency:

When there is to be no hope felt, God can give strength.
For example, some of the prisoners who were in solitary confinement in the Korean conflict owe their sanity to prayers. By

praying and believing that somehow God would help them out of their seemingly helpless situation, they gained strength to go on living. Apparently they were right, for they returned to tell their stories.

When a person is afflicted, such as being blinded, he may feel that he has nothing left to live for. Yet all he needs is to turn to his religion. He will find that he does have something to live for: He can still serve God by following the divine law. This in itself pleases God.

In still "bigger" catastrophes, such as the death of a loved one, the idea of eternal happiness for the deceased brings comfort; that a loved one has entered heaven after death eases the pain.

Where one student generalizes, another will specify and spell out in his own life the ways that personal trial or family tragedy brought him closer to God. A Protestant in the Reformed tradition had spent twelve years in church-affiliated school before entering college. He had taken Bible courses the first to twelfth grade, so that "I knew my Bible fairly well, but I must say I really did not know God." His first encounter with God, as he called it, came the summer after high school, when he found himself penniless and a thousand miles from home after invitation (and rejection) by a major league ball club. "I got so disgusted I got stone drunk and could barely make it back to the hotel. I woke up the next morning, not realizing it was Sunday until I heard the church bells. I went to church and asked God to give me the faith I needed so much at that time. My prayers were answered, and I felt the hand of God upon me."

About the same time, his young sister became ill with a strange malady which turned out to be cancer. The perfect composure in which she died, and the family's resignation to the loss, "made me see how kind God is to those who believe in Him and seek His help through prayer." But he shrewdly adds that it takes more than tragic experiences to insure faith in God. Unless the trials are patiently accepted, "faith in God will falter and soon fail." Sufferings are profitable, but only for those who trustfully receive what faith tells them comes from the hands of God.

Omnipresence. God's ubiquity is a mystery and most people either take it for granted or, if they try to explain what it means, resort to abstractions that have small value for daily living. A striking exception was the study of omnipresence that I received from a senior, who has since gone into social work. She began with the familiar couplet in the catechisms: "Where is God? God is everywhere." Then her comment: That is the answer in the catechism lessons little children learn. It is also in the heart and mind of every person who believes in God.

Every so often, she observed, in talking in the dorm or in class, or when thinking by herself, the idea of God occurs to her. We have our own conceptions of a Supreme Being that rules over us. Yet among these ideas is a common denominator, geographically common in the universality of places we find Him and conceptually in the uniqueness of recognizing His presence.

The pages that follow are the untouched words of this student. They reveal a depth of understanding that forces one to qualify the incredible judgment of those who say that college people are indifferent to God:

Almost everyone finds God in all places at all times. People 'feel' Him in churches, in subways, on boats, in airplanes, in nature. People see God in a towering redwood in California, in the corn fields of Iowa, in the waters of the Great Lakes, in the sunrises and sunsets of the Smoky Mountains. People 'hear' God in the laughter of children, the quiet talk of two people in love, the song of birds in the trees, the rushing of water down a mountain side.

I don't mean to say that people actually see, hear, or feel God, but rather that they see the wonders of His work and the only way they can justify the existence of such creations is by *knowing* there is a God who is all-wonderful, all-powerful, all everything.

I would like to explain some of the reasons which I feel, why there is a God and why I believe in Him. Perhaps the ideas may not be profound or even original, but they are the reasons I believe in God and they are the reasons why I know God does exist.

When I first think of God, I think of myself. Perhaps that may sound a little conceited, but it really isn't. When I think of the way babies are born, I know there must be a superior Being who was 'intelligent' enough to make the complex process.

Each time a person sees a new baby similar words are repeated—'He looks just like Bob except that he has his mother's eyes.' or 'He's the perfect image of his grandfather—look at the chin and the nose.' or 'He's got the bone structure of the Rogers' and the complexion of the Miller's.' What the people are saying is that the baby looks like a combination of the two families of his parents.

The very simple sounding, but very complex process of the union between the sperm and the egg in the ovary to produce another human being is one of the many things in nature that man can never hope to duplicate. It is developed by God and instilled in human beings so that they might continue to propagate.

Even the time of actual birth which is often very painful to the mother is a very special time for her and all those who help her 'deliver' the infant. It is a time of love and wondrous joy. It is the fulfillment of mutual love. He wants us to start life similar to the way His Son started His life on earth.

God wants each of us to know the love that Jesus received from Mary and Joseph. He wants us to know, share, and give the love and understanding, to help the child grow and yet let go when the time arrives, to share the happiness as well as the sadness. None of us can ever have the same deep degree of these things that Mary and Joseph had, but we can have them to a lesser extent.

From the time a baby is created, God is in him. And he grows with the help of God. When he is born, while he is living, when he 'dies,' and when he is 'reborn' in Heaven, God is in each person. God is inside of everyone—in their souls, in their hearts, and in their minds. Every act they do is somehow manifested by their acknowledgement or rejection of God.

God is also love. Love in all its forms, family love, love for one special person (marriage), love for parents, love for children, love for close friends, love for neighbors, love for people.

Love is shown in many ways—by a kiss, by a look, by a touch, by an act. You can see love in a parent's eyes when they look at their children, you can see love in an old couple walking down the street and holding hands, you can see love in the shy way a boy gives a girl some flowers, you can see love in the gentle words exchanged by neighbors, you can see love in an act performed because of love.

There are many shades and kinds of love, but they basically are the same. You want the best for a person you love and you will do anything you can for a person you love.

The many dull and dreary jobs a mother does for her family—the washing, ironing, cooking, cleaning—are all visible signs of the intangible concept. There is love in the father when he works daily to support his family. There is the love of children when they bring a special treasure home for their parents, a pretty rock given with the words 'cause I love you' or a picture painted 'because you're always so nice to me—most of the time' or a bed sloppily made 'I thought I would surprise you.' All of these things mean love in a family.

There is the kind of love you give to your spouse—generous, not seeking reward, giving encouragement. Love is in the special things that you do for your spouse because you know that he or she will receive some enjoyment from it. It is giving up seeing a play to see a western on television, it is going to see the in-laws when you would rather go to a baseball game, it is getting up at 5 a.m. to pack a lunch for the husband when he wants to go fishing with the 'guys.'

All these things are love and God manifests all of them. If God didn't 'so love the world that He gave His only begotten Son' we wouldn't be capable of such feelings. In His tremendous love for His people, God gave us the gifts of life and love.

When I feel the love I have for my parents, I feel love for God. I 'see' Him in my parents—in their thought and concern for me, in their many actions for me, in their love for me. No doubt there were many times when I hurt my parents, and yet they didn't turn against me or disown me. There is little doubt that I will hurt them in the future. And yet they love me now and will love me until the day they die. I feel the same about them. There is nothing I could do that would turn that love to hate.

I grew up in an atmosphere of love, understanding, and trust. There were many times when I could have done the wrong thing, but something always stopped me, and more often than not, (excluding moral concepts and free will) I would refrain from doing the act because of the shame that might be brought upon my parents. I didn't want to do anything that would harm them. I didn't want them to have the opportunity to lose the love and trust they gave me.

In a way I feel that the love I have for my parents, family, relatives, and friends, is also a love for God. Since God exists in all people and I do love them, I also love Him. But the paradox may lie in the fact that since I love God, I love people because He is in them.

Another place where God always comes to mind is in His house, the church. It need not be a great cathedral—it may only be a small, white wooden structure. Huge or small, elaborate or simple, the church is the house of God. God lives here just as He does in our hearts and souls. But a place of worship is something special. It is a home, a house for God, built by his adoring and worshipping people. It is dedicated to God for His many and great works. It is dedicated both in the memory of Him and in the hopes that we, His people, might spread His word and works while we are on earth.

There is something very, very special about the church.

The hushed reverence that surrounds the church for silent meditation. It reflects the quiet ways in which God can perform His wonders. It also reflects the peace and serenity that many people embody in God.

When I do go into a church and no one is there except myself and God I feel very close to Him. I feel that I can talk to Him and that He will listen and try to help me in any way He can. Words really can't describe the wonder and peace that I can find in a church—the contentment of communicating with God can't be put down on paper or even said in words. It is a feeling incomparable to any others. It is peace and serenity and love. It is a closeness with your Creator, the most supreme form of happiness known to man.

There is also something very special about services in the church. The word of God, delivered by His messengers to His people, is wonderful. It brings the people closer to God as they hear of His works, His hopes, and His promises. Hearing God speaking through His messengers is a spiritual rejuvenation for the listeners. They are brought closer to God by their reason, minds, hearts.

One example of the simplicity and complexity of God can be seen in the changing seasons. The entire process of change the earth undergoes in spring, summer, fall, and winter appears to be very simple, but yet it is so complex that the greatest scientists of the world, past and present, cannot explain the phenomena. Perhaps the changing of the seasons illustrates the life of Jesus: spring is the time He was born, summer is the time He matured and bloomed, fall is the time He performed most of His works, and winter is the time He was condemned and died, only to be reborn in the spring.

For me the most wonderful part of the Mass is Communion. When I think of the miracle performed at the altar—the changing of bread and wine into the body and blood of Christ—I feel there is nothing that compares to it. And when I partake of the body and blood of our Lord, a deep feeling of peace, serenity, and contentment envelopes me. I feel as though God is really inside of me, and that it isn't my imagination because I took Him as He told me I should.

When I am in church my thoughts will occasionally wander and other thoughts will enter my mind. But they cannot settle there, there is no room for them. Thoughts of God—His works and mercy and love—erase any other ideas I may have. Perhaps I do not always listen to the sermon or follow each step of the Mass exactly, but that is only because my mind is so involved with God that I have no time for anything else. At times I become oblivious to what is actually going on in the church and think only of how God has affected me. Some people say that this is sacrilegious, but I don't think that it is. All it means to me is that I am so lost in my own thoughts that I am temporarily unaware of what is actually going on about me. I am communicating with God. I feel He can hear me and can understand what I am trying to say even though it sometimes comes out in a confused jumble. I feel that He is helping me, for my thoughts seem to become more organized, clearer, and I know what I am thinking. I feel close to God; I feel He is reaching out His hand to help me on my way.

Not only do I 'feel' and 'hear' God in a church, I also 'see' Him there. I don't actually see Him, but I do see more of His works. In a church, just as any other building or structure, God exists.

Perhaps He doesn't exist in the structure itself, but God does exist in the people who designed and built the building.

No one could ever design a building, no one could ever design the machinery, no one could ever construct the structure unless God were there to give him a helping hand. Without the mind and reason that God gave to us, we would be nothing.

God elevated us above other animals. He gave us reason so that we could accomplish things. Without our minds we are nothing, with our minds we are all.

None of the advances and accomplishments that man has made could have been done without the help of God. Man was able to invent and discover, because God had allowed him to do so. Without God to help us we would be without cars, trains, and boats. There would be no cures for polio, cancer, small pox, and other diseases There would be no love in the world, for we would have no example.

Almost everyone, at one time or another, questions the existence of God. Doubt appears usually at the time of death or in the event of a war. People ask how God can let such a thing happen to persons. How can He allow a war to start and continue? How can He let so many people die needlessly? To me the answer is simple—now that I have reasoned it out to the best of my ability. God allows wars so that we can appreciate His peaceful ways of accomplishing things.

As for death—when we ask why God has let a person die, we are usually thinking only of ourselves. We are angry with God for taking away a person we love. Being extremely selfish we don't want the person to go away from us. We want him there with us, living with us, not merely being a memory. We want to touch him and feel him, not just think of him. We really are selfish, for we want to deny a person the right to see God. We want him with us and not with God. And yet death is much better for a person because then he is with God and not with us.

God is also in nature. Where else can a person see God more clearly than in the many aspects of nature—the trees, flowers, waters, grains, animals, and birds? This is proof of God. Someone or Something had to make all these things in the beginning. Who else but God?

There is so much in nature that reminds me of God that I could write for pages of His many miracles. Take the snow-flake, for example, Each snowflake is individual, no two are ever alike. Each one is distinctly shaped just as each person has his own separate identity. Each snowflake is different from the other—just as a person is different from other persons. The snowflake is so beautiful, so delicate, and so perfectly formed. Science cannot duplicate the making of snowflakes now, and I doubt if it ever will be able to. This is something that God alone can do. I can feel God when the snow is gently falling outside or when there is a full-scale blizzard. The whiteness of the snow symbolizes the purity of God. It can get tarnished when it comes in contact with some of the 'glories' of our civilization, but nothing can ever take away its beauty.

When I go outside after it has snowed, especially in the late evening or night, it seems as if the entire earth has turned into a church for God. The ground is covered with soft, white snow; snow is gently falling to the earth; trees and bushes are covered with snow that reflects the light of the moon and the stars. The soft wind seems to be whispering that God does care for me and He wants me to enjoy another one of His miracles.

One thing I especially enjoy doing is walking, just taking a walk along a country road or a path through a forest and looking. Looking at the ground I walk on, the sky above me, and the things around me. At times like this I can no more deny the fact that there is a God than I could deny the fact that I see these things.

I also see God in the trees and flowers on the earth. The rose is considered to be the most beautiful flower because of its rich beauty and scent. To me a rose symbolizes the beauty of God, a wild kind of beauty which all can enjoy but which none can hope to duplicate, as beauty that puts a catch in the throat of the beholder and even a tear in the eye when the beauty is first seen.

Not only the rose, but all flowers that people enjoy were created by God to give us beauty and joy. We cultivate them so that we may enjoy their beauty. They have no practical value for us; they do not clothe us, nor do they provide food. Why do we continue to grow them, except to enjoy their beauty and to remind us of God?

Animals too remind me of God. God gave them to us for food and companionship. We kill many animals so that we may live, and we have other animals so they might give us companionship when we are alone save for God.

I also see God in water: in streams, lakes, ponds, and sea of the earth and in the water of the rain. Each drop is separate but each works with the others as God wants man to work with Him. The stormy seas with high waves and fierce-looking whitecaps or the peaceful serenity of a mountain stream show the wonder and power of God. Water is a force that man has not completely harnessed and its wild free-flowing beauty is similar to that of God's. He loves all of us and I think He wants the best for us. Yet He gives us free will and conscience so that we may make choices for ourselves.

In that respect I can compare God to my parents. They want the best for me too. I know that they are 'standing behind' me in all that I do, hoping for the best, offering aid when I cannot complete a task on my own yet hoping I can choose and make my choice the best one possible and then follow through. God is the same. Through my parents He has instilled many things in me—the way I use them is up to me, but He always hopes it is for the best.

But most of all, God is in each one of us. No matter how alone we may feel, we know that He is with us. He never leaves us. We can turn to Him any time of the day or night and find Him there.

These sentiments are not unique. They are only better expressed than most students could describe them. They reveal what an educator may be years in the profession without truly appreciating—that the deepest hunger of college people is their search for meaning, and they are impatient with anything less than authenticity. Many, like the one quoted, discover the ultimate meaning in terms that few theologians could improve upon. Others are less accurate, though not less articulate, in talking about "what really matters in life." Yet all types, even the most beatnik variety, tell you they are searching for identity, by which they mean for a purpose in life beyond what they can see or sensibly perceive. They are frankly looking for God, whom they discover in different ways.

THREE

PRAYER

Awareness of Need

THERE is no better index of the students' religious commitment than their pratice of prayer. It is like a barometer that shows how strong or weak is their faith, and how actively their religious principles influence daily life.

All of this would be a platitude except for another dimension that the formative years of college bring into the understanding of one's religion. For most young people, even those with only minimal church-affiliation, religion has meant some kind of communication with the unseen and spiritual world. The communication may have been sporadic or only occasional—though generally more constant than we might suppose—but it was there from childhood.

As they approach adulthood and mental maturity, one of the first things they try to make intelligible is this business of prayer. No student is exempt from the self-examination, although naturally some take it more seriously than will others. They want to make sense of this "talking with God" which their parents and Sunday School teachers considered so important.

I wish I could do justice to what college people think

of prayer and how prominently it figures in many of their lives. It would prove better than almost anything what responsibilities the teaching profession has to respect this crucial area of the human personality.

At least I can quote at length from what they told me about their notion of prayer, of its influence on their conduct and ideals, of the need they feel to commune with Someone above themselves, and how satisfying they find every intellectual support for a practice that instinct tells them is near the heart of man's relations with God.

Man's Encounter with God. A sophomore whose family comes from several generations of highly cultured people came to grips with the essence of prayer as neither psychological soliloquy nor magical superstition but, in his own words, a human encounter with God.

He began by pointing out that if we take our cue from the Bible, prayer is an offering up of our desires to God for things agreeable to His will. So conceived, the stress is placed where it belongs, on God and His will. For no matter how sincere the desire or devout the form of words, a petition is not prayer unless God and the doing of His will are at its center. This rules out the mechanical parroting of words, even great words like those of the Lord's Prayer, that one's own will may be done by God. It also gives the lie to those conceptions of prayer that reduce it to "informing God" or trying to "move" Him to do what we want:

To pray rightly we must let the Lord "open our lips." Prayer is not informing God of something He does not already know or pleading with Him to change His mind. Prayer is the opening of the soul to God so that He can speak to us.

There is also in prayer communion and response in which we speak and God responds. Prayer, as I have stated before, is the offering up of our desires to God. This means the voicing

92

before God of whatever is deepest within the soul with expectation that He will hear and answer. The answer comes in many ways—in the strengthening of soul, in direction for action, in quieting of anxiety, in assurance your sins are forgiven. The answer does not always come as the person who is praying expects or desires. However, unless the person who prays believes that in some way God can, does, and will answer prayer, he stops praying. No intelligent person will continue to pray if he thinks he is merely talking into the air.

What makes prayer possible from the side of man? Assuming that when a person prays he effects something, what basis is there in reality for supposing that anything he can do will "affect" the Almighty? Those who question or deny the validity of prayer have a strong case, if you grant their first premise, that the whole universe (with man included) operates according to fixed and immutable laws. But once grant that man at least is not absolutely determined, then you have an intelligent basis for prayer. "Prayer would be meaningless apart from the existence of human freedom. God has not made us mechanical robots or puppets; and because He has not, He expects us to see our freedom in co-operation with his righteousness." On the other hand, we are not so free that whatever we want or ask God to give us is automatically granted. The "naively confident" suppose that "prayer defies the restraints which surround us," of which the greatest is our dependence on God's will. Mistakenly thinking that prayer is a sort of talisman to be waved in God's direction, and presto He responds, they are disappointed and "likely to end in frustration and despair."

Some do not pray, and college has its quota of cynics who ask if praying for rain will bring down water from the skies. No two people are alike, and it is impossible to give more than general reasons why anyone resists the desire to call upon God:

Many people do not pray at all, and I believe there are many factors involved. The most common barriers to prayer are found in personal attitudes, social environment, and the frustration of unanswered prayer.

The most difficult barrier, not only to prayer but to religion in general, is the lack of any real awareness of the need of it. Our society with its multitude of competing claims crowds religion to the wall.

It is by getting lost in rivalry with competing interests that prayer slips out of life. Relatively few people deny outright the validity of prayer. Ask at random a dozen people if they believe in prayer, and what are their replies? Perhaps one will deny it is anything but wishful thinking, and another will give a strong affirmative testimony. From the rest you might hear something like this. 'It seems to make people feel better. It's all right if people want to. I suppose it's a good thing to do; I haven't thought about it lately.' Until trouble arises, the matter will rest. Self-sufficiency is the particular temptation of the strong, for as long as one has good health, a good job, social standing, and a fine family, one is apt not to think much about needing anything from God.

Self-sufficiency takes many forms. The most common form is the satisfaction with one's own integrity. Nevertheless, this is no barrier of slight proportions among people who think they are as good as other people, and therefore think they are good enough.

On the practical side, a grave hindrance to prayer nowadays is the noise and bustle that surround us. More than once students complained that what they most wanted, and often lacked, was quiet—just plain quiet, not only to study but to pray:

One of the aspects of modern life most detrimental to personality and prayer is that the individual person is seldom alone. Everybody needs certain areas of privacy for his best enrichment for social living. Where in a life like this is there any quiet solitude?

Prayer is not easy under such conditions. In a life of such tension and strain, prayer is esential if areas of calm are to be maintained. If one believes in prayer enough to make the effort and has learned the presence of God, inward prayer in the midst of the most crowded environment is possible. This takes self-discipline, and continual reliance on God. That one can pray in a subway, at a machine, in the midst of confusion, is demonstrated by the fact that many people have done it.

Aloneness, therefore, is not essential for prayer, although it helps. Yet in another sense the company of others may be of great value, if the group prays together. "If people can pray together and lift their desires to God, there is no firmer cement to bind the group together. When each member of the family goes his own way without much concern for the interests of others, there is no deep foundation on which to build a common life. This is why the last trace of family worship, the saying of grace at meals, ought to be maintained if there is any possible basis on which to keep it without its seeming to be a mockery."

Praying together among close friends can be a rich and rewarding experience. Prayer in the smaller and more intimate surrounding of those we love could work wonders. "Many friendships which thrive for a time and then go on the rocks could be cemented for eternity if there were spiritual depths at the center to be shared. Friends who live together but who have not yet formed the practice of praying together have great treasures yet to be discovered," as the student himself had learned.

A man of faith has no exclusive times for prayer, but he does pray regularly. "Apart from public worship in church or chapel, the most important times of private prayer are

upon awaking, at bedtime, before meals, at regular intervals through the day, and during an uninterrupted period
which can be fixed for any convenient time but must not
be left to circumstance." Each of these has a method or
technique that will differ for different people:

When a person first gets up in the morning, his first
thought ought to be of God. This shouldn't take any longer
than a few seconds before one gets out of bed to start the
hurried scramble of the day.

There are various ways to do this. One can look out of the
window and see nature in all its radiant beauty and thank
God for it. One can thank God for his wonderful family and
care throughout the day. This morning prayer is a vital setting
for the day. If one gets up tired, cross and blue, there is no
better way to bring sunshine and happiness to one's inner
being.

For most people bedtime is a time of relaxation and
leisure and thus offers more opportunity for unhurried
communion with God. It is the proper time to thank God
for all the blessings of the day. It is also the best time to
think of one's shortcomings and bring them before God.
"Quiet bedtime surrender of the soul to God releases all
the tensions and anxieties which have developed through
the day. So just as the first thought in the morning ought
to be of God, the last thought should also be of Him."

Above all, everyone should "take time out during the
day for communion with God." Call it meditation or just
plain spiritual reflection, "the only essential principle is
that it must be a time of leisure and free from interruption." Another recommendation is that "it should not be
limited to the words of another." Better speak to God in
your own words, because "to say a prayer without inwardly
responding to it is no more useful to the devotional life
than to read the newspaper." This is the danger of confin-

ing prayer to memorized formulas, and not cultivating the art of praying from one's heart.

To offset any impression that the man who wrote so clearly on the art of prayer was a starry unrealist, it is worth closing his testimony with a reference to his story (told elsewhere in this book) about getting "stone drunk" after rejection by a major league ball club. When his "kid sister" lay dying of cancer, he saw the hand of God in the visitation, but only after a terrific struggle. He quietly attributed to "Judy" the fact that several agnostic members of his family "found and accepted Christ as their own Savior," and that he was "brought closer to God through this faith-trying experience." Among other things, he learned how to pray.

But it cost him. Not everyone in college was as devoted as he. "There is probably no point at which the spiritual life is more affected," he admitted, "than by the fact that one's friends and closest associates either scoff at religion or just are indifferent to it. It is very hard to keep up a habit of churchgoing and private prayer when no one else with whom one has common interests does it. If there is open ridicule for being pious, only the strongest can face it and keep going." Social pressures have enormous power.

Another man, in graduate school, approached the subject of prayer from a different angle. He conceived prayer as "practicing the nearness of God." In prayer a man lifts to the care of the Almighty all the disharmonies, shortcomings, thoughtless decisions and concerns of daily life, on the assumption that God is interested in these things.

More than useful, however, prayer is necessary if the man of faith is to survive in a world of unbelief and not be smothered by its weight:

The believer must pray to keep spiritually fit, to exercise his soul and mind as he exercises his body through movement.

97

He must pray to develop spiritual fibre and backbone, to keep himself in top shape for the race of life.

The believer must commune with the invisible, spiritual world in order to escape the humdrum of daily existence. The noises, the gadgets screaming for attention, the chatterboxes, the gripers, the gossipers, the activists, the routine clicks of the clock which toss him from one engagement into the next, are all part of that inescapable segment of life which fosters anxiety and confusion, often stifling real growth. While carrying contemporary life to its extreme, the believer may develop an actual fear of the quiet hour, a fear of facing God and himself.

Unless a man prays, so this pre-theological student felt, he will go the way of all flesh and become too preoccupied with the "duties" of daily routine to grow or, perhaps even remain alive, in that deeper life of the spirit which alone is worthwhile.

In Time of Need. Less eloquent defenders of prayer can yet be poignantly graphic when they tell how this practice carried them through the "dark hours" of personal conflict and trial. In a few sentences, the most painful experience of a lifetime may be summarized.

Throughout life everyone is confronted with moments of mental confusion. College students especially may undergo a test of faith. It may shake the foundation of the truths they have learned.

I experienced such a disaster this year. It was during a period when depression, due to various reasons, had set in. I began to question the laws of the Church, and even protested disbelief in them. Only now advice was not easily accessible. Boarding at school is quite different from living at the closeness of the parish priest. At college, religious indifference is very possible because no one compels us to pray, go to Mass, or receive the sacraments.

For several weeks I became lax in my religious duties. I was too independent and felt that I could straighten things out alone. It was as if I were waiting for an angel to come and tap me on the shoulder and say, "All right, you can wake up now. The terrible dream is over."

But nothing happened. More unbearable situations came into focus, thus causing my spirits to hit rock bottom. One day while sitting on my bed, I mentally reassembled every incident which led up to my condition. Nothing was getting better and it never would, simply because I hadn't turned to the only person who could really help me. Someone who knew my every thought, namely, God. At that moment God was the only friend I had.

And so I poured my heart out, even though He already knew my troubles. I prayed harder than I ever had before. My immortal soul was on the verge of death, and I refused to seek assistance. How close I was to losing the Faith.

Immediately, my morale was lifted from the depths of emotional instability. I became motivated both spiritually and physically. How fortunate I was that God listened to my plea and elevated me from my sad state into tranquillity.

Her struggles with doubt came back again, but by then she had learned how to deal with them. The quiet confidence that came from prayer allowed her to look at the faith dispassionately and profit from reassessment.

A married woman who returned to college in middle age had a more prolonged conflict. Six months after marriage, she was informed about her husband's chronic illness which the doctors said would not give him a life expectancy beyond the early thirties. He was twenty-seven then. "Words can never explain the turmoil and the sleepless nights that took place. Many times these words flashed through my mind: 'In sickness and in health,' a part of the marriage vows."

The only hope seemed to be in God. "Prayers were countless. Not only mine but those of his mother and others. Evidence showed, I felt, that prayers are not answered. As the years went by and he lived beyond the middle thirties, outliving the doctor's prediction, and we had three children, it was clear that all this was because prayers were answered. Christ shows the way, and many times we are blinded to the little things."

Lesser needs have also been found to be satisfied through contact with the spiritual world. With only a brief Sunday school background, a coed confided that praying had never been easy. But once she learned from experience that prayer is a personal communion with God, she began to practice what could only be called meditation and since then her life has not been the same:

I feel that to pray is the most personal, sacred act a human can perform. Each of us prays in a different way, for we are all different individuals with different wants and needs.

For some reason my prayers seem more thoughtful and satisfactory when I am alone. I find it rather difficult to pray while in church. A person must worship God on the Sabbath and this is done by attending his church. I feel this should be done, but my praying time is not just on Sunday morning. This may sound strange, but I feel closest to God when I walk alone in the evening. I somehow know that He is listening and I can talk with Him.

Praying also makes me feel nearer to my family when I am away. I know God will watch over them and guide them. Perhaps I am close to them because I know they are praying for me too. If prayer can unite loved ones, I see no reason why it cannot unite the world. God loves us still, and we all have our place within this life.

Prayer has given me strength at times, and perhaps it has given me more than I realize. I feel God gives me much, and I return so little in comparison. I know I am lacking in many ways, and I have failed him many times.

The best guidance in the world is God, if you will let Him into your heart and life. But we must be willing. Prayer is the answer. It is the small man that finds it meek and humble to pray. We should humble ourselves to God in reverence and enduring love. I feel God will guide me in the right direction during my life if I, as one of His children, never find my life too busy to pray.

Implicit in these affirmations is a philosophy of life that admits man's inability to work out his destiny without divine help. Not many college students have heard about Pelagius, and when they do they are spontaneously repelled by his theory of man's independence. Most of them know, as by instinct, that happiness somehow depends on prayerful dependence on God.

Divine Assistance. A workable definition of God for many young people would be "the Being who responds to our prayers." There is a personalist approach to the Deity that practically avoids theological analysis, and when I find it I usually suspect plagiarism or unwitting quotation from some speculative author they had read.

This is so true that people whose faith has grown dim or who are struggling for religious identity find it hardest to accept the notion of a God that actually condescends to listen to puny, little men.

One junior thought he would canvass the opinions of some of his friends on the subject of prayer. He made recordings of a discussion with three others, among whom was one that said he was an atheist. The first question raised was, "Why do you think you should pray?" The "atheist" regularly objected to the idea that he should have to call upon God when he needed something, or be grateful that something had been received. "I definitely do not believe it," he claimed. "I don't believe that God has any effect on me. Do you think God listens to every little prayer that goes on every evening." He was told, "yes." "He hears every little kid in the world that says, 'Now I lay me down to sleep,' or whatever way they pray at night? Do

101

you believe that?" Again, "yes," "How? What can you base something like that on? That He's got 150,000,000 ears?" Neither side convinced the other, but both recognized that to admit the necessity of prayer is to affirm man's complete reliance upon God.

Many discussions about religion end in a stalemate because neither party knows enough about the subject to convince the other. For this reason I recommend that students first think through and then write out their ideas on a topic like prayer, forcing them to reflect and read further in the field. The result is always greater mental clarity and corresponding ease in the sharing of convictions. One upperclassman gave me the fruit of his reflections:

As I sit back and think about my spiritual life, I wonder how I would be able to exist through tomorrow if I could not use prayer to back up my spiritual beliefs. A good friend of mine who considers himself an agnostic, although I have my doubts, tells me that prayer never actually helped anyone. He argues that all it has done for mankind is to confuse the minds of world leaders so the decisions they make become twice as difficult. He might use any method approved by Robert Ingersoll to argue the point.

But I think that prayer, or the power given to men through prayer, has kept the world from being completely dominated by madmen. As individuals, we have the desire to maintain our personal motives, and as a nation we have been given the strength to live under a constitution written by men who worshipped God and prayed to Him for guidance. Therefore, religion and prayer have proved necessary to a nation that has many times been denied its freedom.

He argued from the continued survival and prosperity of the country built on the principles of prayerful invocation of the Deity. How can anyone still claim to be agnostic and hold that "prayer has served no purpose" through almost two centuries of the nation's existence? Then he applied the same principle to every person individually, and urged that without prayer religion is quite meaningless. It is like a clever theory that has no impact on real life. "When I think of religion," he explained, "I always associate it with prayer." The two are (or should be) inseparable:

Religion without prayer would be the same as the earth without the heavens, if I might use this comparison. I feel very deeply that the person who really prays has crossed the threshold of spiritual consciousness and has reached a higher relationship with the Almighty.

Whether we look up to God as a person or whether we regard Him as the infinite source of life working through everlasting laws, our final contact with Him must come through consciousness. No matter how we interpret His relationship to us, we can only enter into conscious relations with Him when we cross our own spiritual consciousness. Men may feel they are religious, happy, and useful to the world, but without prayer they will never truly acknowledge God.

It seems quite clear to me that all serious men, whatever their natural ability or intellectual training, must pray. They should pray not only for natural help or even primarily for strength to live rightly, but to know God.

He had found out from practice that prayer opened the mind to a deeper "consciousness of God." It changed a speculative knowledge of the Deity into something personal which, he said, taught him that God is someone you experience.

However, this attitude is a bit unusual. The more prosaic concept of prayer is that it gives people access to God in time of need. "We are so vain," students confess, "we feel that we do not need Him. Instead of being the last place to go, God should be the first. We all need faith and courage, and by praying for God to guide us, He gives us the strength."

When talking about prayer, college people seldom use the familiar categories. A junior in the General Curriculum said it was hard to write on the subject because information was lacking. So "I may be somewhat shallow in expressing my feelings." The reader may judge how shallow these feelings were:

I regard prayer as a very intimate and spiritually fulfilling conversation with God. I regard prayer as a privilege given to me by God in order that I may help myself in addition to the helps He gives me through His other gifts.

When I give my mind completely to God's attention, I am able to reveal my most inner thoughts and feelings without embarrassment, because this union with God is with Him alone. With this gift I am not only allowed to make myself known to God, but through these revelations I am able to see myself in a more subjective light.

After disposing of this psychological value of prayer, there were recollections of early childhood when God was mostly thanked for blessings He conferred. "During the slow process of growing up, these prayers of thankfulness remained, but they expanded to include prayers of adoration, penance, special intentions, and seeking guidance." Over the years it became a spontaneous activity. "I find it almost impossible to regard praying as a burden. Nothing comforts me more than to know that at any time I choose, I may engage in a union with God, and each time I open my mind and heart to Him, He is willing to receive me."

A senior who went to Europe after graduation sent me a dozen pages from Switzerland that are at once a prayer and, as the title indicated, a "manifestation."

Addressed to "God," the statement reveals more than the student ever guessed. Coming from a person in the

Protestant tradition, it shows the conflict that goes on inside the souls of most college men and women—perhaps less pronounced but equally crucial, even when they cannot express themselves adequately.

Somewhere in college, undergraduates get the idea that faith in God is a crutch to support their weakness. They rebel against the insinuation that they must go through life leaning on some abstraction of the mind, which their parents and Sunday school teachers told them was needed to achieve happiness.

Some never get over this rebellion, or at least they never fully recognize the contingency of human nature and its built-in necessity of calling upon God in frequent prayers. Others, like this education major, discover that invoking God can be practiced without denying one's autonomy; that prayer may be elevating, and dependence on the Deity a form of self-realization:

About two months ago I started writing about you, rather than to you, but I couldn't finish my writing because you changed. You changed so much. I couldn't understand you or keep up with you. My thoughts began to contradict my words. I became more and more confused. You're terribly hard to understand, you know. I'm sure I'm not the only person you have confused either . . . why do you do it. I imagine your reason would be something to the effect that this confusion you instill in the minds and souls of so many of us is healthy for us and makes for stronger and more understood values and characters by the time we've untangled our confused minds. Well, you're right and wrong.

I should probably be saying "Who am I to tell God he's wrong?" But I think you are wrong. You're right with people like me. I'm not as confused anymore, and I feel all the better a person for it. I know pretty much what I believe about you now, and I feel better. I doubt I'll ever be completely unconfused, but at least I know where and how to look for my answers now. My complaint is that there are people who don't

105

have the patience or maybe who don't have enough faith or guidance in the first place to guide them into finding their answers, and becoming unconfused the way I did.

You aren't fair to these people, God. They are the ones who mentally do not become stronger. They sometimes become mentally deranged when they can't untangle the confusion you instill in their minds. It's horrid to be deranged. I hope you know what it is like in a whirlpool of feelings and emotions, falling into eddy after eddy, spinning through an abyss of bewilderment—not knowing where the light is or even if there is any. I'm not caught up in any eddies now, so I can see. I can see how bad it is for people who become so deranged that they give up on you. They give up trying to find out who you are. They get to a point where they don't care. They don't give a damn anymore, God, not a damn! Help them! Please help them! The ones that give up are the ones who need more help.

It's terrible not to have faith or believe in good. You're not a person anymore, you're just a vegetable—an unhappy vegetable rotting away to the point where you're not even good fertilizer anymore. You think you're happy, but it's just a rationalization. The good you know is a selfish good. You look for selfish motives behind anything nice. Anything good that is done appears to have a petty, selfish reason.

I must tell you here, the context of what I previously thought and started to write about you. The following is out of context:

I hate this idea called God. He is a termite helping to rot away the foundations of man, of his mind. Man's mind is his most precious possession and the greatest part of the human form that he has. This God theory has helped deteriorate the strength of this mind. Man looks to God as a religion. In the United States this religion has become another tool used in the class struggle. The middle class family doesn't go to church to pray to God, but to see who is there. They use it as a social tool. They don't choose their place of worship according to sought out beliefs. They choose them according to social directives. If they are a certain income bracket they certainly must go to the church on the hill in the woods where the others in the forty-thousand dollar income bracket go.

There are even families who chose their church according to convenience. A church was built on the corner of a new suburban housing development. Before the church was built, members went from door to door to see how many people would join their congregation regardless of previous religion. The majority of the neighborhood joined and they got quite disgusted when one man said he had no objections to their building the church, but that he wouldn't join.

Religion in America is pretentious, phony, and hypocritical. God is a figure for use as a scapegoat. He has lost much of his association with good and right. Middle-class materialism and selfishness would not be, if these people had a God. Juvenile delinquency, illegitimacy, and abortion rates wouldn't be at an all-time high if there was an unpretentious and unselfish belief in God—if God was what he is supposed to be. People don't really want a God unless He can be selfishly used as a scapegoat, nor do they want a religion unless it can be used as a means to material success. This is not God.

No, I can't believe that there is a God. God is love, or God should be love. But there is no real love left. All we have is phony love. Selfish, bogus, and misconstrued love. Love today is not God. It's dirty, filthy, writhing people in the gutter. It's words used to obtain personal satisfaction. It's corrupted humanity—grimy, specious minds that aren't humanity anymore because the most precious part of humanity is the mind and now it has been used and controlled by the physical part of humanity. Distorted, bogus humanity. Minds writhing with their bodies like mad dogs. To Hell with humanity . . . but I'm humanity. I am what makes humanity. My mind must be writhing too.

God is a spider. He crawls in and out of crannies instilling beliefs and not making them work. They never prove themselves, or He never proves Himself! So why not doubt him? People today need material proof! No, God doesn't need to be a magician. He needs to be a rational reason. There must be reason to him. There must be visual material proof by reasonable, rational means to prove that faith and God are real. He's easier to use as a scapegoat. It's easy for the belief in Him to turn into visions of a spider crawling through minds just biting and spreading turmoil and disease resulting in corruption. Big business is a large scale case of what is not only a result of this misconstrued God, but what is actually going on in individual minds.

I tried speaking to you God, but it never seemed to work. I didn't think you ever heard me, so I gave you up. I couldn't believe in something that was supposed to be good when all I saw was bad. All that presented itself to me was corrupt, cant, specious humanity. And you were supposed to make and direct this humanity. From what I had seen, you had done a dreadful job.

The last time I had tried to speak to you, you still turned your back. My mother! Like a serpent you inflicted the worst word in the English language upon her . . . cancer. I asked "Why, why?" Do something— let *me* do something—someone do something! I pleaded, "Don't hurt her. Hurt me. Hurt our dog. She doesn't care about our dog. But don't hurt her bird. She loves her bird." But no, you let a forty-two year old woman's bones go on deteriorating. I could see no reason, no why or because. Just hate. Hatred is all I saw and began to feel. In a world so corrupt and antagonistic there couldn't be a God, at least not in the true sense of your image.

Any studying I had done did nothing in the way of faith for me. I classified anyone who believed into one of two categories. The first were the ignorants. They were more or less mystics belonging in times before Christ. They're people who blindly believed because their parents and grandparents did. They never questioned a thing to find out for themselves what to believe. They only knew what was true according to what they had been told was true. The second group were people making up our materialistic society. They are the ones with a bogus, selfish belief in God. The ones who call themselves a member of a certain sect and don't know the Ten Commandments or the Creed they supposedly believe.

With this, my walls were built and my mind almost shut to

any alternative explanations. There was no real God. The God I'd learned about when I was little was not to be found. He had gotten lost in the shuffle of contemporary materialism. There was no real love, or uncorrupted good in the world I saw. This proved there was no God. If he was real—I wouldn't see selfish, filthy, petty, grabbing hands and minds everywhere I turned. He wouldn't let children starve all over the world, from hunger for food and hunger for love. He wouldn't let guns fire so loud and so long. I only read about international conflicts and it hurt. If I had actually seen them, I think I would have started a crusade against you.

With no God I wondered where people put their faith. Security is an innate need in human nature. With no faith in God, where does security come from? I tried a hypocritical faith in you like the others I saw, but the security derived from this was also phony. Real security cannot be pretentious. This only bred more discontent.

I must have retained some faith subconsciously, or at least the want of faith. Since that period I found some answers to my questions. Maybe I just found some new questions! Moreover, I did find someone I thought didn't exist. You knew all along that you were there! Why didn't you tell me sooner?! It doesn't matter. I'm just thankful you showed up at all. I just have one request . . . Please show some of the others who you are. Please, God. Those others who think you were blown away by the first atomic bomb. They need you too. They need to know you are here. Help them! Help me explain to them that they need to hang on to at least a milligram of faith and you'll prove yourself. Even through reason! I never thought I'd see you through reason, either.

It's amazing. Maybe I'm extremely ignorant and only believe in you because I gave up finding my own security. But I don't believe this could be so. You see, I had this theory that since there was no God, I had to find all security within myself. To get this security meant developing immense self-discipline and consequently self-satisfaction which would result in security. I could not put faith or trust in anyone or anything else, so I had to put it in myself. I did not approve of those who said they believed in you and who I knew were only using you, or what you represented, as a crutch to develop their own self-discipline. I could not imagine what kind of self-reliance this was when they used this fictitious thing they called God as a crutch to develop their own self-satisfaction.

How wrong could I be! I know now that if you can be a crutch to someone and help them develop a better and stronger character, you are doing good. If you can help them be self-reliant and self-disciplined, you are helping man use his human facilities to their fullest. When man uses you as a crutch in the sense of a scapegoat, then he is wrong . . . but only then.

I was wrong. I want to argue with my old beliefs and tear my irrational and blind defensive reasoning to shreds. It took common people, innocent people to show me the answers. I didn't have to go on reading and comparing great schools of thought, which only beckoned to confuse me more. Nor did I have to watch or listen to those "great people" anymore. Those successful ones (when rated in accordance with their materialistic values) who aren't really so great or successful when it gets down to bare values.

I realize people are the same all over the world. But I had to go to the other side of the world to find people who knew the real you. I didn't go searching intentionally for you or someone who knew you. That is what was so confusing at first. You crept onto the scene. It started when I saw so many old churches in England, Scotland, and Wales. The rolling, rich, green country-side was abundant with twelfth to eighteenth century churches. I looked with satisfaction at first when I saw so many of them abandoned. But then an elderly Welshman explained it was due to the rot eating away the foundations. This little man still worshipped in one thirteenth century church. He lived for this church and two others in the vicinity under the same conditions. They were abandoned in use but as he said . . . "they weren't abandoned in faith." I thought at first what a sad life he must lead, in such illusion about his old churches. But they were built in your faith and even though they were decayed, to the little old man they were still your houses.

You made me hesitate about those old churches. But you made me stop when I saw more and more of them on the continent. Here I saw many of them rehabilitated. I wondered why the people in such a backward and poor country like Spain spent money on the rehabilitation of churches. Then, a bewildered waif in this backward country, I was taken into a home in the Basque country and cared for. I completely forgot my distrust and was caught up in a generating atmosphere of love and heartfelt good intentions. They were not educated people, and at first I doubted the validity of their religious beliefs. These people had faith and believed in God, but it had been handed down to them through generations. They didn't question it or contemplate another religion. They just believed. Their belief was so good and so real that I became more and more convinced that American advancement made the perfect setting for the corrupted mores, norms, and values we have. I decided it was the smaller people who are good. Not the striving, materialistic, class-conscious maniacs we have at home!

I left my "little people" and proceeded to Lourdes. I soon found a contradiction to what I had just decided about the so-called "little people." It makes no difference what part of the world someone is from, or whether they are materially "big" or "little" persons. At Lourdes I saw "little people" misusing the central meaning of the Grotto. They had set up souvenir shops, several deep, surrounding the Grotto. These were my "little people" acting like the "big people" I had run away from! As pathetic as it was to my eyes, I learned something else at Lourdes. Cripples, sick, old, and young were sitting, lying, and even crawling near the Grotto.

I would have thought before, "How blindly ignorant of these people. What mental derangement that they should come from so far thinking they will be cured." But I cannot say that now because I see something else. These people have faith in you. So much faith they can't believe you'll let them

111

down—ever. I realized that all people: the blind, the crippled, the rich, and the poor, regardless of education, can legitimately believe in you and find love, understanding and good. There will be corrupt people in every culture. I cannot generalize and put them into categories as I did. I know I could go home now and find honest believers in you, people with faith, and people who know what real love is. I cannot condemn people who have not questioned you but just believe in you. They know their belief as good, as truth . . . as love. When you give such happiness, such peace of mind, and such faith, all as a way of life to people, I cannot question or doubt your being.

I now have proof of you. I complained I had no proof so I couldn't believe. What better proof could I have than that you heard me and gave me the support I needed. I can't ignore the many ancient cathedrals I have seen. Nor the tiny chapels hidden in every old castle. You must be real! People are not strong enough to have kept religion and faith alive by themselves so many centuries. I think I also understand the people I met in Hungary, now. The government won't rebuild their churches. Everything else is being rehabilitated, but the churches are being left to ruin. But the people keep these churches alive. They may be damaged from the wars, but the people's faiths aren't. If anything, they are stronger. I couldn't frown upon these people for the way they diligently pray every time they pass a church.

Before I would have thought they should have given up their faith in you since it had not gotten them anywhere. I see now, if they did not still have faith in you, many of them would not be able to bearably live their new way of life.

You need not worry, God. I understand now. But please don't forget to talk to those who still don't understand. I'll try to, but you must help me. I know you are here ready to help those of us who want your help. It's just that some people use your help in an evil way. They often do it innocently too! Help them and help them to help themselves. They think they are happy, but if they were to experience unselfish love, they

112

would experience a new happiness. Only you, God, can help us to know this happiness.

Thank you, God, for listening. It's helped me to understand even more.

Not the least value of reading such self-revelation is the evidence it gives of people grasping the inner meaning of prayer without being able to analyze its theology.

I have scarcely met a single student out of hundreds, who did not occasionally reflect on his need of a supramundane power and express this dependence in the depths of his soul.

FOUR

CHURCHES

Why Institutional Religion?

IT IS impossible to be indifferent to organized religious enterprise, whether Catholic, Protestant or Jewish, for the simple reason that "religion" in the abstract exists only in peoples' minds. The religion of real life is organizational, and whatever respect or its opposite a man has toward the church is a good index of his faith.

College students are vocal about the churches. They may be slow to express an opinion about God or His providence, and they are not so ready to philosophize about such things as grace or predestination. But they are never at a loss for words when it comes to talking about their own or someone else's religion, as they call it, by which they mean church affiliation.

For most young people before they come to college, the church of their parents is the form of religion which they know best. It is also the one they were taught to cherish above every commitment; to regard as a philosophy of life and, perhaps, the indispensable means of salvation. Small wonder that a common topic of conversation in the student center or residence halls is a "comparison of notes" on the relative merits of institutional religion. Practically every argument on the subject occurs in this context, and some students claim this exchange of ideas is more important to them than almost anything else in the university.

Whatever else a university is, it becomes a melting pot of religious denominations by the sheer coexistence of so many traditions on campus. Every type and level of church connection is brought together physically, and for four years the psychological miscegenation continues—to the detriment of some, the profit of others, but to a change and mental stimulation in every one.

Roman Catholicism. In many ways the prototype of religious institutionalism is the Roman Catholic Church, whose representation in American colleges is above its national average in population. Even in secular and state institutions, Catholics are as much as thirty percent of the total student body. The situation has so radically changed since the Second World War that a veritable crisis has set in, with consequences and ramifications that may affect the whole country. With the increased Catholic enrollment in state universities has come an increased demand for strengthening chaplaincies on campus and the development of instruction courses to meet what the Church considers a grave spiritual need. This in turn has given Catholic students a sense of belonging that a generation ago was quite unknown, and a desire to become integrated with the academic life of the university which they often find incompatible with their religious beliefs.

How do Catholics look upon their own commitment? Do they rebel against its indoctrination or at least chafe under its restraints? What do they make of the freedom that others enjoy in matters of faith and worship, and how many compromise when faced with the choice between conformity and isolation?

Under the limitations of this book it is impossible to do any more than suggest a few answers. One problem is that

Catholics vary so much, in their past education and home training, in native intelligence and fidelity to religious practices and, above all, in that deeply personal thing which makes every believer an individual. Persons are unpredictable, and Catholics are no exception.

As a rule those who had more Catholic education before college are better founded in their faith and more constructive in their criticism of the Church's policies. Those with less formal training are not only more critical but sometimes at variance with basic doctrinal positions.

One coed recalled when she began going to catechism as a child. "We learned prayers, and the nuns read stories to us. We learned new and strange things about God and angels. Then it was time for my First Communion. I was so proud and excited to be able to go to Communion with my mother." But things soon changed:

After the excitement of my First Communion wore off, I began considering catechism a bother. I couldn't go outside on Saturday morning to play with the kids. I had to go to catechism. At that time all we were learning were the same things over and over again: "Who made me? Who is God? Who created the world?" I felt I had to go to catechism because I heard the priest say in church one Sunday that it would be a sin for the parents if they didn't send their children to catechism.

When I began junior high, my religion became a problem for me. I was embarrassed to admit I was a Catholic. Had I learned the history of my religion and how the other religions broke away from Catholicism, I wouldn't have felt the way I did. I felt inferior and odd. Each time the topic of religion was brought up in class, I would sit as tense as could be, dreading the next sentence when the teacher might ask how many in class were Catholic. I had it all set in my mind that I would not raise my hand. I would sit there with that horrible fear until the topic was finally dropped.

By the time she reached high school the situation improved a little. At least catechism was more interesting. "We were now discussing how Catholicism pertains to our everyday lives, and the students were finally given a chance to voice their opinions." Then disillusionment again. The trouble was "it was too late to be learning those things. When I reached my junior year in high school, we were just beginning to discuss sex." And she had been dating a Jewish boy in the seventh grade!

Another thing she missed was even a rudimentary knowledge of other people's beliefs. "I wanted to learn about other religions. At no time in any of my catechism classes did I ever learn anything about other religions. Yet, when I talked to other people my age, they seemed to know their own religion and something about Catholicism too. They were also familiar with the Bible. I was never taught anything about the Bible in my catechism classes," with the result that she felt helpless (like facing a brick wall) "when discussing religion with someone who was not a Catholic."

A saving feature, in her opinion, of the twelve years of Catholic instruction while attending public schools was that her parents never once constrained her. "I was never pushed into my religion," she described it:

I think that is why I have such a keen interest in my religion now. I'm not tired of it. In my senior year I went to Mass every morning during Lent. I also went frequently on weekdays during the summer before I came to college.

I often wonder if I had gone to a Catholic school if I would have been so interested in religion. I know quite a few girls who went to a Catholic school and who were tired of going to Mass every day. They said that Mass on Sundays held no special meaning for them, like it did for me. They just regarded it as something they had to do and connected it with school work.

Other students had less religious training, and came from less formally Catholic environments. A sophomore whose father was Catholic, divorced and remarried, had never been confirmed. Her only religious education outside the home was for a short time before First Communion and then irregularly during high school. In spite of this meagre upbringing, she soon found out that "Catholicism is not just a religion but a way of life." It was tested and proved satisfactory:

During the last few years, I have had mixed emotions about my religion. I turned away from the Church (by turning away I mean stop going to Mass) at intervals only to come back unhappy. I have had trouble believing the Church's teaching only once that I can remember. It was a question about confession but I understood after it was explained.

I have never quit going to Mass because I didn't believe in it or in the religion; it was my idea that God couldn't accept me. It bothered me a great deal, and I finally went to talk to a priest, which helped me. The thought now of how this question haunted me and the many heartaches it caused seems like a waste of time. It wasn't a waste of time, though, because I learned of God's existence, and His love for all creatures. If Catholicism were not to be my religion, why then would He have bothered to keep me coming back to it. Perhaps this was His way of testing me.

Firmly rooted in her faith, she still believed that not all the Church's teachings are mandatory. "I have had the conviction for some time," for example, "that it wasn't necessary to attend Mass every Sunday to be a good Catholic. I always thought it was enough to love God and try to live the kind of life you should." She was trying to understand how this love of God and practice of virtue include the obligation of assisting at Mass when so many obviously good people do not participate in the central act of Catholic worship.

118

Catholics who have given up the practice of their faith while in college are numerous enough to cause churchmen alarm. Their life histories are not easily accessible, and they are not the ones who normally take courses in the Department of Religion. A recent study at Harvard and Radcliffe showed that twenty per cent of the Catholic undergraduates left their faith; and estimates among the Big Ten universities range between ten and fifteen per cent defections. Some return to the Church when the ethics of Catholicism become less imperative in later years, but it would be a mistake to suppose that all (or even the majority) leave because they find Catholic morality too demanding. Acceptance of ecclesiastical authority and the duty of believing beyond the mind's capacity to understand are dominant pressures to which the faith is subjected.

"I have always been greatly attracted to the papacy," an honor student admitted. "However, as much as I was told to believe that the pope was infallible—and nuns can be very convincing—I could never quite understand and accept it. I rarely asked questions because I knew what the answer would be, and I kept quiet most of the time probably out of fear. I did little to find out about the nature of my discontent" until coming to college. For the first time in his life he encountered "troubling facts about the papacy." Two years of exploration finally convinced him that "the papacy is a conservative, reactionary force clinging to its spent glory and, unless Vatican II succeeds, the Church will fail to keep up with the forces of modern times, many of which are tearing man apart." Then a brief conclusion: "I do not accept the papacy as the mainstay of my faith."

Those with little religious education sometimes discard the faith outright. They tend to equate the Church with authoritarianism and, in their search for autonomy, reject what to them is a threat to independence of thought:

To me there is no such thing as religion. I believe in a God, but I feel that it ends right there. This is the only thing I really believe in. I think that God created us, but everything else depends on us. We have to get to heaven on our own, if there is a heaven. I think also that man has to set his own code of ethics for himself for his relationship with society. What a man does is up to this code and nothing else.

Besides, there are too many conflicts in religion. Roman Catholics say that Calvinism is wrong. Why? Predestination is their answer. Roman Catholics also say that God knows beforehand what everybody will do. He knows all things, past, present, and future. Therefore what is the difference? It is things like this that make me cautious about a specific church. This is what religion means to me—nothing!

Another man claimed he had often discussed religion with priests but was unconvinced. When asked by a fellow-student if he believed in the Trinity, he said he did not. Life after death was uncertain. His main contention was that the very concept of God was under suspicion. It was something that men have conjured up as a "rationalization for the unexplainable." Religion has some value in helping people live decent lives; but even this implies a weakness to which the strong personality does not confess.

At the other extreme are Catholic students from every background, with or without parochial training, whose faith and principles are severely tested but whose commitment becomes stronger in the process.

A senior gave me a complete rundown on his four years at college, and the variety of issues that forced him to reexamine his beliefs. They began with his family.

One of his sisters was married to a man who left her five times in eight years. She would like to have gotten a divorce, but the priest advised against it. Her brother did not know what to say. "She is a good Catholic and is raising her children to be the same. At times I feel she wants the divorce. But then again she is much against it because she would not be able to remarry and receive the sacraments. I feel the Church should make some concessions in cases like this." However, he admitted the wisdom of the Church's severity. At school he was seldom allowed to forget his religious affiliation:

Whenever I am in a group discussing religion, I become a target for all the questions concerning Catholicism. One thing that I noticed here on campus is that many of the Catholic students seem ashamed of their faith. They will agree with a non-Catholic view that is contrary to Catholic belief because they do not want to admit that they believe. But really they do. Many times I have this feeling myself; but after thinking it through, I see the light and feel that I am right in my belief.

Also while here at school, I noticed that many students who are Catholic do not attend Mass on Sundays and days of obligation, and they don't fast or abstain on days appointed. I have had two Catholic roommates, and they were both lax in their faith. I got to know them both quite well, and their families were not like this. It was hard for me to see why they acted this way away from home.

Every basic belief and practice of Catholicism was brought into the open and scrutinized. He tried his best to satisfy every question. A "strict Methodist" told him she could not understand how Catholics could sin and then go to confession and be forgiven. "I then asked her what Methodists do when they sin." She told him they pray to God for forgiveness. He assured her that Catholics do the same. Birth control was a favorite topic of discussion. It was unlawful by Catholic standards, he would say, because the use of contraceptives is a means of preventing preg-

121

nancy by unnatural means. Then why rhythm? It is permissible because "this method requires self-restraint." He was often asked why Catholics do not eat meat on Friday. "I explain it this way. Christ sacrificed His life for us on Good Friday, therefore we make a sacrifice for Him by not eating meat on Fridays." Many times he was tempted to ignore the laws of fast and abstinence. He decided they were only feelings that have to be reasoned with to be overcome. Anyone can overcome these feelings, he believed, "if they would just think of all that God has given to them." There was no respite invoking such motivation:

Until I came to the university, I never realized that such feelings were held toward Catholics. Many, many times I have sometimes wondered what it would be like not to be Catholic. I get a real empty feeling when such a thought enters my mind. I suppose if I were not born a Catholic, I would most likely not be one today. However, I am a Catholic and very proud of the fact. Many of my Catholic friends in the dorm are doubtful of their faith at times. If they would only sit down and think it through, I am sure they would rid themselves of such doubt.

This man had no Catholic instruction in parochial schools. Besides receiving catechism lessons as a boy, he was privately tutored in the New Testament by the local parish priest. Another senior had twelve years of formal Catholic education. She experienced less of the conflict that her classmate described and attributed all the devotion of her faith to her parents' training and example. "In our family going to Church is a normal and natural thing. Our religion is practiced and is just as much a part of us as the air we breathe." Less concerned about defending the faith and more in living an interior life, she went through college with a minimum of friction from her environment.

My love for God is the only motive for my efforts to lead a good Catholic life. Because I love Jesus Christ, I believe all His words. The greater my love for Him, the stronger and more alive will be my faith in Him. In my opinion faith is the foundation of love, and is brought to perfection by love. Love helps me to believe not only with my mind, but also with my will.

If I were given a choice tomorrow between my life or my religion, I would choose my religion because without it my life wouldn't be worth living. I think those people who choose material goods and pleasures in preference to friendship with God do so because they have little or no faith. Their faith blows hot and cold; they believe only what they choose to believe. All the goods of this earth could not satisfy me if I did not have God to bring contentment to me in success and failure. My success would be great if I lost all to gain all.

She concludes with the hope of being able to communicate to others something of her own idealism. "As a future teacher, I will have a great responsibility to guide my students toward a complete education, one that will develop their bodies, minds, and souls. The danger of our future is not in the atom bomb but in the minds and wills of men who hold the power of the bomb in their hands. If I can develop spiritual values and teach what is morally right and wrong, then I will be living up to my duties as a teacher, and at the same time achieving heaven by fulfilling my vocation." While the terminology is Catholic, the ideals are not unlike those of thousands who believe in God and whose faith is deepened in the atmosphere of a state university.

Protestantism. Christian students in the Protestant tradition are in a different position from their Catholic friends. They are normally the majority and in many ways the university climate is more congenial to their way of thinking. This may be accounted for partially by what Paul Tillich calls "the Protestant principle," according to which nothing that is man made, or less than God, may be respected or honored as though it were divine. "Protestantism," says Tillich, "has a principle that stands beyond all its realizations. It cannot be defined by a definition. It is not exhausted by any historical religion; it is not identical with the structure of the Reformation or of early Christianity or with a religious form at all. It transcends them as it transcends any cultural form. On the other hand, it can appear in all of them; it is a living, moving, restless power in them. The Protestant principle contains the divine and human protest against any absolute claim made for a relative reality, even if this claim is made by a Protestant church." He further explains that this principle is the guardian against all attempts of the finite and conditioned to usurp the place of the unconditional in thinking and acting. It is the prophetic judgment against religious pride, ecclesiastical arrogance, and secular self-sufficiency and their destructive consequences.

Consistent with this principle, it is easy to see how students would react to religious beliefs that seem to absolutize dogmatic creeds, or even to secular institutions which inhibit freedom of thought. One of my students in Comparative Religion expressed the Protestant principle (and her faith) rather clearly when she distinguished between the essence and form of all religions.

More than anything else, religion is the means of attaining harmony in the universe. Harmony first of all between man and God, secondly within man himself, and lastly in the relationship with one's fellowman. Disrespect and lack of tolerance for views other than one's own has resulted in making harmony a rare and difficult achievement.

One may speak of two aspects of religion, its essence and form. The essence of religion is directed to us from God and is known clearly only to the soul of man. Essence is that which is infinite in religion, and is not affected by such factors as intellect and culture. Form is the more apparent aspect of religion and the most diverse. Although often of great beauty and inspiration, it would be only vain ritual were it not for the essence.

Let us define the form of religion as the influence of human interpretation on the essence. Paul speaks of "seeing through a glass darkly." In effect, religion as we ordinarily think of it reflects this view. Since man is a complex being, one might expect many factors to influence his interpretation of Divine Truth.

The capitalization of the last two words was not rhetorical. It symbolized a distinct approach to Christianity (and the churches), in which the essential element of any belief is not its external creed or ritual cult but the invisible spirit of God, who is the same and unchangeable in every religious faith. Accordingly, it would be a mistake to suppose that any religion has a monopoly of God's revelation or that one form of worship is objectively superior to the rest. "Each of the major religions seeks true knowledge of the why and how of life and death, of evil and suffering, and of the world as we know it. Each is aware of Something-not-seen that has greater reality than what is perceived through the senses and reason; and each realizes that the link between man and this Something must be found if human life is to have any depth or meaning." If we must speak of superiority of one religion over others, it should be only in relative terms. Thus Christianity may be called higher than, say Buddhism, "and for this reason what one believes is of vital importance." But that is only because the human interpretation of God's nature is more profound in the Christian tradition. If we are truly catholic in outlook, "we must be willing to concede the value of insights in faiths other than our own. All who seek to know God deserve the respect of those who are engaged in a similar quest." Christians no less than Buddhists are questing. Neither may claim to have already found.

A specialized problem for some students is how to reconcile fundamentalist concepts of faith with the findings of science, and adapt certain norms of moral behavior to the demands of college life.

One of the most common issues was evolution. Time and again I was questioned about the interpretation of Genesis, whether it could be harmonized with human evolution. Both sides contributed to the confusion. Scientific popularizers and textbooks left the impression that direct, lineal development of the human species from the lower animals was an established fact; "as well known as the laws of bodily digestion," according to one author. The same sources might digress to point out the conflict between faith and science which this posed, since the churches were unalterably opposed to the theory of evolution. On their side, a surprising number of conservative denominations still teach that evolution in any form is incompatible with the Bible. Students were caught on the horns of a dilemma, either remain Christian and reject science, or take the findings of science and cease to believe in the Scriptures.

One of the deepest satisfactions they received was to have explained to them that so far from being opposed to evolution, Genesis encourages it by the clear witness of the Bible. Where God is said to have breathed into Adam's body a spirit, thus creating a soul out of nothing, He began with something (symbolically slime of the earth) to first form a body into which the soul could be infused. This something might have been a living organism, and in that case the essentials of evolution are admitted. Several upperclassmen told me that it "saved my faith" to know that evolution could be squared with biblical revelation. It was secondarily important that evolution was still a theory, or that ancient writers like St. Augustine thought it more agreeable with divine wisdom that the world should be made gradually and certainly not in six days of twenty-four hours each. The main thing was that a Christian does not have to stultify his intellect to remain a believer.

Although less frequent, tensions in the moral order are more sensitive and difficult to resolve. A young woman told of her conversion some ten years before. Up to that time her religious attitudes were vague. Suddenly one December she was "born again." It was an emotional experience "that affects my character and behavior even today." Immediately on conversion, she was to behave like a new person:

> The church expected me, as a newly born Christian, to show external signs of my internal spiritual experience. Conformity to these external changes was necessary to be accepted by the majority of the congregation. If external changes did not appear soon after being born again, questions were raised as to whether the internal change had really taken place. To be Christlike and remain unspotted by the world, everything having the appearance of evil was to be avoided. Such things as movies, makeup, and dancing were considered to be "of the world."

There were interior changes, too. She soon developed a taste for Bible reading and church attendance. In time she also acquired a sense of conviction that faith really mattered and that God could be spoken to as a person.

But then a dichotomy set in. Socially she excluded herself from the world, feeling that contact with worldly people would lead her into sin. She stopped taking part in school activities and replaced them with social and religious functions at church. Alternately, she felt frustrated because she was cut off from her classmates, and again reassured "in thinking that I was one of God's chosen few." That lasted through high school. At a church-affiliated college she was scandalized by students, ostensibly religious, who ignored their church regulations. Transferring to a junior college, she also came into contact with the local YWCA where the idea first took shape that while moral perfection was impossible, the example and teachings of Christ were to be followed as a "guide for living." Better to confess one's sins, she decided, than try to convince others of living a perfect life. The catalyst for this change was contact with other students:

Questions asked about what I believed caused more questions and confusion in my mind. During discussions I realized that Christians did not all hold the same convictions that I held. I also began questioning my convictions, whether or not they were my own or dictated from the church.

The practice of external signs became less important for my religious satisfaction. The first noticeable change was in the use of makeup. For the first time in nine years I purchased a tube of lipstick. During the purchase I felt like a child taking a cookie from the jar. Attending church for the first time with lipstick on was like walking before a jury. Nothing was said directly to me, but the condemning looks spoke louder than words. However, this type of reaction was expected because I had done the same to others when I conformed to the expectations of the church group.

By the time she transferred to a state university, her mind was made up. She saw that by conformity in certain externals she was acceptable in her church, but "nonconformity resulted in better relationships outside my church." Non-conformity won out and her next step was to find a denomination "that emphasized personal relationship with God rather than dogma," notably in the reception of Holy Communion. A year later she was at peace even to admitting that her previous asceticism had been a valuable preparation for adult religious life.

When Protestants undertake to write autobiographical essays on their religion, they follow two courses in the main: either to explain why they are not something else (Jewish or Catholic), or to affirm the more positive benefits they derive from their profession of faith. Both approaches reveal an attitude towards "ecclesiasticism" that deserves careful attention.

A good example of the exclusion method was the senior in the Christian Thinkers class who carefully analyzed his premises and concluded that Protestantism was the purest form of Christianity in existence.

After a colorless childhood, he had an experience one Easter Sunday that made him a different man. "I woke from a sound sleep," he remembered, "with a profound feeling of remorse that the Son of God had died for men like me. For me this experience was as meaningful as St. Paul's on the road to Damascus. While I would have had difficulty explaining it at the time, I realize now that this was my crisis conversion that made me a Christian." He was a mature man at the time, while serving with the Air Force between high school and college.

If the sudden burst of grace showed him that he was a Christian, it took years of further reflection to convince him that he should also be (or remain) a Protestant:

I think I can best explain why I am a Protestant by explaining why I could not have become anything else. It is apparent that I could not have embraced the Jewish faith. After all, if my faith was based on the sacrifice of Jesus Christ on the cross, I could not accept a faith that would not accept him as the Savior of the world. If my redemption and justification were tied up in Christ, it would require that any faith I accept also accept Christ.

Moreover I could never be a Roman Catholic. I am happy

129

to state that I hold many beliefs in common with the Roman Catholic faith. We worship the same God and the same Lord who gave his life for us all. We also share a common foundation in the early Church. But while we agree on the major points, we are miles apart on the minor ones.

He then proceeds to examine these differences, which he dates back to the first centuries of the Christian era. Heading the list is the Church's administrative authority. "I can find no justification for the elaborate system that prevails in the Roman Catholic Church today. The absolute authority of the pope and the conditional authority of the bishops is completely without foundation. I grant that Peter was chosen by our Lord to be the leader of the Apostles, and that he was to be the foundation upon which the faith in Jesus Christ was to be built. But I find no evidence that this leadership was to be passed on to the bishop of Rome." Admittedly, Catholics make much of the fact that Peter and his successors were accepted by many Christians. "But I respectfully submit that there were also many instances where this authority was denied." In the last analysis, the bishops of Rome enjoyed what jurisdiction they did "because Rome was the seat of secular authority." It was a natural transfer of allegiance from one to the other or, perhaps, a natural absorption because the Roman emperors "established the authority of the bishop of Rome."

More intimately connected with the ministry is the concept of a sacrificing priesthood, which this man excludes from his idea of the Church. "The sacrifice that Christ made is available to all mankind if they will merely believe. It needs no special application by the hands of mortal men." The New Testament discloses a ministry, indeed, but only one that preaches the word of God.

In the most remote sense I cannot conceive of the Apostles as priests. Their office both during and after the time of Christ was to preach the Gospel to the people to lead them into a new life. They introduced the people to Christ and his new covenant. After this, each individual was capable of further conversation on his own. In modern days Protestant ministers function in much the same way. They introduce the person to God and stand ready to assist him in his spiritual growth. But this growth is not totally dependent on the minister; it is free to grow as the person responds to God's love.

Other students in the Protestant tradition expanded on this responsiveness to divine love which their churches promoted, especially through the Scriptures. If they singled out any feature of their religion it was generally the role of the Bible in its influence on their lives. On the statistical side one man in my New Testament class made a survey of seven hundred people in the city and found that Protestants as a group are more familiar with the Bible and read it more regularly than Catholics.

Some of the most eloquent testimonials of faith I have read, were from those who had been encouraged by their church to make Bible reading a daily practice. One young woman summarized the result by saying that the Bible had influenced her life as a guide to conduct, as a means of strengthening her faith in God, as a guide in her family and social relations, as the center of her recent marriage, and as a guide to her chosen career. Covering each impact, she quoted a favorite passage to illustrate the influence:

The Bible and its word has been my daily companion and inspiration. It is a guide to my daily conduct as a Christian. God has assured me that if I love Him and keep His commandments I will inherit life eternal. When it seems difficult to be a good witness to Him, I think of the love He has for me and I strive to serve Him better. I try to look for positive points in those I dislike, to find out what I don't like about them and try to overcome it. It is difficult to do, but I try.

Being human, I worry and fret about many things—will I do good on my next exam, will I find a job when I graduate, what kind of a job will it be, what will I be doing five years from now, will my parents become Christians, what shall I cook for dinner today—to mention a few worries that are common not only to me but to endless other people. God's word comforts me with this thought, when faced with the often trite problems of life: "O men of little faith! Do not seek what you are to eat and what you are to drink, nor be of anxious mind."

Appreciating myself as I am has much to do with the blessings that God has given me. If I were someone else, I wouldn't have the same blessings which are so dear. I have a wonderful family, loving parents, a nice home and all the necessities I need in life. I have good health, many friends, a good education and a wonderful husband. They are blessings that are unique to me in the way that I have received them. God's word, especially in the psalms and praises, has made me more aware and thankful even for the smallest blessings. 'In everything give thanks to God.' I know that everything I have and all that I am I owe to God.

Looking back over her life, it seemed that the Bible became dominant only with her affiliation with a church. The Reformed pastor opened her eyes to the riches of wisdom contained in the Scriptures for her personally. "With the personal inspiration I found in the word of God and the concern of my Christian friends, I found what I had been searching for"—a message from God to her soul and the support of like-minded persons who professed the same devotion to the Bible.

Sectarianism. Outside the ambit of traditional Protestantism every campus has a variety of denominations commonly called "sects," without implying anything opprobrious but only saying they are separated from the main body of the Christian churches. One of the best organized is the

Church of Christ, Scientist, founded in 1866 by Mary Baker Eddy.

According to its own teachings Christian Science is a religion and a system of healing disease of mind and body by means that are unknown (or mainly ignored) in other churches. Since cause and effect are mental, sin, sickness and death can be destroyed by a full understanding of the divine principle of Christ's doctrine.

It is symptomatic of the tensions under which college students labor that Christian Science clubs are among the most flourishing at large universities. They reflect a hunger for sympathy that is often missing among the organized religions. Christian Science gives what other "more respectable" bodies either neglect or delegate to the medical and psychiatric professions. It is not surprising, therefore, that a small group of Christian Scientists can become the nucleus for a "campus fellowship" of several hundred who find in Christian Science a ready answer to their academic and emotional needs. In view of its revealing character I offer the verbatim testimony of one of my students, a "born Scientist," to illustrate a dimension of the Christian faith that might otherwise be overlooked. It desperately wants understanding if graduates are to remember their religion for something more than social activity or a Sunday morning ritual with a pious lesson in morals. Unless religion *satisfies their needs*—and they have grave needs—it is under suspicion and may soon be abandoned:

Christian Science is a religion with two faces. One face is seen by those who do not believe as Christian Scientists do, and another face is seen by those of us who are Christian Scientists. As pointed up so clearly in our class discussion, the differences are great and lead to much confusion and misunderstanding.

We who proclaim ourselves Christian Scientists find that it

is the foundation of our lives. We feel it to be the center around which our activities and thoughts revolve. We dearly love Christian Science.

One thing must be stressed from the very beginning. The things I will be saying come from my own understanding of the various subjects. There is much about Christian Science which I do not know yet. These are the things I will strive to learn in the future. It should also be noted that Christian Scientists have a vocabulary all their own. The words are not different, but the way in which they are used has a very special meaning for us.

When my father was a small boy, he was stricken with a mastoid infection. The family doctor told my grandparents there was great danger that, even with an operation, my father might lose his hearing in the infected ear.

My grandparents naturally were very disturbed. My grandmother sought the help of a dear friend who was a Christian Scientist. My grandmother and father went to her house and lived with her for several days. During this time, my father's mother and her friend "worked" and studied, using the Christian Science textbook, *Science and Health With Key to the Scripture* by Mary Baker Eddy. At this time I pressume they declared that my father reflected the perfection of God because man is made in God's image. And by recognizing that God is omnipotent, they knew that the healing must come from Him.

Several days later the doctor was amazed to find the infection gone. The operation was not necessary and the danger was over.

This religion was a wonderful discovery for my grandmother. This demonstration of Mind over matter was the beginning of her study of Christian Science. Through my father Christian Science has been given to me.

I have found that the thoughts and ideas found in Christian Science are exactly the ones which satisfy the needs I feel I want expressed in my religion.

Some religious groups believe that because a person reaches a certain age or goes through a particular ritual that he *suddenly* has a deeper understanding and knowledge of the Word of God.

As Christian Scientists, we believe this knowledge and understanding of God must come gradually—in steps. We reach a certain level of understanding. Then we must work and study, using Christian Science to the best of our ability, and strive for a higher, more perfect sense of faith.

This is important to me. There is a definite satisfaction in feeling oneself progress spiritually. I enjoy the idea of working for something always higher, always better than before.

A Christian Scientist does not believe in death. Here is the reason, as I understand it at this time.

We do not believe that God has a body or any form at all. Instead, we think of God in terms of qualities. We usually express these as Life, Spirit, Love, Truth, Principle, Mind, and Soul. (Notice that these words capitalized as we consider them to be the seven synonyms for God.) We believe that God created man in His own image. Therefore man expresses these qualities of God just as a mirror reflects the original object. We believe that the *true* man is spiritual and without physical body or form. We know this true man through Mind, God; and we find that as the true children of God we cannot die. Spirit is infinite, with no beginning and no end. We reflect this and express eternal life.

This is one of the things about my religion which I find most helpful and comforting. No one can deny that matter in the form of a human body can be injured and destroyed. It is important to my own spiritual well-being to realize that as expressions of the qualities of God, we need not worry about the destructibility of the human body. Happily, we may fill our thoughts with the indestructibility of Spirit, God.

When a person seems to die, I know that the death comes only to the physical body which is made of matter. The *qualities* which that person expressed will live on forever.

Christian Science is a positive religion. It stresses many truths about God and man and the relationship between them. We believe these to be true for all mankind, and not just for Christian Scientists.

God gave mankind something very special when he sent Jesus Christ to earth. Jesus' purpose on earth was to act as a "middle man" between God and man. People did not understand God or what their relationship to Him should be. Jesus, through his teachings and good works, was to help them find this understanding they lacked.

He helped them by expressing the qualities of God. Although many were receptive to his teaching and healing work, there were many who did not accept this spiritual advancement at this time. These were the people who were responsible for the death of Jesus; that is, the destruction of the physical body.

People eventually have realized more clearly the mistake that was made by mankind regarding Jesus. They soon began predicting that he would come again.

Christian Scientists believe this prediction has come true. The object of the "Second Coming" is the divine Comforter. I believe that Christian Scientists think of this divine Comforter as the religion itself of Christian Science and not necessarily as the person of Mary Baker Eddy. We recognize her as the person through which God sent our religion to us.

We believe that Christian Science captures the essence of the teachings and the healing powers of Jesus Christ which man is capable of having because he is the child of God.

I use Christian Science in as many ways as possible each day. The three most common problems I face as a college student are exams, personality conflicts, and sickness. I would like to show some of the ways I work in Christian Science while meeting each of these situations.

In exams we are dealing with God as Mind. My first thought will be for the teacher. I always try to remember that we all express the same Mind. And because of this, I can say that the same Mind makes, takes, and grades the exams. I can expect to feel a real sense of Harmony.

With this boost in my confidence, I go on to work on my own intelligence. I try to remember that as a child of God I have every right to expect that I can express the intelligence of the divine Mind which I need for this exam.

136

Besides reading the lesson sermon daily, these things usually constitute my work in preparation for an exam.

For personality conflicts I begin by thinking of God as Love. I try to eliminate evil thoughts about the person and replace them with a multitude of good thoughts. I also try to recognize the person as a child of God. Here, also, the use of passages from the *Bible* and *Science and Health With Key to the Scriptures* is one of the methods which helps me the most. These are simply thoughts on love and brotherhood which serve to fill my thoughts with good to replace the evil which had been there.

I use the synonym of "Truth" for God when dealing with sickness, pain, or injury. I know the truth about man's perfection because of God's perfection. It is true that God is omnipotent, omnipresent, and evil does not express these qualities. God fills all space. There is no room for anything which contradicts Him.

God did not create evil, therefore there can be no evil in His creation. There is no possibility that the reflection of a perfect God could suffer from such "beliefs" as sickness, pain, or injury.

When I am studying to overcome one of these beliefs, I read from the writings of Mary Baker Eddy those things which apply most directly to my particular problem. I also read testimonies of healing printed in the various publications of the Christian Science Publishing Society. These, again, serve to fill my thoughts with good and crowd out the doubts and fears brought on by the problem.

May it be noted that at no time have I mentioned a hypnotic trance as a part of a Christian Science treatment. I have never gone into a hypnotic trance, and I do not believe any of the Christian Scientists I know ever have. We do concentrate very intently and intensely. We work and study very hard to reach the level of thinking and understanding which will enable us to handle the problem we are facing. But I will venture to say that no hypnotic trances are used in Christian Science treatments whether given *by* oneself *for* oneself or by a Christian Science practitioner.

I find that Christian Science fills my spiritual needs. I was so pleased to be made more aware of how many thousands of Christian Scientists there are in the world. This past summer I attended the Biennial Meeting of the Mother Church for College Students in Boston. There were college students from all over the world attending this meeting. Naturally we gave a standing ovation to the young man from Poland who came.

I have found a real source of strength and confidence in knowing that as I study my lesson sermon each day and practice Christian Science, young people all over the world are doing the same.

Basically, I am a Christian Scientist because it is the religion of my family. But more specifically I am a Christian Scientist because it so completely meets my spiritual needs.

It is impossible to see this kind of mature judgment and dismiss Christian Science as just another "sect," or treat undergraduates as impersonal ciphers.

Judaism Jewish students have much the same experience in college as Roman Catholics, except that American society has more prejudices against the Jews and they in turn have more problems maintaining their religious identity.

Not the least difficulty in speaking of Judaism is the question of terms. If Protestantism is hard to define, Judaism is even less definable. Etymologically there is no problem. The name "Jew" is derived from Judah, one of the twelve tribes of Israel. Later it came to apply to any one belonging to the Hebrew race, and finally to those who profess the religion of Judaism. The question is whether Judaism is basically ethnic or religious, since there are many Jews who are not lineal descendants of Abraham and many others who may be so descended but do not profess the Judaic faith. Perhaps the best definition is to see Judaism as the mind and Jewry as the body of a permanent moral tradition, which has its roots in the Old Testament prophets and its hopes in a forthcoming Messiah.

There is more than academic value in clarifying these concepts because much of the prejudice that Jews experience is produced by ignorance—certainly ignorance of the spiritual vitality of religious Judaism. Two of my students illustrate the broad spectrum of American Judaism and point up the specialized difficulties which they face.

Although he professes himself to be a Jew, the first man admitted that his religious ideas are far from clear. "My religion is one of uncertainty," he explained. One reason may be that his mother was a Christian, and the Jewish father never provided for a thorough grounding in the faith that he gave to his son:

I consider myself to be a member of the Reform Jewish faith, but there still remain many questions for which I must find the answers. I cannot honestly say I do not believe there could have been such a person as Jesus Christ, but there remains the doubt. I do believe in some higher or supreme power which guides man towards his ultimate destiny. I tend to believe in an eternal life after death, but again there arises doubt.

Religion, I feel, is the belief by which a man conceptualizes the future and a way that governs his attitudes and behavior in society. I do not think it is necessary for a person to attend church every week. Too many people attend church merely to please someone. Some attend services because it has become a social custom and to omit this would violate accepted procedures. Any conception of God or religious doctrine that a person has learned, is carried with him wherever he goes and influences his behavior even if he fails to attend church every week.

He speculates with the idea of becoming a Christian, if

need be, to insure peace and harmony in the family that he plans to rear—assuming that he marries a Christian girl. "I'm not a strict Jew," he confesses, "in the sense that I cannot change my views on some religious beliefs if necessary. It is very possible that I may wed someone of the Christian faith." In that case a variety of adjustments would have to be made.

This will be a problem—after many years believing and practicing one religious concept, having to change to another. The greatest problem here is the religion of the children. If I do marry a person of the Christian faith, I believe the children would be raised Christian. That of course depends upon the woman and if she has strong religious convictions. If I were to go so far as marrying outside my faith, there would be very little reason trying to retain my Judaic beliefs for my children.

Behind his adaptability was the new understanding that college had given him of how much in common all the great religions have. "In this modern day and age," he felt, "the majority of people are becoming more and more liberal in nearly every respect. It amazes me to see the similarities among the various faiths. Most people today have a higher education than they did ten or twenty years ago, and part of this education consists of living and working with people of other races and religions." The effect on him has been a broadening of perspective. He became more tolerant, to the point of willingness to change religious affiliation.

His counterpart in the Jewish Orthodox tradition has a different early training and developed much different attitudes. His autobiography will be quoted at length.

I was born into a family of Orthodox Jews. From my earliest years the principles of the Jewish religion were instilled into me. This religion has given me the basic factors by which

I am to run my life. It has given me concepts and ideals which I have chosen to uphold. What my religion means to me is in essence more than a set of beliefs, more than observing certain days of the year, more than going to the synagogue for worship. It has mainly come to me as the basis for my way of life.

My early life revolved around my family, its social unit, which gave me the fundamental feelings towards my being a Jew. I often remember the days sitting with my grandfather and having stories told to me about our religion. He told me of the many heritages of the Jewish religion that have come down to us through the ages of history.

My father and mother were a great influence in creating within me a strong religious faith. When I was young my father took me with him to the synagogue and explained to me the many doctrines of our religion. I thank my mother for keeping a kosher home and preparing the Sabbath and holiday meals. She upheld the belief of lighting the Sabbath candles on Friday evenings along with practicing the many other observances of the Jewish religion.

Along with these family influences, he was early introduced into formal Jewish education, starting Sunday school at the age of five and Hebrew school at seven. He attended both schools weekly until he was thirteen. At thirteen he had his Bar Mitzvah (confirmation), when he became recognized by the synagogue as a "Son of Command," or more popularly, when, it is said, "Today you are a man."

From the age of thirteen to seventeen, he studied with the rabbi of his synagogue, who helped him "broaden my concepts and ideas concerning religion." Before each conference he would come armed with questions that occurred to him or that others suggested. The rabbi went over each question carefully, and tried his best to give answers that were "logical and conclusive." Gradually he developed a system of values which he called the virtues or "ways that I should react and feel toward other people." They were

soon put to the test, for at least four years before he came
to college.

The hostilities which I received set me back in amazement.
I had never before run across people who would try to run me
down because I was a member of the Jewish faith. At first I
just did not know what to do. I went to my parents and told
them. They told me this was common among boys of that age
group, and not to worry because they would soon tire of harp-
ing on me. I did tolerate this for quite a while, but soon realized that I could not take it without trying to do something.

I knew I had to fight back, not physically but verbally. I
found that in some manner I would have to gain the respect of
these boys and prove to them that they were wrong in their
assumptions about me, the Jewish religion, and the Jewish
people. The way I handled the situation was to slowly talk it
over with the boys, and after a short time they stopped their
hostility.

I tried my best to answer their questions. Their basic problem was a lack of understanding of the Jewish faith. All they
needed was clarification.

He would soon learn that the issues were deeper, and
that something more than "slowly talking it over" was
needed for a complete adjustment. It dawned on him that
he had to live down an image that was not of his making.
People around him would say that "Jews were mercenary,
clannish, and always taking something away from another
person." His first reaction was to admit the stereotype but
defend himself that American Jews were different. Then
he realized that what was really at stake was survival in an
atmosphere that was alien to his sense of values. "I now
had to evaluate myself on the basis of belonging to a minority religion in a very large society," where minority
meant fidelity to his religious convictions.

The problem was compounded by the dietary laws

which he had been careful to observe, but which made him appear singular and forced him constantly to re-examine his motivation:

To the best of my knowledge and ability, I was obeying the strict laws and customs set down by the Orthodox pattern of the Jewish religion. Under obedience to these laws, I would eat only in my own home or in the homes of people that kept kosher. I observed these laws out of respect for myself and my religion. I was proud of the fact that I was able to do this, and was not concerned with what other Jewish people did, because it was their own business.

After my entrance into college, radical changes had to be made, which again caused me concern and proved to be a real test of my religious faith. The first conflict arose when the type of food that I was used to eating had to be changed. Why? Because I found it impossible to get and maintain a kosher line of food while attending school. I ate most of my meals in restaurants and in the school cafeteria. I did not eat pork or mix milk with my meat, but I still felt a great deal of guilt over my new eating habits.

On his first visit home, he told the family and rabbi about the crisis. Their explanation left the matter up to his own conscience. "They said that if I really wanted to uphold the dietary laws, it would not be impossible. The choice was mine." He took the cue and decided to distinguish. "I justified my actions (on not eating kosher) by saying that I still had not lost my identity, I was still Jew. The circumstances I was under did not allow me to uphold this tradition. I was forced to make the best of it."

In the second year of college another, more serious conflict arose. He met an attractive girl that he thought he might want to marry. Then one day the question of religious differences came up, "and we were both put into a frenzy over what to do." Should they continue the relationship in spite of these differences and risk an unhappy marriage?

The way we handled our problem was to go and talk with our respective religious leaders. They each told us of the possibilities and impossibilities. As more and more explanation was given to us, we finally saw that we could not live a rich and full life together without a firm religious foundation.

Our families also entered the situation. They explained the great differences between us over religious and family backgrounds. So inevitably we broke off our relationship. This was not an easy thing to do, but a realization of the probable end result made it much easier to understand.

This event left me with stronger feelings towards my religious belief. Having the choice put before me, I chose my religion. I found that my emotional feelings towards my family and religion were stronger than those I had for the girl.

Even though I was hurt in many ways, I was also strengthened. I now know one thing for certain, that if I am to marry in the future, the first qualification the girl must have is to be of the Jewish faith.

Although his mind was made up on that point, he still had to find himself socially on a university campus. He tried two approaches, one of identifying himself as closely as possible with his own coreligionists, and the other of entering into the full stream of college life.

After a year's experimentation with the "closed circle" method, he reluctantly gave it up for reasons that he called religious and sociological. The two reasons were closely related. "By being associated with this group, I found it hard to broaden my spectrum of knowledge concerning other people" That was sociological. "As far as my religious values were concerned, I felt that they were being infringed upon by the people within the group. Their beliefs in the Jewish religion seemed to be based on entirely different values than mine. The main difference was that they used the term Jewish to signify a type of person rather than a person that was associated with a religion. Thus there was a conflict between what I believed and apparently what they stood for in relation to my feelings."

More recently, and mainly "for the purpose of re-evaluation," he tried the other approach of mixing by preference with students who were not Jewish. But he found that while one problem was solved, another was created. "I have managed to maintain a certain amount of individuality," was the advantage. Isolation from his own people, however, was impossible. As he approached graduation, he could look forward with new confidence.

There have not been many changes or modifications of the basic doctrines given to me by the Jewish faith. I believe in it strongly as my way of worshipping God. I also believe it is the right way for me to run my life. I know it has given me many things of which I am justly proud, and I do not in any way regret that I am a Jewish person. I feel it is an honor and a privilege to be born of the Jewish faith, and I will be thankful for this throughout my life.

His conscience assured him that he had not compromised on any (not merely many) of the essentials of his religion. The adaptation he felt constrained to make was on things that he considered modifiable to meet the higher demands of social life. As he recalled the sacrifice he once made of a mixed marriage, he now believes that "marriage outside of my religion would be a very great sin." By comparison with that sacrifice, and strengthened by such a resolution, the future seemed promising.

FIVE

PARENTS

Family Influence

THE psychology of religion is still largely unexplored. When the field comes to be better known, it will show that early home influences are the most important, single factor in the development of religious character. What parents believe and how they worship, their attitude towards God and the moral law, and the whole complex of family life are powerful elements that shape the growing child.

College students know this and the knowledge is not always salutary. They may feel that because their religious outlook has been so strongly affected by parents and the home, it is therefore suspect and needs to be radically revised. From the valid assumption that childhood practices and beliefs should be critically examined, they are prone to question their whole philosophy of life.

But they can rise to maturity in the light of a questioning present that builds on the influences of the past. They can develop a balanced appraisal that must be assisted, however, at the risk of their becoming intellectual snobs whom I have known to dismiss the accumulated wisdom of centuries with a shrug. Much has already been said about the role that family upbringing plays in forming the average college man and woman. Yet it is impossible to say too much. Students are remarkably keen observers, and they have long memories when it comes to recalling how much (or little) their mother and father contributed to giving them a foothold on life. Even when the memories are not pleasant, they are not exploited to debase parents for whom most students have the highest respect. But the failings and limitations are not spared, and would make a fine catalogue of "things to avoid" by those who are training the young.

Religious Foundation. Unless they are directly questioned or required as part of class work, students do not easily go back over the past to ask themselves what factors were operative in their religious development. Once faced with the issue, however, they respond with alertness. "In order to explain my feelings about the relationship between God and myself," they tell you, "I must explain my past environment. This determines whether the habits we acquired are good and lasting, or bad and later should be cast off."

Quite typical is the criticism that "in my case, I feel that my early environment was too strict and inelastic." It kept her from really understanding her faith and "this inelasticity caused feelings which were to result later on in religious instability." She specifies:

My parents thought it necessary for me to obtain my education from a religious order, partly because of my father's experiences with education from Jesuit priests. He felt that education by a religious order best satisfied the purpose of discipline and learning, as well as offering religious instruction.

I attended an all-girl school for my first twelve years, under the supervision of nuns. My feelings toward religion during this period were more of fear than anything else. It seemed at the time that there was always the threat of punishment hanging over my head if I deviated from the behavior proposed by

147

my superiors. These guilt feelings were fostered by my immaturity and lack of understanding of the basic religious concepts. Little did I realize at the time that this was to help me later in life to form a more unified relationship with my religion.

Since childhood she considered religion so essentially a part of her life that the only comparison possible was with bodily hunger. "Just as my physical appetites are satisfied by food, so my spiritual appetites are nourished by religion." It was not all clear sailing, however, and there were plenty of compromises:

At times I have fallen away from my beliefs, as I have also let bad practices at times control my behavior. I have even questioned the existence of God and wondered if religion might not be just a creation of man. Maybe there isn't a God—I have asked myself.

When I first had these feelings, I thought I was falling into atheism. I became ashamed and afraid when I couldn't answer the questions I posed to myself. During this period I was tied to my religion only by fear. I was afraid of the retribution from parents, from religion, and from God if I strayed from the norms set up during childhood. I seemed encased by these fears and hesitations.

Now I realize that these fears of religion were one reason I couldn't find the answers I asked of myself. As this fear changed to love, I found that I gained a permanent religion and a kind of stability in my life. I suddenly matured and believed more deeply. I then began meeting these challenges by confronting them and relying on my religion to give the answers. This new insight helped me keep the bad habits down to a minimum, but more than that, it gave me a self-identity and satisfaction in myself.

This discovery opened up new horizons and gave her the conviction that religion is not only obedience to a code of morals. Above all it is not mainly an object of fear. "I understand now," she concluded, "that religion is not to be feared, for a friendship with God on these terms is not very deep. Fear only teaches you something, but you do not really learn it and are not able to apply it to your daily living. I didn't understand my religion until I began to love it." But not all students come through the experience unscathed:

These struggles which I had are by no means special or witnessed only by me. Everyone meets such obstacles and conflicts in life. Some fall away from God because of them. They do so because they were never able to love and confront their religion face to face. They were not able to take their problems directly to their religion. They have not learned to apply God to their everyday life. In a word, they have not learned to love Him, treasure Him, and most of all they have not really sought Him. I am only glad that I did not cheapen myself by losing Him.

Men make the same observations. Is religion true belief in God or is it merely a tradition handed down from one generation to the next? According to one physical education major, it is mostly tradition:

Take myself for example. I started attending church when I was a baby. I had religion pounded into my head as soon as I was able to understand things. I attended church almost every Sunday until I was eighteen.

But there was one big problem: attending church was not my own choice but my mother's. At that time I could see no future in attending church. I did not try to learn anything about religion, and anything they tried to teach me I would not accept. I was actually rebelling against religion. My father did not attend church so I could not see why I had to attend.

I believe that church should be an important part of every child's life. The child should be taught the importance of

149

religion early in life. Both parents should attend church with their children. They should not attend just for the sake of taking their children, but in a reverent and obedient manner towards God. The parents should dedicate their children to God in thanks. I believe that proper family life is part of religion. I had no religion during my childhood, but something you might call a tradition in my attendance of church.

Regretting that he had not received more positive encouragement in the practice of his faith in childhood, he had to go to the army to learn the value of family prayers. "I believe that prayer is another important part of religion," he explained, adding the slogan "that always sticks in my mind: A family that prays together, stays together." He missed this at home:

To have someone to talk to in time of need means a lot to me. Not just any ordinary person but to a superhuman person, God, who is real. I will never forget August, 1961. I was in the Army and was stationed in Kaiserslautern, Germany. We were awakened early one Sunday and placed on stand by alert with orders to be ready to move out at anytime. The Eighteenth Infantry was moving by convoy into Berlin and the brass were expecting something to break loose at any moment. Everyone was scared and everyone prayed. The next day, President Kennedy gave his Berlin crisis speech and the thing I most remember about it was his closing words to pray for him. I have always heard that all things through God are possible.

Perhaps his "compulsory" attendance at church every Sunday had more effect on him than he supposed. It gave him the idea that religion cannot be compartmentalized. "You cannot thank God for something on Sunday morning in church and then forget all about God while you are in class or while you are at home or work. Religion must be a continuous part of our lives."

He would draw a moral from his own experience, to be

applied to church affairs generally. "One thing," he insisted, "that I would like to clarify is the idea of the Church being a part of everything. The idea that the Church is the center of everything and therefore everything should spring from the Church. I do not believe that the Church should control, run, or have anything to do with the government of any country. I believe that there should be a distinct line drawn between the two." By all means "the officials of the government should be religious and not just men of high moral standards. But these two organizations, the church and the government, should run and function separately." Without further explanation, it can only be conjectured, but a case could be made out for a subtle transfer in this man's mind from childhood constraint to a reaction against church "interference" in the secular order.

A Mother's Role. Every so often in the volume I have found it useful to interrupt the cadence of quotation-and-commentary to give a full-length statement from one of the students. I have felt that in these cases I would spoil the effect by interposing my own reflective thoughts. After all, my purpose is to have men and women speak for themselves.

A music major with extraordinary sensitivity gave me a penetrating analysis of the role of motherhood in its relation to religion. I have not changed a syllable of her study, which begins with her own family situation and projects the lessons learned at home into the hopes she has for college women as mothers of the future.

The word "family," she says, much like the word "home" has very special connotations. It may be that in many ways they are synonymous, for where there is a family in the true sense of the word, there is indeed a home:

Family is a deeply emotional word for me; it indicates a

151

feeling more than an actual, physical relationship, and it implies a togetherness which is essential to make the feeling real and alive.

Since it is the mother who is the heart of the family, it seems to me that it is primarily her job to foster this kind of togetherness and to help the family learn to share their experiences in such a way that each member will feel that he belongs to all of the others through a special kind of love and respect.

I say that this is primarily the mother's duty, and I do not mean to imply that the father has no part in this. His is a very important role, because he, as head of the family, serves as a strong leading and unifying force, and he can contribute in large measure to this feeling. But it is the mother who spends the most time at home with the children, and in many ways it is the mother who serves as a catalyst, helping the many personalities of the family to adjust to one another.

In today's world, unfortunately, there are too many mothers whose idea of married and family life is that they are mothers in name only. This results in an overabundance of houses and a lack of homes. Because of our mothers' lack of interest in their families, family life has become a day-to-day rat race in which parents and children rarely see each other for any length of time. The unity of the family is becoming a thing of the past; the sharing, the togetherness, the respect which make a group of people truly become a family are becoming passé.

This, I think, is tragic. In fact, it is disastrous. It is tragic because one of the most wonderful blessings in any person's life is that of being a member of a closely-knit family and knowing the love that abounds within that kind of group. It is disastrous because it indicates a breakdown of family life, and when family life has been destroyed, society has been destroyed.

I can speak of family unity with a great deal of knowledge, for my own family has proved the importance and meaning of true family life to me more and more strongly through the years. There were four children in my family, and although that is not large by most standards, it was large enough to make us aware of the responsibilities of one member to another. And it was large enough for us to develop the consideration and cooperation so essential within the unit.

The children in our family are as different as different can be—physically, emotionally, and intellectually; in talents, abilities, and interests. We are considerably separated in age, and now, with our various professional interests, we are widely scattered geographically.

Yet I don't believe that a closer family exists. We have always enjoyed the excitement of doing things together, and we have learned to sacrifice individually either for other individual family members or for the family group. There is love and respect in our family which is not a product of carrying the same name, but a product of ties woven throughout our lives.

The important thing is that these ties were not automatic; they *were* woven. We did not merely love and respect each other because we were brother and sisters; we learned the truest and deepest meaning of that love and respect within and through the family. We were drawn together by the experiences we shared and by the common interests which my parents were careful to draw out and nurture in each of us.

This unity existed not only in feelings and attitudes, but also in actions. When we did things, we did them together. There was very little of the scattering of individuals in all directions which is so common today. My parents both felt that their most important duty was raising their children, and they took the time to see that they were around enough to do a good job. And so our separation came later, when each of us left to find our own place and to build our own home.

This family unity undoubtedly resulted, to a great extent, from the natural bonds of family affection which my parents had known. It has always seemed significant to me that my parents' own families have never lost the "family touch." Even more significantly, I know they never will, because there is a pride, a feeling of worth and unity that was developed in them from the beginning.

How different this kind of feeling was from that which I find so prevalent among the young people—especially the young women—with whom I am in school. For too many of them, home has become a meaningless word and parents are a liability. The idea of family life is disappearing; in fact, the whole desire for a family with which to share and through which to build a significant future is becoming "old-fashioned."

As a college student, I am, so to speak, "at the marriageable age." And although I do not intend to enter that state of life, most of the girls whom I know do anticipate that in their future. So the air, especially now, is literally filled with the excitement of engagements, showers, and weddings.

Rarely is it filled with the excitement of children and families. I've spoken with many of these girls whose future lies in making a home. "Children?" they say. "Oh, not for a long time. And when I do, not more than two."

The saddest part of this is that these girls mean what they say, and I know that they will see to it that they get what they want, regardless of means. This, of course, is in a different area than family living, and it is more a question of morality than anything else. And yet it is definitely related to the problem of the modern family, because these young women will miss their greatest joy—the joy of giving their lives to raising a family. And they will miss the joy of seeing that family grow strong in bonds of affection; they will miss the joy of knowing that they have helped to make the foundational structure of life a meaningful part of their children's futures.

What has happened to family unity? Has it gone out of style, or does it now seem like some sort of Victorian philosophy, dusty with age?

Let us look at some of the ways in which the family has changed. Some of these changes are recent; some are more the products of changes made many years ago. For some of them, we young people are responsible; for others, older generations are responsible, and we are the products of their ideas.

One of the first changes in family life came with the independence of women. For many years, a woman's place was in the home, and she accepted that fact—whether with enthusiasm or not is not known—and did the work that was expected of her. Finally, driven by a desire for freedom from her "drudgery" of the home and by a desire for equality with her mate, she rebelled. Very soon, the woman's place was anywhere she could go, and her job was any one in which she was interested and which she was capable of doing.

This change probably would not have created the havoc it did if more and more women had not become interested in working as a source of independent income. Gradually, women began to comprise a larger percentage of the working force, and families were left unattended while the mother worked. Women found this kind of independence and freedom much more attractive than being tied down at home and rearing a family.

Another change arose, in great measure now to compound the problem. Families moved to suburban communities, and they soon found that the activities available in a large city were considerably more numerous than in the smaller areas in which they had previously lived. And since people are interested in those things which are enjoyable and satisfying, mothers and fathers began to find their afterwork pleasure in social life, clubs, theater-going, and cultural ventures instead of in the old-fashioned family activities.

Perhaps, in the beginning of this movement away from the home, there was not a noticeable change. But gradually, parents began to evaluate the importance of their activities above their children. Today, the result is obvious. The modern family is too often taken care of by a baby-sitter rather than by parents, and children are left to fend for themselves as soon as they are old enough to do so. This divorcement within the family unit, this consistent separation of parents and children has destroyed much of the respect which not only should be but must be present in the family group.

I am convinced that we as young people have contributed to this attitude. We have become more and more interested in the work we can do, or the organizations we can belong to, or the fun we can have, and we have allowed our interest in and concern for our family relationships to wane. So, in this way, we are also at fault.

And yet, there is another force at work here which cannot be overlooked. Much of the change in attitude, even from one generation to another, can be attributed to the fact that we learn what we are taught. In other words, although some of our older families may not have believed in the down grading of family life, they nevertheless taught it to their children through example.

Many of the college students I know come from very small families, that is, of one or two children—which resulted from the first great movement toward increased parental independence. As a result, this is the only kind of family life with which they are familiar. It is significant that these young people usually feel that small families are the most convenient for providing the best and most of things for children; they themselves were rarely denied anything on the grounds that there simply wasn't the money or that "one of the other children needs something else more." They have enjoyed a lifetime of asking and receiving, and they are very much aware that a large family would have created problems in this regard.

Of course, the question of providing for children all of the things which they deserve (and, for so many parents, "the things which I never had") has become a matter of primary importance. In a society which demands certain achievements of its citizens, most parents want to see to it that their children attain the heights expected of them, in order for them to belong to society in the most formal sense. And so, parents' concentration has turned from instilling in their children the most fundamental and important ideals to attaining the highest social status possible and impressing the children that this and this alone is of value.

Our generation has definitely inherited this social concern from our elders. Because we have been given a different set of values on which to build our lives, we are aware, almost excessively, of economic situations, and we are striving for the most money and the highest social standing, because that has become our measure of success.

The concern is so overwhelming, however, that we have turned away more than we should have from what is really the measure of success—that is, what kind of a society are we building right in our own homes?

The social problem is not the only one, of course, although it is the most obvious of the contributing factors. Another difficulty is the expansion of our personal horizons, not only in the area of jobs, but in the growing of our worlds. Today's young people have discovered that there is a world to see which their parents had little or no opportunity of seeing; they have found that there are a million things to do in that world. They are unwilling to give up or at least forego the enjoyment of all those newly-discovered opportunities in order to concentrate their lives and work in a family unit. Unfortunately, they have not learned to forego the pleasure of marriage for a few years in order to enjoy the available opportunities before settling down to a family life.

All of these social and ideological changes have affected us to a considerable degree. There are, of course, moral problems involved in the situation, the primary one being the question of the means which are used by families to limit their size. But the moral problems are better left to theologians; most of the young people will have to be reached from a different standpoint than that of morality. But where do we start?

I think we start in school and in church. It doesn't seem to me that it was made clear to us in either of these situations how important the family structure is. For some, the attempt would be a futile one; the difference between what they see in their homes and what they hear from their teachers and religious leaders would be too great. But the majority could be reached in this way.

Education on this point must be clear and decisive. It must be explained what a family is, how it works, how important its unity, indeed, its very existence is. It must be made clear to these future parents that if family life is lost, society is lost. They must be taught that position and money are poor substitutes for humanity as important personal values. They must learn the sacredness of marriage, and the virtue of the family.

157

And we must begin to teach them now.

I wish that I could tell the young people who are facing the future with the hope of marriage and families strong in them about the deep joy and satisfaction that comes from true family unity.

I wish especially that I could convince today's young woman—tomorrow's mother—that nothing she does can ever be more important than this. I wish that I could convince every young woman I know that her place is still fundamentally and primarily in the home, helping to weave the unbreakable bonds of family unity. For it is through her that the family truly comes to life.

There must be this change, this swinging of the pendulum, back toward the old-fashioned ideals of family living. If there is not, we will soon find ourselves facing problems as a society that we will simply not be able to cope with. Unity must begin in the fundamental society; unity must begin at home.

Broken Homes. In contrast to the social consciousness that arises from strong family ties, the opposite is also true. Where the home has been broken by death or divorce, a tension is created that has to be experienced to be believed. Torn between affection for mother and father, a child has the difficult option of choosing one or the other long before separation takes place; and after the rift has to adjust to living with one parent and maybe accepting a stranger as a substitute for the one who is specially loved.

No wonder some students are happy to be away at school. "I hate it at home," one of them confided. "I can't explain exactly why, but I can't stand to go home for the weekend, let alone for the whole summer. It's as if I were a stranger in a completely foreign household. I sleep on a rollaway bed, formerly used for company. There's no place to put my clothes away since my cousin lives at my house and he occupies my closet. There's no place or thing to call mine. I realize that a big step is taken when one departs for college, but I never thought I would feel like company in my own house."

Although he says he cannot explain why, the explanation is clear enough. His first father used to be chronically ill, which forced the family to move from place to place searching for a hospital where the father might be cured. This left no time to settle down anywhere or attend church regularly. Outside of a few basic beliefs instilled by his mother, his religious education was neglected almost entirely. When he was twelve years old, his father died.

Life was not pleasant under these circumstances. Illness brought worry and worry produced tension. His mother had to earn the living and money was short. Her small weekly paycheck was supplemented by county welfare. The children grew up without normal companionship and were discouraged from bringing friends to their home. "There was very little affection displayed between my parents, though I'm positive there was much love between them. I rarely saw them together. My mother was always loving and affectionate toward us kids but my father, being ill, did not have much time for us. When I got older I had difficulty expressing my feelings toward other people."

After putting up with what must have seemed an impossible situation for years, the mother divorced her husband shortly before his death. When he died, his children did not even go to his funeral, although the mother insisted that the oldest child go to the funeral home as a representative of the rest of the family. There was one more token of respect. "About a year later I visited his grave with my grandmother. This time also because my mother thought it was fitting that I should at least know where my father was buried."

Soon after her first husband's death, the mother remarried. This was her third marriage, and for a while it looked as though the family would find the peace and happiness they had never known before. But there was no peace for the college freshman who felt that coming home for a week end was like entering a stranger's house.

One result of this estrangement was the decision to give up the faith of his parents, which he admitted had not been easy to make. "It's taken much thought and prayers, There's really no one I could talk to, to help me make the decision." So it was made quite alone, with the cryptic observation that "the consequences, good or bad, remain unexposed."

Other cases of broken homes have been less tragic. Here the man's father was divorced by his wife when their two sons were only a few years old. Writing about himself, he admits he was fortunate that divorce struck their family when he was very young. "I didn't remember having a father. It's like being born without an arm; you don't miss it as much because you never have the use of it."

The mother tried, and in most ways did, give her boys what they would have had with a father. But no matter how hard she tried, she could not give them everything. There were certain things that only a man could provide. Many difficulties arose because there was no man's guiding hand:

One experience that immediately comes to mind is when I first started school. I never tried to hide the fact that I didn't have a father. My mother always said that we never had anything to be ashamed of. Kids would ask, 'what does your father do?' I would reply, 'I don't have a father.'

Children at that age don't understand words like divorce and separation. It was a hard thing to try to explain to a schoolmate that I didn't have a father. Lack of a father's guidance also affected my school life. When questions would arise concerning why the little girl was different from me, I had no father to ask. When I learned, as all young boys do, that I had to defend myself, I found that nobody had taught me to fight.

Consequently I was always the one that the little bully would pick on. I had to have my face shoved in the mud a few times before I learned what it was all about. I also missed the camping trips, the baseball games, and all the other events that make up a good father-son relationship.

There were certain things that I didn't want to discuss with my mother what would normally be discussed with a father, so I just kept them inside of me. In the process of repressing my thoughts, I developed a strong set of values at an unusually early age.

The mother encouraged this self-reliance. She let her sons decide things for themselves. She hardly ever said, "No," because she respected their judgments. But the boys also knew not to ask for something they could not have or do. The development of this attitude played a major role in the development of their personalities.

As a sophomore in college, his fatherless boyhood and the self-sacrifice of his mother left him with strong convictions about the way children should be reared. He would give his children the things he never had, and "fulfill some of their desires that, for me as a child, could not have been fulfilled." Above all he wanted to make sure they will know how to make up their own minds. He felt that parents bring their children up in too sheltered an atmosphere. Proof of this can be found on any college campus. You can see people walking around who seem not to know anything about life. "These are the people who have been brought up in an atmosphere where their decisions had been made by their parents." When they leave home, they find the change difficult. All of a sudden they are left alone to shape their own lives. Some make the adjustment, but many do not. Teenagers are not given a chance to develop their sense of values, so that when they get to college they hardly know what their goals should be. They have trouble in school, with many dropping out of college; and even those who graduate may become liabilities to society. Long before they stand in line for their first college registration, they should have been trained in the home:

> In bringing up children I think it is very important to have a close-knit family. This means functioning together as a family. I also want my children to feel that they can come to me with any problems they might have. This is what I missed most in being brought up without a father. I will want them to feel free to tell me anything and to know that I will understand and respect their opinions.
>
> I also have a strong philosophy about explaining the so-called facts of life to my children. I feel they should know these vital facts as soon as they are mature enough to understand them. A large percentage of sex crimes could be avoided if parents would explain these facts rather than have them learned in a pool hall or school corridor. When I was a child, I never had these facts explained. It was hard for a woman to explain them to two boys. Although what I learned was from the neighborhood boys, I realized the seriousness of the subject and took it maturely.
>
> Probably the most important factor in bringing up children is religion. I feel that a child should know and understand God as soon as possible. I wish I had. It is very important to possess a strong knowledge of God, though I don't feel it is necessary to send children to a parochial school. I feel that a public school has much more to offer in extracurricular activities. This philosophy stems from my own personal background.

He summarizes by admitting that "divorce is a terrible thing, more so when children are involved." But just as people are human, so is divorce! Better in his judgment, a divorce where the marriage is unhappy than to continue pretending and making matters worse. No doubt a divorce indicates the failure of a marriage, but the absence of divorce does not indicate its success.

Trial and Temptation. Part of a child's training is to be educated to virtue. What the parents believe and say is important, but what they do is paramount in teaching their children. Youngsters are great imitators and no greater benefit can be given a child than to have a father and mother whose conduct may be followed.

A senior recalled the behavior of her own parents from as far back as she could remember. "They always set good examples for us to follow. Neither of them smoked, drank, or swore, and they attended church regularly. I guess there's nothing wrong with smoking or drinking, but I know I respected my parents so much more because they refrained from these." This pattern of asceticism paid off in time of crisis:

When I was eight years old, I was attacked by a sex pervert. Though I wasn't old enough at the time to realize the full implications of this or its effects on me, I did realize that what had happened was wrong. I had no guilt feelings or guilt complexes, but I knew that this in some way was part of my life. I learned from this the importance of control over the sex urge.

I certainly don't recommend such an experience to everyone who has this trouble, but I am saying that through this experience I knew I had to control myself, so that I never was caught in any situation that I couldn't handle. I definitely feel that this had a strong bearing on my being good as far as sex is concerned. The results of my being good led to many happy fun-filled dates. More important than that, it led to a happy courtship and solid footing in my married sex life.

She credits her parents with the fact that she came through the ordeal with such ease, and was able to use it to great profit even though the memory would never be erased. Their moral conduct may have been overstrict, but it proved a happy balance to weathering a storm that

163

might have broken any spirit trained in a less demanding discipline. Among the ideas she learned from it (but through father and mother) was that "to be good as far as sex is concerned is to receive many rewards and personal gratifications which can in no way be filled by premarital sex relationships." Example and experience told her it was wiser to wait.

Another girl's experience was less traumatic but equally rewarding in a different way. She philosophized on the three stages through which most people have to go in their quest for the *ideal life*. They must first have some notion of what this *ideal* is, then have some practice in the value whch the *ideal* implies, and finally begin speculating on the inner meaning or theology of the *ideal* itself.

She defined the *ideal* as a personal God, who is Love. "It has never not existed and can never cease to exist. It is the creator of everything. It is, just as the name suggests, the *all*." So much could be found in books.

But the practice in the values demanded by the *ideal* was not so simple. It took years to cultivate, and then was only beginning. Yet even the beginning would never have been made except for a great trial and the help of her family.

Her father was a frustrated small-scale farmer who drank excessively. That was about five years before she entered college, right at the time when she began having doubts about the "childish conversations with that *something* up in heaven." The more her father drank, the less she could fathom the meaning of God, for "how could He let my father feel so alone, so much a failure, that he would become the sickly-spirited person he was. Why wouldn't this 'loving God' *do* something?"

All the while, her two younger brothers, who saw their father drunk and often senseless and heard him "yell twisted, terrible things," could come to him the next day with smiles on their faces, unafraid, and without feeling an ounce of bitterness toward him. The boys followed the example of their mother who "always had faith in him." She taught them to ask: When will he overcome his illness? It was never: Will he ever overcome his illness?

The ties that hold a family together are curious ones. I doubted; I felt bitter, but not toward dad, because I had knowledge of his sickness and the cause of it. Rather I despised that which I could not understand—the *power* which would allow my family to go through so much hell, if there was any *power* at all. I quit praying, quit confiding in anyone, and quit crying for the entire worst and last year of his drinking problem.

But at the point which seemed to be the last bearable point for us all, the faith which these two little fellows had in their father was finally justified. He somehow found enough courage to admit the need for assistance. I shall never forget the impact of the words when he humbly said, "I need the help of each of you and I need all of the help I can get."

He had been searching for an answer, and because he had the courage to realize his human limitations and recognize a power above him, I too became aware of the need for accepting God as the *great helper*. There was a loving God, and He did do something. In fact, the five years have brought our family much closer together than ever before, for now we all realize how wonderful a real family can be.

She could afford to speculate from there on, and formulate her concepts of God. He is a loving personality from whom men have received everything they have, but He is also their Creator who requires obedience to His laws. Obedience implies freedom, and this was the main lesson that her father's drinking and mother's faith taught her. She discovered that "God is not trying to give us an easy way to completeness with Him, for there are many things which are pleasing to us but not means to ultimate happiness. Not only do we have to contend with the good which is pleasant, but also with the good which is unpleasant." Patiently bearing the cross, she found out, was not pleasant; but it was rewarding.

SIX

SEX

Pleasure versus Love

MAGAZINE articles about campus morals are misleading. They leave the impression that sex is the main interest of college students, and that virginity or male restraint is a Victorian relic in American university life.

Actually sex conduct among people attending college is no worse than among American youth generally. If there is any cause for concern it is not that some students are promiscuous or that many find sex morality their most difficult challenge. It is the insight their problems with chastity give us of a new dimension in Western culture, and the need for a drastic re-assessment of higher education which is supposed to prepare men and women for real life, including a life of sexual enjoyment in marriage.

These problems are a compound of elements as deep as human nature—the desire to be loved and wanted, the hope of security and family joys—and of elements peculiar to college life—the impersonality of a university metropolis, the mad scramble for recognition and urge to conformity, the faceless competition for grades and often the doctrinaire philosophy of self-assertion which ignores when it does not ridicule a lifetime of moral ideals and principles.

Join these with the enclosure in dormitories where

people of the most disparate background live together in such lack of privacy as never obtains in normal homes, where ideas are exchanged and changed through endless hours of conversation, and the wonder is how chaste the university population really is.

Campus Morals. With rare exception, students are brutally frank about morality on campus. Yet what they have to say is nothing new, certainly nothing that national magazines have not featured in a dozen ways during the past ten years.

I have in my files enough details to write another book, that will never be written, describing the sex patterns of the students, all on their own testimony and so sincere it is impossible to question their veracity.

What may be new and worth telling is their analysis of what is taking place. Depending on their moral outlook and religious training, they are either shocked or merely surprised at what they first experience. Sex on campus, according to one man, is an "uncontrollable plague." If he is a bit loose with his adjectives, at least the impression he gets is unmistakable:

It spreads among the students either by direct or indirect means, and leaves them either in a state of distress and depression or in just the opposite state of personal and pleasurable satisfaction. It depends on the student's sex, on his or her attitude toward sex, and on the way the sexual act was performed and with whom.

I would venture to say that the majority of women fall into the first state mentioned, and that at least eighty percent of the male students fall into the last. A sexual act with a person of the opposite sex tends to have a more demoralizing effect on women than on men. This is because the male student regards sex as that which makes his friends take notice and look up to him. He is actually proud of himself if he seduces a girl.

On the other hand, most women students look at it as

168

being used. They have lowered themselves to the pleasures of men and are now just a call number and a name that isn't respected. They feel guilty and degraded because of their action, because they used their bodies for impure and immoral acts.

This problem of sex on campus is uncontrollable in that it cannot be stopped or solved, because, in short, association brings on assimilation. The incoming freshmen are orientated to the sexual opportunities and happenings on campus just as well as they are to the school itself. This orientation is passed on from year to year, and the more students enroll the more widespread the problem gets.

Surveys of sex conduct are only minimally reliable. They are either too selective to give a fair estimate of the whole picture, or those who reply to questionnaires mentally qualify the answers to a point that negatives their response, and always in such delicate matters people are not likely to reveal themselves. The two Kinsey reports are consequently suspect in their major premise, that the replies he so carefully tabulated are truly representative, in his case of the students at Indiana University.

Nevertheless some stock may be placed in these surveys, when they cover a large segment of the enrollment (over a thousand students) and are repeated with different groups over a period of several years. The pattern that emerges I think is less shocking than most people might expect. Half the students believe that heavy petting is acceptable, one third that intercourse is allowable between those who are engaged, yet only one in ten claims that premarital relations are necessary to insure a well-adjusted marriage.

When they come to analyze sexual permissiveness, the women offer more extensive and incisive criticisms than men, no doubt because the moral factor plays a larger part in their estimate of sex. Those who come from a sheltered environment invariably find the college situation challenging, and their attitudes undergo a corresponding change. A sophomore coed expected her friends at college to be no different than those she had known in high school:

Little did I know that my new friends at college, my own roommates, students from homes like mine, the new boys I dated, and even many of the teachers would openly profess ideals so contrary to my own. I was totally unperpared to meet and have close association with the people who were profound atheists, and others preoccupied with nothing but sex. I was really unsuspecting, wasn't I?

But now that I have been in college a year and a half, I have met these people. I'm in college now and nothing shocks me any more. Things still sicken me, make me feel ashamed for my fellowman, make me feel alone in what I stand for, make me wonder if perhaps I've been wrong all along. But things have ceased to shock me. I like these people. They are my friends and I have learned to accept them for what they are. I don't exactly approve of most of them, but I like them and care for them. Their good qualities certainly cannot be denied. Besides my old friends from high shool are just like my college friends. They brag about their latest sex experience and wild parties. It doesn't just happen to be the crowd I'm mixed up with. It's all college kids, all adolescents out of high school. I do think we're still adolescents.

I would be pretty alone and miserable if I didn't communicate with these people, for they are my friends. I can't get away from them. It is because they are my friends that I find their morals so disheartening. If I didn't care for them, I wouldn't care what they did. But I can't just shut my eyes to the situation. I can't ignore it.

College students are under a strain and get depressed. Even those with the healthiest attitudes have their problems. And during college one is not always sure where to draw the line between right and wrong. Many questions arise and as many different answers are given. It isn't always easy to know just what is decent. Ideals are distorted by majority rule—

what everyone else is doing. Loving parents are not close at hand to guide. Understanding friends are just as confused.

But I also realize that students know the difference between kissing and petting. They should have the sense to find the right answers to their questions, to seek help from the proper source, to be individuals and stick up for what they believe. There is no excuse for the student who believes only what he wants to, who won't listen to reason. Just the other day one of my roommates said, in complete sincerity, "Sure I admit that I've petted with Joe, Bob, and Danny, but I don't do it with every Tom, Dick, and Harry." How she consoles herself with such reasoning is beyond me.

So many of my friends enjoy their immorality, and have seemingly no regrets about it. They have every intention of doing it again. This is what really scares me. But it doesn't bother them.

We who have stuck to our principles are definitely in the minority. Maybe this is not just in college life, and not just a reflection of the times we live in. It may be true in all levels of a society, and perhaps the same situation has existed throughout the ages of mankind. But it is true now.

She returns to the theme of fearing there may be some mistake. "So many times I wonder if maybe I haven't been wrong, if I'm not missing out on a lot of fun. Yet I know I could never live with myself if my standards were lowered to any degree. I would be in a state of misery." Every once in a while she is encouraged to believe she is right after all:

I pray to God and ask for His help, and now and then someone tells me they wish they could be more like me and not give in to their weaknesses. They say they respect me and wouldn't want me to change. Little things keep me going, keep my head above water, relieve doubts from my mind and renew my faith in mankind. It is then that I want to be better than ever. It is then I think my fellow students aren't so bad after all. Maybe this is just a stage they have to go through, of experimentation before reaching adulthood where they will have to settle down. I can at least console myself with this thought.

Then on a sobering note, "I only wish they could all make it, for the tide is turning against them. I hope that my generation, our generation, can instill more faith in God. I hope we can produce individuals who are not afraid to be individuals." She would like to see young men and women who can profit from the independence that society gives them, who believe that independence and maturity go hand in hand. "I would like to see students who are not afraid to stand up and say, 'This is against my beliefs and ideals,' who respect other people and their rights. Most of all, we need students who are better Christians, for surely good Christians are good people. Renewed faith in Christ is the key to the problem."

Another coed made almost the same discovery. Her parents gave her the basic information about sex, but she was not prepared for dormitory life, where "sex is the main topic of discussion." However, she does not think the intention behind the talk is reprehensible. "It is usually out of curiosity that girls talk about sex—not immorality. They often read and discuss materials written on the subject and help one another by giving advice." Many of them were too embarrassed to raise the issue with their parents back home, but they feel perfectly free to ask or say anything among women of their own age.

Time and again I have been told, as one student put it, "few of the girls approve of premarital intercourse or don't admit it if they do. The few known girls who have engaged in intercourse are the center of all the gossip, and are not wholly accepted by the others."

172

This judgment sheds considerable light on several distinctions that are not always made in appraising campus morals. Men and women differ radically in their moral sensitivities on sex. Allowing for exceptions on either side, men are generally more lenient in excusing men, including themselves, and more severe in judging women. Women speak of weakness when they give in to sex activity; men will boast of their strength. Men are more likely to demand as much as the woman allows and condone even intercourse; whereas woman may permit sex play, but are reluctant to engage in relations which symbolize the full giving of self and then only to the man they hope to marry.

Critical Appraisal. No matter how personally involved students may be, they are not sparing in their judgment of the moral climate that produced the sex hydra in what should be mainly an academic atmosphere. They quote the dropout figures for college, upwards of fifty and more per cent in some institutions, and point to the shambles of American family life (reflected in the mounting divorce rate) that colleges should be, but are not, helping to save by developing a stronger sex responsibility.

One man sizes up the situation by noting the obvious, that practically all studies indicate premarital sex is more prevalent than ever before. Many believe that only the lower classes are responsible for the rising index. Not so. The highest social castes are involved and college students are included, with some ranking universities taking the lead. The behavioral sciences suggest that what college people are doing today will be the ethical pattern of the next generation. "The problem, then, is reflective of our society as a whole, and as such concerns everybody." Colleges have a grave duty to do something constructive:

Many colleges are too lenient in their curfew hours for women students. Some allow too many opportunities for couples to be alone (and) even allow men and women to study together in the men's dormitory. I don't mean to imply that I am against college men and women being given opportunities to be alone. Those with affection for each other should have the privilege.

However, I believe that if the administration is to allow this freedom they have the responsibility of bringing the students to an understanding of and respect for moral and spiritual values. It's all right to allow togetherness and probably impossible to prevent. But it is also necessary that the students feel some sense of responsibility

This is probably the biggest task facing American higher education today. Students will have to be shown the difference between what is morally good and morally bad. They will have to be taught reverence for spiritual insight so they can better judge the morality of their actions. Colleges and universities will have to provide the means necessary to instill in their students a respect for the virtue of premarital chastity.

Another man is more comprehensive. Curbing the sex surge on college campuses, he thinks, is the joint responsibility of parents, churches, and universities. Parents have the gravest obligation because, no matter what faith they profess, if their actions contradict the teachings of their church, the children will instinctively follow the example of mother and dad, as naturally as "they acquired and speak their parents' language."

The churches should also play their part in developing a healthy attitude towards sex. They supply the parents with ideals and principles, offer their children opportunities for religious and moral instruction, and surround the teaching of morality with religious motivation for which nothing can supply.

But the universities, too, have a share in the responsibility, especially since many of the students and often most of the women live in residence halls on campus property ostensibly under some kind of moral supervision:

In my mind, the university is a place for higher education. It is not a place where sex morals are to be raised, and therefore the administration feels that whatever the students do is up to them, as long as they follow the rules. If they are not mature enough to conduct themselves in a respectable social manner, the consequences are on their own shoulders. The university has nothing to do with it. But doesn't it?

I'm not that well versed on the programs a university could incorporate to curb the overpractice of sex on campus, but I know a few practical things that could be done: 1) Eliminate all student ownership of vehicles on campus, unless a valid reason for having one is had, 2) Impose stricter regulation and enforcement of rules governing fraternities, 3) Impose stricter regulations concerning the checking out of women students for the weekends.

I think the car is the largest, single asset in the quest for sex. It is a means of escape to privacy, and it serves to help students get what they want because it serves as an influencing factor. If students do not have a car, they are practically immobilized. They are compelled to take their dates only to activities on campus or downtown; they can't go out and drink or park; they can't go to the beach or to parties out of town; they find it quite inconvenient when they have to walk to and from an apartment or a motel; and they also have trouble getting any kind of alcoholic beverage.

Fraternities can be an asset to university life and, properly conducted, they offer students opportunities for social development closed to those who are not Greeks. But the same power of organization that may assist can also demoralize if the membership is not well screened, or the wrong characters take charge, and sponsor events, or set a pattern that a man with conscience cannot morally follow.

Stricter regulations on the checking out of women is easier to advocate than implement. Enforcing regulations off campus is next to impossible, and the whole tenor of college discipline is to reduce instead of to increase the number of restrictions.

As students see it, the crux of the sex problem is tied in with the delicate balance between student rights, and college responsibilities. How far can the administration invoke "the welfare of the student," and in his interest impose limitations on freedom that he may not even experience at home?

Some reflective undergraduates are willing to admit they are not yet fully adults, and therefore the college may exercise a certain amount of control over them. Absolute freedom cannot be declared on issues where irresponsibility hurts not only the individual but also those around him. Yet they also feel that prohibitions cannot be rigidly applied to everyone without discrimination, especially when so many people in college are no longer teens, and married, and in any case, differ immensely in their relative maturity. A serious issue is transformed into low comedy, they tell me, when campus rules for those just out of high school are unsmilingly applied to the private lives of mature adults only because they are enrolled in the same university.

Spokesmen for the student body sympathize with the usual outrage over administrative action in trying to regulate morals. But they are also self-critical:

Students are typically still dependent on their parents who, in most instances, are financially sending them to college. Whether we like it or not, most parents, like mine, under American ground rules, hold colleges responsible for our intellectual, personal, and moral development. Whether this is as it ought to be is beside the point. The fact is that colleges are still given the task of acting 'in place of our parents.'

Many students, my own friends, have been fighting this doctrine vigorously, but they must consider it in effect until the colleges and American society jointly agree to declare it void. Realistically, the colleges cannot safely stop acting in place of our parents until such time as enough parents have in their own place and at the proper time prepared and conditioned their sons and daughters for the mature responsibility that is the greater part of freedom.

Another consideration should be the fact that American society endorses certain official standards of behavior. Since even adults are subjected to 'supervision,' it is hardly realistic to expect college administrations to give up policing their dormitories and their students' sexual behavior. Perhaps this is why campus life, once considered a luxury for the privileged few, is now increasingly considered restrictive. Now a growing number of campus dwellers would like to turn commuter mainly to escape from campus-regulated morality.

A deeper issue underlies this matter of external discipline. Too many college students are not ready to drink the heady wine of freedom that colleges traditionally offered. Their numbers preclude the likelihood of most of them being sufficiently inner-controlled to obviate the need for some (or as they think, too much) legislation. The watchword is "regimentation." If only it could be "guidance" or "direction," and not regimentation, so at least one woman undergraduate thinks:

It is the absence of clearly stated standards that leads to the progressive deterioration of conduct. The majority of young people are not irresponsible, weak, and impulsive; they are seriously concerned with the major problems of human life and are earnestly seeking some kind of guidance. In the absence of such guidance the exploiters of permissiveness exert the strongest group pressure. This is especially important in the domain of sexual morality among young adults. Unless the authorities strongly condemn immoral behavior, pressure by the 'fast-living' set becomes irresistible.

I have learned that "majority rule is never a norm for morality." I have taken this as a sort of personal motto. Just because so many people I know have no regard for their chastity, most certainly does not mean that it is a signal for others to follow them and head for 'ye olde necking grounds.' Chastity is something sacred, something worth-while. A girl, as well as a man, who loves and treasures purity, knows that there is nothing to gain, but there is a lot to lose. Once human beings seek one exception to the law of nature, they start down a steep precipice ending in general ruin.

We cannot uphold the dignity of chaste wedlock unless at the same time we defend the absolute necessity and the high dignity of extramarital chastity. And we can uphold our chastity, because each of us has our own 'personal code of conduct.' It certainly may not be something which we have written down, but nevertheless we have standards of behavior by which we live.

This is especially true of girls. There is probably not a girl in the world who doesn't know how to say, "No!" So, that is not really a problem, saying, "No!" The real problem—the one that most girls don't seem to realize is the basic problem—how to avoid having to say, "No!" For the chances are, if a girl has to say, "No," she has already gone too far for her own standards. If girls would stop to think about it, they would realize that if they had to end an evening by saying, "No!," then it is probably their own fault. A girl is given many opportunities to stop a situation at any point earlier in the evening. Even if she allows the fellow to park a car, she can still avoid a bad situation by insisting that it is time to be getting home. He may not be happy about it, but he will respect the girl for it.

Young men and women today have been reared under pressures, exerted from an increasingly early age, to render them socially 'mature' long before their time, with the accent on physical rather than intellectual and moral growing up. It is an odd thing that the most normal and natural thing about the teenage years is so often completely overlooked—the opportunity for growth. Those who claim readiness for early

178

marriage are often lacking in the very character and personality resources which ensure development toward maturity. They base their claim, however, on biological maturity, which most young people can claim in their very early teens.

It is, as everyone knows who has ever dated a single person for some time, natural to want to go farther than just kissing. But it is a great mistake to talk yourselves into the idea that it is not normal not to go farther. No doctor or psychological counselor will ever tell you there is any necessity to go farther, no matter how long marriage has to be put off to ensure a sound start. Especially is there no real need for sexual relations when both boy and girl are emotionally immature and insecure in their love.

It is true that the tendency nowadays of so many young people to make their relationship a frustrating one by going too far makes marriage seem like a necessity. But isn't it a bit ridiculous to get so excited about love-making that you cannot wait to get married, when by rushing marriage you may be spoiling your chances of having your love last? It is certainly the great mystery of human love which makes two hearts beat as one. It is a sacred flame; but one which has too often been abused.

The preparation for the sacred vocation of marriage should be started while teenagers are still in high school, since the majority of them do not go to college. That training must of course be amplified and intensified for us who do go to college. In college we are faced with a greater challenge to our moral ideals. I know that many of my moral ideals have changed. I no longer am afraid of being part of the "college generation." I feel that I can realistically face the challenge that is facing me; and this most certainly does not mean lowering my ideals to fit in with those which I have learned are immoral. Just because a person is thoroughly convinced of the worth-whileness of chastity, of its sacredness, does not mean that he will be leading a 'borderline' life. Just because I am now twenty years old does not mean that I have to make every date into a 'game' so I can catch a fellow. I have no fear of becoming an 'old maid,' because my friends say that I will

179

never catch a man if I don't let him make out. I feel that if a fellow really wants to spend an evening with me or any girl, it won't matter to him whether they spend it together at her house studying, provided her parents are home, or if they just go out for a walk, and talk. If his call is just an invitation to a necking session, then the girl is better off knowing the truth beforehand.

College is a challenge to everyone who goes. It is a challenge to us scholastically as well as morally. It is a time when we find out if we are ready to tackle the problems of the adult world; a time in which we will do things that will indeed be a test of our moral ideals. Even if there are times when we give in to the demands of our 'social group,' we can still avoid adding to those 'too late' situations. Only by restoring our values, if we have lost them, and forming sound goals can we hope to have a bright and happy future.

So much for idealism, yet an idealism that more college people put into practice than Sunday supplement philosophers would lead us to expect. Men and women exposed to the raw wind of sex every day, and almost every hour of their social life, still manage to keep chaste, except that their chastity is not the milky type associated with "nice people." It is of such fibre as only those who have access to the human conscience can appreciate.

Sex Appeal. In their analysis of sex conduct, young persons can be shrewder than their elders, if for no other reason than that experience is the best teacher. Men and women differ in their explanations of why sexuality has reached an all-time high, and the crest seems not to be yet in sight. Roughly speaking, men believe the principal factor is stimulation and women put it down mainly as commitment.

As men see it, the rising tide of sex activity among their peers is due in large measure to the atmosphere in which they live, which is literally charged with erotica to the point of suffocation. Wherever they turn, no matter what they see or hear, everywhere the libidinal drives are stimulated and the marvel is how self-contained men remain in spite of this hyperexcitation.

Women feel their main problem is not external stimuli, but internal emotions which are pulled to the breaking point by men who speak of love but often want only lust. And once a woman has committed herself to a man she loves, or thinks he loves her, she throws caution to the winds, even at the price of her chastity.

The men are usually not elegant in talking about the subject. But they make up for elegance with clarity. Speaking of erotic literature and entertainment, one married student put it bluntly: "It's almost to the point where mere fornication and adultery are mild. To insure your book financial success, you have to throw in some incest, homosexuality, and any other perversion that comes to mind." In the movies, "Nudes are becoming the vogue now. There are also pictures where premarital and extramarital relations are presented in a light comedy vein. You're supposed to laugh when you see some Don Juan bungle an opportunity to corner an unsuspecting girl in his apartment. It's funny to see Dad get caught having an adulterous affair. If you're supposed to laugh at this sort of thing, what do you get serious about?" Then he philosophizes:

The great harm done here is that the movies and books are seen and read by many of the younger generation. The type of activity they depict serves to overstimulate these young people sexually. This is especially so for boys. The stimulation does not last just when they're reading the book or viewing the movie, but comes back to them as their memories bring the scenes to mind. Most boys do not know how to handle this stimulation properly, and so they engage in some perversion to release sexual tension. Of course, the older the boy gets the more likely he is to use a girl for sexual release.

Stimulation continues into college, and, if anything, is stepped up to meet the more sophisticated, male appetite. In reflecting on these pressures, the men singled out one magazine as symbolic of the trend. *Playboy*, with a monthly circulation of over two million, is the most popular reading matter on campus. Each copy goes through at least a dozen hands before its pinups adorn the walls of the one who paid the subscription. It features complete nudity and through more than two hundred pages an issue offers every form of titillation that its staff of professionals can conjure up. The stress is on sex play and the impact of a single reading on the average college man, I am told, is to build up erotic tension that few can resist. Its publisher advocates the removal of all restriction on pornography in language and picture, including "a detailed examination of a couple engaged in various forms of sexual activity and intercourse—produced with the single and obvious intent of sexually arousing its audience." Within the limits of civil law, he succeeds admirably.

Women on campus become the objects of release, and, depending on their character, either add to the male stimulation because they enjoy the sex experience or allow themselves to be carried by their feelings because they cannot bear to think of living without the man who victimizes them.

In the nature of the case, I will not use confidential information given me by the students, in writing and at length, describing their involvement in this pavlovian web of conditioned reflexes: from erotica to arousal to heterosexual satisfaction. Only God knows the turmoil these young people experience, in several cases ending in pathology. My record was dealing with three attempted suicides in one month.

But one coed gave me permission to quote her story in part, changed only in such details as were necessary to shield her identity. It is eloquent in its simplicity and tells how a girl trusted too much, unwisely, unaware of the forces at work around and within her. Only a coincidence of circumstances and a strong faith in God save her from what is often a lifetime of tragedy:

On March 8, 1963, around one A.M. I entered Wilson Hospital to deliver my baby. The baby I could never have, as I wasn't married.

The first feeling I had when entering the labor room was one of relief, my trialed times were finally coming to an end. Then the hard labor began and the pain seemed as though it would never cease. All I wanted was relief as I had never known such pain existed. The thought of praying suddenly came to me, so rather than screaming I orally said every prayer that I knew again and again, and over the preceding months I had acquired quite a few. I soon discovered that talking to God relieved the pain—or so it seemed to me.

My thoughts went back to the night that began my worst months yet probably the most profitable ones of my life.

Ron and I were in love and planning on marriage after our completion of college, which was another year, and although I knew it was a mortal sin—I'm human—we had intercourse, to my unwillingness at first leading into desire and living for the moment.

I had been building up my courage for days to approach my mother; the notion only terrified me. She and my father would surely disown me. Their only daughter among five children letting this happen to her. They had done so much for me all my life—how could I tell them? I kept remembering the time that Mom told me that if I was ever in 'any' trouble she and Dad wanted me to come to them, not to try to handle it myself. I had never thought too much about her words. Now I desperately needed their help. Hanging onto these words I told Mom one night that I thought I might be pregnant. Of course she was quite speechless.

The tests came back the next day, Saturday, with positive results. Mom broke the news to Dad, which I found impossible to do myself. Dad, who had a prominent position in the city, who had worked so hard for his family, and who was so proud of me.

I'll never forget the look on his face when I finally talked to him. He suddenly looked so much older than his years. A man who had tried his best yet felt as though he had failed. He was as diplomatic as he could be. I knew I had deadened a part of both of them.

I went back to school in a daze of depression. I seriously knew that marriage wasn't the answer. Neither one of us were really ready for marriage. We both had another year of school and I knew that if Ron quit to work until after the baby was born, that consciously or subconsciously he would hold his postponing his education or possibly not obtaining it all against me. And myself—I wasn't so sure I wouldn't feel the same way, as I had worked all my life to go to college, putting myself through, and now I had planned to do my student teaching in the fall. I just had this very strong feeling that marriage wasn't the answer. I knew it wouldn't work.

That weekend Ron came and we discussed, contemplated, and discussed some more. We decided at that time that marriage would not be the answer. The following weekend we thought we should marry. This went back and forth for several weeks, time rapidly slipping by with no decision in view. My folks considered marriage the best way. I was feeling the pressure placed on me to the extent where I reminded them that it was a decision that Ron and I would have to make.

The decision was made when Ron informed me he didn't think he was ready for marriage. I replied that if that was the case I would never want to see him again—not for reason of punishment, but simply that there was no future in it and I couldn't see continuing a relationship where I wouldn't be keeping the child of the man I was dating. I knew it would be a long and rugged time ahead, I would have to go it alone.

I was putting the baby up for adoption through a reputable, church adoption home. I knew I could never give the child the home, parents, and love that it deserved and needed by myself and I knew that this agency would find such a home for this child. The child's welfare was naturally a major concern of mine and I wanted it to have a chance for the best. I had to condition myself to think that this child that was developing in my womb would not be mine. I was carrying it for someone else. This was very difficult to do as I became more and more attached to it as the months went by.

The social worker that did the arranging for a home was very helpful to me. I went to her countless times, each time giving her more information of Ron's background and mine, including my parents and four brothers in order for her to find the most suitable parents and home for the child. The agency was exceedingly thorough.

I went to the clinic at the hospital for my prenatal appointments which were experiences in themselves. I didn't realize how fortunate I was to have such a wonderful family until for instance, when one girl (age fifteen) told me that her folks had disowned her completely along with all her relatives save one aunt, who was letting the girl live in her home only until the baby was born. Then the girl would have to find a way of supporting herself and the baby. The poor child, only fifteen and no help from anyone. I might add that she had had cancer at one time and was far from a very strong person.

Another girl, also age fifteen, failed to realize the sin of her act and really found it quite humorous. She was dating other fellows besides the father of the child and on numerous occasions told of the fun she had had at some party the previous weekend. I failed to see the humor in her situation.

I had never before actualized the number of girls who were unwed mothers. The amount is staggering. The most awakening fact, the age element. The majority under seventeen. In fact, I was the oldest one they had in the group of girls going to the clinic at that time, myself being twenty-one. There were times I felt older, seeing the girls without a decent future to look forward to, with little education, and for the most part, less ambition to do anything about it.

I was repeatedly reminded seeing the girls almost every week of what might have happened to me if it wasn't for the strength, faith, and desire to go on given to me by the sympathy and kindness of my family and friends. I know I couldn't have done it alone. Faith in God can give one a great deal of strength, yet I believe one has to have loved ones standing beside them at the same time. I certainly had both.

I had the prerogative of seeing the baby or not. At first I had chosen not to, then after contemplating the matter over I realized that this was my only chance. I felt strong enough in my decision to give her up so I didn't think seeing her would affect me in anyway. Now I'm glad I did see her, for I knew for sure then that she was a healthy and, I might add, a beautiful child, a child that would make some couple very happy.

The day I left the hospital, Mrs. Swanson, my social worker and I had to go to court to finalize the giving over the child to the adoption agency. It was indeed an onerous task. I thought the worst part of the past months was over. I was wrong. The hardest part was yet to come, giving up my baby—never to see her again. I had known from the beginning that I wouldn't be keeping the baby but when the final time came to sign papers and swear to God that I would never see this child again, I discovered that this was the most difficult thing that I would ever have to undertake. It was like signing part of my life away. In fact, I felt the strong desire of screaming, "No you can't have my baby, I carried it for nine months and I brought her into this world, she's mine!" I forced myself to do the opposite. Mrs. Swanson assured me that she had already found a home for the baby and that she would be living with her new family in a couple of weeks.

I have periods of depression when I think that I have a baby somewhere and I shall never see her or know what she will be like or what her future will be. I then have to remind myself that she is undoubtedly very happy. Happiness she wouldn't have known with me. It is not an easy thing though, going through life knowing you have a child somewhere, an illegitimate child no less. I have survived presently due to my strength based on the faith I've acquired over the preceding months. My past is an experience I have to live with and overcome, becoming a more knowing and better person by it. I believe I am accomplishing this slowly, but surely.

I could let my experience control the rest of my life, and possibly ruin it. Life has too much to offer to sit by and not take advantage of it. Every experience teaches. In such a strong experience one either falls one hundred per cent or lives one hundred per cent better.

She was fortunate. Other women on campus escape the trials of pregnancy but also never learn to control their impulses. Some believe they are in the minority, but not one staff assistant who turned over to me some of her letters home, to be used in writing this book. "Living on such a short corridor," she wrote, "most everybody is aware of what is happening in others' rooms. Out of sixteen rooms on the corridor, the number of girls who have frequent intercourse is sixteen. This means an average of one to a room." Then she reflects on herself.

I'm beginning to think I'm definitely in the minority and some even look at me queerly when I ask some 'ignorant' question. Please don't misunderstand me, I wouldn't have it any other way. Not everybody is like this, thank goodness, but it sure is a switch from high school. I can remember when a girl could be ostracized for getting married whether she had to or not. Now, if a girl has to get married it's 'no big thing.' It's just that they were unlucky enough to be the couple who got caught. With everyone accepting this so readily, it is no wonder that girls don't think twice before succumbing. There's little or no social stigma attached to being compelled to marry.

The most confusing part of all this is that these girls have no compunction, bragging about their feats or complaining

about the treatment they receive after they have been so oblig-
ing. They have absolutely no conception of what they have
done and seem quite naive in their expectations of the boys.

Remember how surprised I was when I wrote you about
the dates I had had. These fellows seemed so appealing and
yet after a couple of dates—and drinks—they seemed to think
they had a right to make all sorts of demands on you.

Maybe I'm just naive, but I expected no noticeable change
between senior boys in high school and freshmen in college.
But there certainly is! The college boy seems more serious in
his intentions, that is, he *thinks* he is in love; and he *says* he
wants to marry you. Therefore he assumes he has a right to be
more demanding. There seems to be less of a physical attraction. The high school boy certainly doesn't have marriage on
his mind and is not even sure of the meaning of love. I still
wonder what brings on this change. It almost seems as if the
college student is compelled by some desire to relieve his tension or build his deflated ego. It is easy in a large university
for a person to become quite unidentified.

Surprised at the ethical standards around her, yet realistic enough to take them in stride, she admitted being
shocked "to find that most girls think you cannot possibly
go with a boy for any length of time without petting and
that many girls have intercourse before they are married." However, "when you see the drastic adjustment in
their environment you may more readily understand why
the sudden change in attitudes. As the extent of the adjustment is lessened, the shifting of attitudes will narrow."
Desperately in want of acceptance and urged by their
deepest instincts to conform, "these girls need someone
they can talk with and trust, especially if they are in trouble." But the metropolis of which they are anonymous
parts can hardly be expected to help—if only because it is
so big and they are so small.

As a rule men take a more detached view of sex conduct. They see that "some students have set high ideals and

live by them. Others have developed a low set of moral standards. Which type is prevalent? Neither." In this fraternity man's judgment, "Most students play the game of life fairly straight. But these same people will be tempted and many will fall." So much for the past. "Do they live their life like this after they made the first mistake? No. The average student has a few experiences of immorality but does not set his goals by them." He profits from the exposure to challenge and, if nothing else, is a wiser man for the experience.

SEVEN

MARRIAGE

Ideals with Realism

W HEN you receive an invitation to speak at a woman's residence hall or sorority, you can predict in four cases out of five what they want you to talk about. It is either "marriage" or "birth control," with a preference for marriage. The reasons are obvious. Many young women enter college with the avowed purpose of finding a marriage partner. Others believe that college will better equip them to marry successfully, or at least the experience of one to four years on campus is useful in choosing a mate.

It is hard to generalize, but it seems that most women are seriously thinking about marriage from the day they enter college. They may not be planning on matrimony as freshmen or sophomores, but they are more realistic than men in seeing the opposite sex as a potential spouse, and their attitudes are heavily colored by this concern. Often the men are blind to this feminine bias and act like school boys in their treatment of women, reflecting an immaturity that girls are quick to spot. In fact, coeducation in college almost creates the anomaly of two sexes vying with each other for mastery: the men trying to get a degree and some basis for future security and the women (while getting a degree) looking around for someone to marry.

Consistent with their realism, women distinguish between sex and love to an extent that baffles most men even when they exploit a woman's desire for affection and compromise her chastity in the process. Depending on their ability to communicate, women differ in the explanation, but they are quite clear that marriage should build on more than sex attraction. They learn very soon that sex is too passionate in men to be trusted apart from something higher:

It is in a woman's nature that she wants to be loved and to think he feels for her. I realize this may be a childish attitude to have because if he loved her truly he would not ask her to submit to his demands. Some men put sexual relations on such a high level that if a girl doesn't submit, they will quickly drop her as immature.

Another excuse or reason given is that they should find out if they are sexually compatible. They want to know this before marriage, because marriage is an important step and they do not want to ruin their future. Many girls fall for this routine, perhaps out of love for the fellow and find that giving in to his demands is the only way to keep his 'love.'

Perceptive men say the same thing, like the English major who describes the situation in terms of Ian Fleming, the creator of James Bond. As he sees it, Bond is the "All-American boy" type, super spy, super lover, and generally the greatest thing the British have going for themselves. His feats are told in a series of books in which Bond is always confronted with a countersuperman, an enemy of the English people, and several women, most of whom he must inevitably seduce before the end of the book:

Mr. Fleming seems to be the English Hugh Hefner (publisher of *Playboy*) as far as his views on sex are concerned. Bond has countless affairs with women, whom he often has just met. His view that 'sex is something to be given willingly whenever one feels like it' is not much more than a man's wishful thinking. Sexual experience is gratifying, truly gratifying, only when it occurs with someone you love. Sex relations other than this place a person at an animal level, a fairly obvious characteristic of James Bond.

Through all the personal testimonials written by women, they insist on the distinction between love and appetite. They are willing, sometimes too willing, to go along with the appetite but only because they hope (often naively) to foster the love. One of the most poignant statements came from a girl who was caught in the dilemma and could not extricate herself:

I really felt I loved him, and that he loved me. After another month or so, he made his first move, which he told me later took a lot of courage. I was startled, dumbfounded, hurt, confused. Nothing like this had ever happened to me before. I had never dated one boy for this long a period at one time, just different boys casually. What he did really made me mad. I ignored him the rest of the night and most of the next week and warned him never to try anything like that again. He promised over and over he wouldn't and how sorry he was until I forgave him and we were finally back to normal. I had believed him.

It didn't last long though, until he tried it again and we went through it all over. I put up with it because I felt I really loved him, and that he loved me. He said he did it because he loved me, and I said, "Don't do it if you love me," and kept insisting like the books said. "Prove your love by controlling yourself."

Each time we broke up I couldn't stand it without his company, so finally one day I gave in, and petting became the normal once or twice a week occasion. I felt it was wrong, I knew it was wrong, I couldn't help doing it, though, because I wanted to show him that I loved him, wanted him content, partially wanted to satisfy my own curiosity, but did it mostly for his sake.

This girl, with high ideals, was victimized by the prevalent mores. As she put it, society almost expects young people to have sex relations before marriage and frowns on their activity only if the girl becomes pregnant. "Then it is a mistake if it happens. We are expected to use contraceptives or relieve the sexual desires in other ways, if we're to stay out of trouble." Her own principles were against this. "I don't like the idea of satisfying sexual desires out of marriage, and there are others that probably feel the same way, but get hooked into it the same way I did. I think if marriage could be made possible sooner for couples who are seriously considering it, it would be better than having to go through what I did." She plans to marry the man, but regrets the mental anguish which the pressures of a sex-stimulated culture had brought her.

Christian Ideals. In proportion to their Christian upbringing and the depth of religious commitment, college men and women have high ideals of marriage and its responsibilities. Catholics and Protestants differ in their understanding of marriage as a sacrament, and they may not agree on such things as family planning, but they are not much different about the basic meaning of the married state or the essential conditions for marital happiness.

A Protestant coed soon to be married frankly believed that one of her main goals in life had always been to marry and have a happy family of her own. She was conditioned to this by years of experience. "Our home," she recalled, "has been one of comfort, understanding, happiness, and wonderful memories. It was home where we, the children, have been able to express our feelings, were taught right from wrong, and always received encouragement and guidance." Out of this atmosphere she developed a philosophy of marriage that is all the more remarkable for its authenticity. Except for the Scriptures, there are not two sentences of quotation:

Marriage is a holy union of two people as one. In a successful marriage both partners must learn to understand and tolerate the other's differences; they must acquire tact and the ability to sacrifice and, most important in a successful marriage, God's advice and guidance must be pursued through His word and through prayer. In the Bible God has established guidelines for couples to follow and rely upon. He has given them a set of goals and standards for married life, and He has instilled in them the ability, desire, and courage to reach these goals, if they truly believe in Him and His word.

Marriage is a life-lasting union between man and woman. It is a sacred union and one that has many reasons and purposes behind it. The partners in a marriage are joined by a mutual love and understanding. The two people work as a team in rearing their children, in managing their home, as citizens of the United States, and as Christian members of the church of Christ. In teamwork, conflicts may arise, but the team members must have the courage, faith, and strength to admit that a conflict is present and work on the problem until a solution is discovered. They must be able to discuss freely, easily, and openly with each other. If they aren't able to communicate with each other, more serious problems may arise and eventually divorce may result.

In the formation of the team in marriage much consideration must be given to the choosing of one's mate. Many times one may feel that he is in love, and this one is the one forever, only to realize later that it was infatuation. Fortunately the majority of the people are able to distinguish between infatuation and love before the marriage contract is made. In seeking a mate, God's guidance must be sought through prayer. He will guide and direct one to the one meant for him, He will aid in the development from infatuation to a beautiful, spiritual love. I thought I was in love twice before I met Jim, but due to God's guidance and help I realized, after three years of acquaintance with Jim, that he was the one for me. It was important to me to find someone who would treat me as a lady; I wanted someone my parents enjoyed being with and one they would approve of; it was also my desire to find someone with interests and beliefs similar to mine so that we had activities, goals, and aims that were similar; and very important to me was if he would go to church or not.

It was in Jim that I found all the above qualifications plus many more. He is ambitious, faithful, attentive, understanding, and a Christian. We are in agreement as to the rearing of children and practicing our faith. I know that without God's help I never would have seen Jim's qualities. It was through faith in the Lord; facts I learned of Jim and a feeling of understanding, desire to be with him, and a feeling of devotion that I discovered a devotional love for him. In worshipping together we have discovered that our love is strengthened and that a deeper understanding and admiration develops. We are determined to raise our children under such Christian love, to teach them that it is through faith in Jesus that our questions are answered and that we receive direction to the path of love and devotion. Through the love of Christ I discovered the love of the man I am soon to marry. There have been several times that Jim and I disagreed, and during such times I have turned to God in prayer asking for His guidance in doing the correct thing overcoming the difference, and asking forgiveness for feeling disgusted and unhappy with my loved one. He has always answered my prayers.

The old saying, "marriage is a fifty-fifty proposition" may be classed as a falsehood. Many times one may find he is required to give ninety to ten. It is true that compromises must be reached, but to reach a compromise one may have to resign himself completely to the other. Even though one has been wronged he must be willing and ready to forgive. He may find that he has to forgive many, many times but when one's mate asks for reconciliation, the other must pardon him.

In order to be so willing to forgive one must have faith, strength, and understanding; these necessary qualities may be obtained through the reading and believing of God's word. Only for the asking, He is willing to forgive us no matter how many times we may sin. If He can forgive us, we certainly can forgive our fellowman, especially our loved one. Because a problem may arise between partners, marriage and love do not cease. Through understanding and forgiveness the marriage is enriched and the love is made stronger. If a person can maintain the above qualities through pain and strife, he is a Christian depending on God's word and guidance.

She is old-fashioned enough to think her husband should be in charge and is concerned on the eve of marriage to make herself selfless enough for the role of a Christian wife. Her ideas must seem strange to readers of *Feminine Mystique* or to champions of the emancipated woman:

In less than two months I will be the wife of a wonderful man. It is my desire to make him happy and to have a happy home and married life with him. I am a very possessive person and at times very bossy, but I have made a great effort and have been quite successful in overcoming these habits. I firmly believe that the husband should be the head of the household and that major decisions should be made by him. I don't mean to say that I should not be consulted or that I should be completely submissive. I feel I should have the privilege of expressing my opinion and being a part of the final decision. Today a woman has more independence and freedom than she has ever had before. For many it is difficult to submit themselves to a man; for others it is a joy and an honor to please the man they love.

A married woman can still remain independent to a certain extent; however, she is dependent upon her husband in many respects. He is providing for her physical, emotional, and social needs and desires. She can belong to various organizations as she chooses, but these organizations should never interfere with her duties as a wife. She can be a leader in society but her leadership should not be practiced in the home, for this is where her husband is to lead. A woman who marries, as I myself will do, is choosing to give up her independence; and, instead of living as one, she is choosing a life as part of a team. She is choosing to submit to her husband, who is worthy of her submission. Her ideas and abilities are to be used in establishing the policies of the home, policies that are not to be made selfishly but in the interest of both members of the team. Policies made under such joint decision govern and satisfy both partners.

The husband has an important role of responsibility and leadership. He is also dependent upon his wife for satisfaction of certain physical, emotional, and social needs and desires. He does not consider her ideas and suggestions as detriments to his manliness if there is a feeling of good will and understanding between them; rather he seeks her ideas and suggestions and considers them in making his final decisions. The husband, as leader, is sensitive to the needs of his wife and family. He does not do as he wishes, rather he carries out the plans and policies made by the two of them as a team in the interest of the team. Christ came to earth not to do as He wished, but to lead in carrying out the plan He and His Father had decided upon.

Sex is an essential part of marriage, but she does not consider it everything and least of all the normative principle of a happy union, as though successful wedlock is to be measured by the amount of pleasure the couple derive from intercourse:

There is a mutual dependence in marriage on the satisfaction of the sex drive. This satisfaction is by no means the most important part of marriage. Marriages that are based on physical love and attraction only are not likely to last, for understanding, sympathy, and comradeship are also necessary for a successful marriage. Sex is not to be treated lightly, especially in our society today where there is a definite problem with the

197

morals of the people. God created sex, He is the one who fashioned the bodies of men and women to match their personalities. He meant it to be an enjoyable act between two people who are in love. The reason for the completion of the sex act is the procreation of offspring, it is not only for enjoyment. Sex is wrong when it dominates a marriage, when everything revolves around it. It is beautiful when it is a uniting factor, when it brings two people who enjoy each other in all situations closer together.

To be a virgin is a virtue many women no longer possess. To most women who are no longer virgins, sex has one reason: satisfaction, or pleasure. Most men who are involved in premarital sex-relations have one goal in mind: satisfaction, or pleasure. It is the terrible truth today that too many men and women have only the one reason for sexual relations, the true meaning and feeling of sex is removed. In a Christian marriage sex is a very personal thing, it is a uniting factor, it aids in the growth of love between two partners.

Convinced that selfishness is at the root of all marital unhappiness, she has no illusions about the difficulty of adjusting to her husband. With a woman's intuition, she plans on ways to avoid needless friction and above all to include God as a partner in the marriage. Knowing her personally, I can vouch for her delicate practicality and absence of anything suggesting girlish immaturity. Her piety is not sentimental:

The most important mutual role that husband and wife play is the understanding and satisfying of the other's needs and desires. As a wife, I want to be able to recognize the needs of my husband, and upon realization that a need exists, be able to satisfy that need. It is my firm belief that many marriages fail because each partner is so concerned with his own desires that he can't be bothered to realize that his mate also has needs and concerns.

In this respect marriage is a fifty-fifty proposition. Each

member of the team must be able to give and take, each must be aware of the other's needs. If one's partner is not aware of his needs he should feel free to bring it to the other's attention. It may be a temptation to say nothing concerning this desire, but it is usually better to bring it out into the open for discussion rather than harboring it. When little things mount up a very unnecessary disagreement may result; this disagreement may be avoided if the partners are able to communicate freely with each other. We bring our concerns and problems to the Lord in prayer so that He may aid us in the solutions of these perplexities. So must we also go to our marriage partner when we have questions. Yes, there are many roles that a man and woman acquire as they become a husband or a wife. No matter what one's role may be, as God's advice is requested, He will aid in the determination and administration of this role.

A Christian's view of marriage is determined by his faith in God, and the facts and his feelings about and towards his mate. My goal is soon to be reached, and as the day approaches when Jim and I will be united as one, I turn to the Lord many times in prayer, asking for solution of a problem that has risen, and His guidance in making of such an important decision as marriage. I pray He will watch over us and guide us in raising our family and establishment of our home. Christian partners form a Christian home where their beliefs will be transmitted to their children and confirmed by their actions. A Christian marriage and home is the answer to my prayers.

A Catholic view of marriage differs in two significant ways: it is considered a sacrament which confers grace in the form of divine light and strength for husband and wife, and it is irrevocable until death, which precludes remarriage after a sacramental union between two Christians, whether Catholic or otherwise.

Shortly before her wedding, a Catholic coed wrote a personal commentary on the ceremony for marriage, and applied its ritual lessons to the life ahead of her. "Marriage is a sacrament," she begins. "A holy union of two people blessed by God. My marriage is not to last for a day, a month, a year, or years. It shall not terminate because of a quarrel, incompatibility, or lack of love. A lifetime of sharing, giving of one another, building upon the love we have as long as we shall live."

Reflecting on the importance of perfect love, which means sincerity and sacrifice, she anticipates problems, no doubt, but also the help from God which a common faith will insure:

I'm twenty years old, what do I know about love? Am I willing to deprive myself to make sacrifices for my husband? The man kneeling next to me is about to become my husband. We've known each other over two and a half years. In that time we've become very close. This closeness has not been limited to a physical closeness. We have also grown together spiritually. We both have a deep faith and strong trust in God. I, to date, have benefited more from our relationship.

Our mutual belief in the Catholic Church has nourished our love and is the basic communication between one another, and foundation upon which our marriage is built. Another very important factor in our relationship and in fostering love is our honesty with one another. Developing a trust in a person and feeling free enough to be completely honest with another person is a quality in friendship that should be treasured. To be able to discuss feelings honestly and incidents with your spouse without fear of offending him or destroying his trust in you is a great boon to a marriage. The priest said only love can make self-sacrifice easy. How true this is. Because in loving my husband making sacrifices is not a painful task. There's a feeling of wanting to give up things, a feeling of pleasure in knowing that you can give up something in order to make your husband happy and ultimately making your relationship a happier one.

The ring is a symbol of a pledge of fidelity, promising to be faithful to one another. During the marriage ceremony it seems impossible to fathom unfaithfulness by either of us. But in thinking, I know the possibility exists and in our society unfaithfulness in marriage is prevalent almost to the point of becoming an accepted norm. Also living in a society where we both will be acquainted with many people and will be meeting others frequently the feeling of being attracted to certain personalities is normal. But temptation if it ever became too strong must be avoided. By giving in to one temptation of unfaithfulness I'd be risking my marriage, my husbands's faith and trust in me. Without faith and trust, for me, I'd have a marriage in name only. We will both need God's help in preserving us from falling into unfaithfulness.

Although her husband is entering a financially secure profession, she knows the pressures placed on women in the United States to continue working after they marry. As a wife, she believes, "I will have certain duties. As a helpmate, I will do what I can to make my husband's homelife comfortable. This, for me, does not include the taking of a job." She argues from some experience.

I have seen many families where the wife, who also may have a few children, is out working full time. The home is deprived of the feeling of being a home. It becomes just a house where husband and wife share two meals a day and both are exhausted everyday when they return from work. Numerous arguments can arise as a result of the double income. First arguments are more likely to start because of the irritability and tiredness of both parties. Moreover the wife instead of being interested in her husband's work and encouraging him in his job, can become more self-centered because of her interest in her own work. Finally, the money that the wife earns gives her a sense of independency. She no longer has to depend on her husband for her comfort and security. If her salary is higher as in some cases, it might be that her husband will be made to feel inadequate as a provider and as a husband.

Today more than ever, the home is not centered around the emotional or intellectual needs of a family. It is centered around finances and material wants. A lot of young couples today both work for a number of years and keep from having children, at least not more then one or two, in order to buy everything they want for material comfort. The necessity of the big rush in both working is so they can afford to buy things while they're still young enough to enjoy them. Somehow to me, their purpose is defeated. When they're first married they're working, indulging their own self-interests, plus eliminating the primary goal of marriage, the procreation of children. Finally when the money is gained and material goods obtained enough to satisfy both, as a married couple they have lost the communication and relationship they had at the beginning of their marriage. They've both been so busy working at setting up an ideal family through material comforts they've forgotten to build on their own relationship, and for some reason unexplainable to either of them, they've drifted apart. I believe, the wife's place should be in the home, at least as long as she has a growing family.

She looks forward to the children that will hopefully enter her married life. "Children," she exclaims, "what more could a couple ask from God than this gift?" If a child is the symbol of love between husband and wife, it is also a responsibility on the parents and especially the mother. "A mother must love her child and fulfill its need for emotional gratification. Of course, a child's physical needs must be taken care of too, but this is a small part in comparison with the love and affection a baby needs. All through childhood, it is necessary for the home to be a place of security. This is more the obligation of the father."

Besides physical and emotional stability, the child

needs to be developed spiritually and mentally. Again the mother's role is primary:

> A child readily accepts the fact that he is loved by God. A young child's mind is open to learning and guidance. It is up to the mother especially, whose time is spent in great lengths with her child, to teach or guide the child's mind in learning about God. I believe, it is possible to teach, in simple terms, a child of three about God.
> The best possible way for a child to learn is by imitation. The cliche of 'do as I say not as I do,' cannot apply. Some form of daily family devotion is very important. A father and mother must set examples, good examples. This applies not only to religion but every aspect of day-to-day living. Religious and intellectual education can then be furthered upon entering the child in a parochial school. But still the family is important. The family's end is union with God. This union must have its roots in the family in order to gain its end. As both wife and future mother I must see these duties fulfilled.

Knowing her character, she expects problems. "My greatest weakness," she admits, "is lack of patience. In married life I will have to work at controlling my impatience, in coping with situations different from what I'm used to." But again, "with the help of God," she looked forward to the future. In the two years since she married, she had more than her share of difficulties and more demand than she ever dreamed on her patience under trial. Her confidence, however, was not disappointed.

Mixed Marriage. A university is pluralistic in the extreme. Students come from every kind of religious background, or none, and among these with the same church affiliation are the fervent and the lax, with the majority in-between.

Interfaith marriages are, therefore, inevitable, and among the pressing decisions that young people are called upon to make, the choice of marrying outside their faith is for many the most painful experience of college days.

Men are usually more pragmatic about these things. They tend to underestimate the possible tensions or the corrosion of all belief that conflict over religious differences can produce. But there are exceptions, as the senior who has since entered a divinity school:

The fundamental question regarding interfaith marriage is: Can two people of different faiths effect a complete and satisfying marriage while retaining commitment to their own religious orientation?

At the outset, we can say that this amalgamation is not ideal. It is obviously desirable that a married couple agree in all important matters. If religion is, as most of us will agree, of basic (perhaps greatest) importance, then it follows that it is better if there is common agreement on religious commitment.

The question then takes on two possible forms. First, can the basis for a successful marriage be other than religious. Secondly, we have the possibility of an agreement in which religion has a central place but each of the partners expresses the common commitment in different ways.

The first of these alternatives seems less than desirable since it relegates religion to a relatively unimportant facet of the lives of both members of the marriage. The second of the alternatives seems to me to be the most desirable solution under the given circumstances. It does, however, presuppose a relatively high degree of intellect on the part of those involved. The whole problem is to respect the validity of your spouse's religious commitment while preserving your own.

Most women do not speculate about the principles involved, but they are greatly concerned about how the marriage will work out. Even those who enter mixed marriage have their misgivings, and, according to their own commitment, are more or less prepared to make the best out of what no one denies is a risky enterprise.

One girl who was contemplating marriage with a Protestant planned her life in such detail it would be a pity to cut her analysis. Based on experience and written with an eye to her own married life, it leaves little to the imagination. She assumes good will and strong faith on both sides, and more than average ingenuity on the part of the Catholic wife, which she calls "tactics," and not without reason:

The strain of different faiths is obviously more acute when children result from the marriage bond. However, the friction can be kept to an absolute minimum or completely eliminated by the right tactics. For purposes of illustration, I will use a Catholic wife and an average Protestant husband.

Upon rising in the morning, the Catholic recites her morning prayers before she begins her daily duties. More likely than not, her non-Catholic mate does not have this practice. If this is a source of irritation, the prudent wife will not make a big display of saying her prayers. And while not necessarily hiding the fact that she is praying, she can do so rather unobtrusively.

Another step is waking the children and leading them in their morning prayers until they are old enough to do so themselves.

Grace is said at every meal, and any form of thanking God for the food which He has so generously provided is acceptable. It is not necessary to use the generally accepted Catholic form of giving thanks. This practice may take the edge off, or completely remove, any tension that may otherwise arise at mealtime. It is possible that the family may wish to compose their own prayer of thanks and this could possibly bring them closer together and make mealtime a pleasure instead of a secret dread.

If the children attend a Catholic school, it would be advisible for the wife to take her husband to see the school and meet the nuns. Many non-Catholics labor under the impression that nuns are 'different' in the sense that they are weird and may not like the idea of them teaching their children. A short chat with a nun that perhaps the wife is familiar with will quickly relieve the other partner and show him that the good sisters are merely dedicated women who have given their lives to God and manifest this in their teaching. It will serve to point up that nuns are, indeed, 'human.'

If the children attend a public school, they should be enrolled in a weekly catechism class. This religious education should also be supplemented by home training, as is necessary even when they attend a parochial school, but more necessary in the former case. This training should not be done outside of the husband's sight or hearing unless he is engrossed in something else. If the children were taught their prayers and given moral guidance away from their father, he would surely feel left out or slighted, as if the rest of the family had something that he could not share. Even though he does not participate in the religious education, to relieve him of a feeling of being an outsider will lessen household tension considerably. And it is well to remember that he may have a favorite prayer that the children would enjoy learning. It is the little things like this that will strengthen the family and the marriage bond.

Husband and wife should definitely agree before marriage on their values and ethics which will be transmitted to their children. In this way, they will both have the pleasure of training the children so that they grow up to have high ideals and morals and will be a credit to both parents, the product of mutual love and understanding fostered in their offsping.

The time of Sunday worship may present a feeling of tension between the two partners. In some cases the Protestant may not regularly attend services and find it hard to understand why his Catholic mate has to go to Mass *every* Sunday. It should be explained that obligatory attendance is a safeguard to the faith, for the Church knows human nature very well. It is easy to fall lax in practice, and weekly Mass renews the faith at least a little and tends to enrich it and bring it clearly to mind. Also, a good practice is to stress clearly that one enjoys going to Mass, that she likes it. *Never* should the remark be made that 'I *have* to go to Mass.' Regard it as a privilege and a pleasurable task rather than a drudgery into which the Church forces its members.

A wise and rewarding point to make is to heartily encourage the non-Catholic to attend his own church regularly. He will surely gain much, for he can't possibly lose. And the thought would definitely be appreciated. When the spouse becomes accustomed to regular church attendance, it will make it much easier for him to understand why his wife and children appreciate going to church. Maybe, just maybe, in time he will come to ask if he too may join in the Catholic services on occasion. It would surely be a good idea tactfully to invite him to attend, maybe at Christmas or Easter, or perhaps on just any day. However, the matter should not be pressed if he declines, but rather dropped and suggested at a later time.

It should definitely be explained to the children why their father doesn't go to church with them, that he was brought up in another faith but that he believes that they should go to church with mother and learn her religion. Never tell children false stories about parental religious variances but be truthful and tactful. It would be gratifying to encourage the children to say a secret prayer that their father may someday appreciate and embrace the faith as they do. But it is definitely wise to explain to children when they are old enough to understand that God does not give the gift of faith to everyone and perhaps their father may never acquire it, but never give up praying for it—witness the faith and endurance of St. Monica. When children are able to understand, it is advisable to ask the non-Catholic to explain a little bit about his faith to them, not to an extent that they will become confused; but rather to deepen their understanding of the difference in their parents' religions. In this manner, the children will grow to love their own faith more, and to appreciate and respect the faith of their Protestant parent.

Religious objects in the home may present a source of conflict in a mixed marriage. Most non-Catholic homes do not display religious statues, pictures, and the like. If this is true, perhaps a mutual agreement can be arrived at. A picture of the Last Supper, a tasteful crucifix or some other nondenominational religious work may be placed in a modest location in the home. If the non-Catholic partner is strictly against other forms of religious objects displayed, a bedside stand or kitchen shelf would provide an unobtrusive and unoffensive place for a statue or picture of a favorite saint.

Certain religious practices, such as reciting the Rosary, could be performed while the husband is at work or after Sunday Mass if it is the cause of strife between husband and wife. This is certainly not to say that the non-Catholic party must not also strive to be tolerant and understanding. Indeed, he should make as many concessions as the Catholic member, and should realize his marriage promises must be fulfilled. But because religion touches on so many aspects of life, every effort should be made to avoid conflict whenever possible.

It is imperative that the subject of birth control be thoroughly discussed before marriage. When the non-Catholic enters a union with a Catholic he is entitled to know the full viewpoint and regulations of the Church concerning this most problem-forming subject. When he fully realizes that rhythm is the only accepted method of birth control, and willfully enters into the bond, then he should never alter his decision. However, many problems do arise and should be settled by thorough and frank discussion between the spouses. If this is not enough to clear up the trouble, outside help may be advisable. It would be helpful perhaps to have the husband on good terms with the pastor or assistant—does he play golf?—or a good Catholic friend with whom he could confer if the occasion arose. A man's point of view can often be very helpful and would more than likely be an unprejudiced opinion, yet a frank one, and from the Catholic viewpoint. This could bring the non-Catholic to a clearer understanding of the why's and wherefore's of the Catholic faith and help him to adjust better.

Subscription to a Catholic magazine in the home could offer a small opening to the interfaith couple. Occasions will undoubtedly arise when the Protestant will leaf through it and find articles of interest. Maybe there are questions about the faith that he has always been curious about but never asked. Be quick to answer any question a spouse may have and if the answer is not known, make it a point to find out promptly. The surest way to squelch a budding interest in the tenets of the faith is a disinterested "I don't know." It is much wiser to state that you are not positive but that you would be more than glad to find out because you are a bit hazy on the exact meaning too. And while ordering that subscription to the *St. Anthony Messenger* why not an order for *Presbyterian Life* (or whatever), too?

The sacrament of confession may be a cause of dissension in the family. So many people of other faiths find it extremely difficult to comprehend why Catholics tell their sins to a man instead of directly to God. Naturally, an explanation of this fact could clear the air, so to speak, and prevent an extreme distaste for the children, especially, to go to confession. It is easily explained that the clergy descends directly from the Apostles and that Christ gave them the power to forgive sins in His name. Pointing out that the priest works through the power Christ has placed in him will help to set the matter straight.

It would also be extremely prudent for the Catholic to explain any difficulties which the non-Catholic in-laws may have. They may hesitate to bring up a question for fear of interfering. If this hesitation is noticed, information cheerfully volunteered would certainly be a nice gesture. Parents definitely influence their offspring even after the children have left home and are married. To try to ease any religious qualms they may have will improve relations considerably. It is evident that non-Catholics do not accept most Catholic ideas, ceremonies, and practices. Otherwise they would also be Catholic. But to have them understand why certain things are done is only courtesy and is also wise. It is a good practice, too, to be a thoughtful listener to a telling of last Sunday's sermon on, say, virtue that mother-in-law would enjoy relating. A reciprocal, brief notation on, perhaps, grace possibly might be in order. But it is unwise ever to press religious issues in family circles or ever state religious debates that could lead to family troubles.

At all times the Catholic should set examples of high ideals for her children and husband. She should outwardly convey what she inwardly feels. This is of course not to say that the non-Catholic should not set good example. On the contrary, he should proceed the same as his mate. His image and example is irreplaceable in the forming of the character of his children. Both parties should endeavor to express themselves to the best of their abilities.

In conclusion, I feel that a mixed marriage has an excellent chance of working. It is a much more difficult state, granted. But the difficulties can be surmounted if both parties are willing to put forth their entire effort and if their love and understanding is boundless. It is well to be remembered that although their prayers may take different paths to God, both do reach Him.

Every so often a student tells a less encouraging story, where his own parents had entered a mixed marriage and their children were the victims of a familiar tragedy—loss of faith for everyone in the family.

Under the title of, "Why I Do Not Go to Church," one senior traced his nonaffiliation to the fact that mother and dad had bartered their respective faiths for the sake of marital harmony. So their children had nothing religious to inherit.

The last time he had gone to a church, and the first time in a year, he felt guilty about even entering, as though he had misused the chapel by indulging in thoughtless observation rather than by piously worshipping. When people ask him why he does not go to church, he is embarrassed. It provokes self-evaluation and a rational explanation. As far as he can tell, the whole thing stemmed from home:

My mother seldom went to church to worship. In fact, the only times I ever saw my mother enter a church were for special occasions such as weddings. The main reason why she did not go to church involves her relationship with my father. Before marriage, my mother worshipped regularly in the Catholic Church as did her parents and their eight other children. Thus, she had grown up and lived in a strongly religious, Catholic family. When she married my father, who is strongly anti-Catholic, she sacrificed her affiliation with the Catholic Church for something she thought was more important, my father's love. She thought that my father could teach her to gain the same satisfaction from his form of worship as she had experienced in the Catholic Church by helping her to understand the Protestant religion as he believed it. She thought my father could 'show her the way' in his religion.

Her religion deteriorated from practice to memory. This memory included an image of the church as she once knew it, of family worshipping together, and it was permeated with sentimental feelings. It was this memory that supplied my mother with an image of what the religious life of our family should be like. She thought we should attend church regularly and did much to influence us to go to church. She had forfeited her affiliation with the Catholic Church, however, and she could not derive suitable satisfaction from attendance at Protestant services. Therefore, she just stayed home.

In terms of going to church, my father's example was not much better than my mother's. His was a Protestant background. He believed, strongly, that the most important factor in a man's religion should be how he lived every day and that church attendance was a secondary factor. Under the influence of my mother, he did gather the family, occasionally, and take us to church. For me, this seemed an heroic experience. I felt strange and uncomfortable in church. From my mother, I inherited a kind of guilt complex because I did not go to church often, and I wished I could hide from the eyes of the regular church members. I thought they must have known we seldom attended church and I was ashamed that I should be there only on special occasions. I felt guilty if my mind wandered to thoughts of anything outside the church or if I could not be interested in what the preacher was saying. I even pretended to be sorry for the time I had sinned that week, even though I knew the sorrow would not last long after I left the church. In short, I felt guilty, ashamed, and sometimes, afraid. I suspect these are the symptoms of a shy, young person who seldom sees the inside of a church. Needless to say, I was not disappointed when my father failed to make church attendance a regular habit.

As I grew older, I learned to understand my father's beliefs and prejudices more fully. He was an independent person and highly critical of his own church and, even more, of the Catholic Church. He believed it was good to worship in a church, but he was most critical of the hypocritical nature of many of the people he met there. It seemed to him that the same people who frequented church also frequented the local bar. The people who were so stingy at the time of collection were the people who indulged in luxuries outside the church. The people who prayed on Sunday were, too often, people whose profanity was outstanding on Monday. Such hypocrites, he thought, were too great in number at church, and the church, rather than teaching the people, was simply accommodating them. The church had become a place of social gathering, a place to make a social impression, rather than a place to worship.

In the Catholic Church, it was the autocratic nature of the hierarchy and the material wealth of the church that my father most often criticized. He could not understand how the members of this hierarchy live in comfort when so many Catholics lived in poverty. He charged that the priests were mere mortals who possessed no special powers of insight and whose judgment was not much better than his own. He guessed the hierarchy was of a political nature, more interested in itself than the people in the church. Many of these feelings were based on misunderstanding and prejudice but they were the basis of deep and frequent criticism. My father, then, felt that the final and only judge of a person's conduct of earth was God. He felt that a man needed only to live according to the Christian rules of morality to pass the final judgment of God.

Obviously, I seldom went to church as a child, and, consequently, never formed any habits of church attendance. I was strongly impressed by my father's independent attitude, but, at the same time, my mother made me feel guilty that we did not often go to church. I had a false impression of the purpose of the church and the place of religion in my life as indicated by the discomfort I felt when I did go to church. It was not infrequently that my mother expressed her dissatisfaction with our church attendance habits and there were frequent conflicts between her and my father whose views differed. I am critical of this type of marriage, then, mainly because of its detrimental effect on the formation of a sound religious philosophy in the children raised in this environment.

During my elementary school years and throughout high school, I gave little thought to the formation of some religious philosophy or to the place of the church in my life. The memory of my childhood experiences in church were still fresh in my mind and it seemed easiest to avoid the issue. In spite of the conflicts indicated by my parents' differences, mine was a closely knit family. If ever I experienced a personal conflict which was too great for me to solve, I could easily go home to my parents, brothers, or sisters for guidance and advice.

When I entered the university, however, I realized that I could no longer turn to my parents or a coach for answers to questions, for, here, I experienced greater conflicts which only I could solve. I was asked questions that other people could not help me to answer concerning morality, religion, and my way of life. I lived with a boy who, at various times, claimed he was existentialist, Hindu, and Buddhist, but never Christian, and, who went home on weekends in anticipation of intercourse with a Catholic girl. I listened to accounts of drunken fraternity parties and orgiastic motel parties. At Easter time, I watched an ever increasing number of students heading for the 'Fort Lauderdale blast.' In the midst of these moral and religious conflicts, I realized that I must make a decision as to the place of religion and the church in my life.

It took very little thought to realize that religion itself had a definite place in my life. I had only to observe the examples offered by those people around me to realize the importance of

213

religion. It seemed that the people who had no religions affiliations were those whose moral standards and degree of success
were low. My existentialist friend, for example, dropped out
of school, lost his job and was forced to marry a girl he made
pregnant. People who had strong personalities and who ac-
complished greater projects were those guided by a stronger
religious faith. Many times I have felt alone and overpowered
by the facts and events around me, and realized there must be
a God. I have often felt the need to pray and to ask for help
and enlightenment from God, but I have seldom done so. I
felt guilty when I prayed because the only time I prayed was
when I needed help. As I once heard it expressed, 'We often
pray for help, but seldom give thanks.'

These feelings seem trite now that I understand more fully
the purpose and reasons for prayer. It is easy to understand,
though, in the face of my background, how I got so confused
about the place of religion and prayer in my life. As I studied
and learned about the massiveness and orderliness of things
around me, I became convinced there must be a God. The
more I realized how fallen is the nature of man and how easily
I am influenced by others, the more I recognized the importance of prayer.

I am convinced, then, that the church and prayer should
be an integral part of my life. I am confused, however, as I try
to decide in what church I should pray. I have often thought
of postponing the decision and accepting the religion of the
person I marry. In general this has been the pattern followed
by my sisters who have adopted the Catholic faith and my
brothers who have adopted some form of Protestant religion.
These facts suggest two ideas. All my brothers and sisters have
faced the same decision I am now facing which is good evidence that my parents' mixed marriage was instrumental in
producing the confusion we have experienced. It seems that
the boys in the family have been most influenced by my father's example while the girls have been influenced by my
mother. I could easily follow this pattern. This would not only
reduce the confused feeling I now have, but would reduce my
chances of becoming involved in a mixed marriage.

On the other hand, I feel that a personal decision as to my choice of church affiliation is essential to the development of a mature philosophy of life. Without such decision, I can hardly consider myself mature enough for marriage. When I have not begun to make a decision which is so essential to the development and assurance of a stable view of life, how can I ask a woman to depend on me as she would in marriage? I feel that too many people marry before they have made similar decisions and before they have established a similar level of maturity and stability. Too many *boys* and *girls* are married in our society. How, then, must I choose the church within which I will worship?

I feel that the decision concerning the church in which I will worship must be based on an intellectual study and enlightenment of the doctrines of both the Catholic and Protestant doctrines through which I will choose my place of worship. Too often, I have observed people who seem religious enough, but when asked to explain their beliefs or the reasons for their devotion to the church, they can give no satisfactory answer. They go to church regularly and live their life accordingly, but they cannot explain why they do so. Similarly, people who do not go to church or express little religious devotion indicate the same ignorance. As one friend recently stated: 'People who are raised going to church, go. I was not raised that way, so, I do not go.' I feel I must avoid the mistakes made by these people, that I must avoid the blind acceptance and, at the same time, the blind rejection of the Church. I feel I must cultivate, through study and observation, an intellectual understanding of the religion that I accept or reject. I feel that I must evaluate more thoroughly the influences which will have an effect on my decision. I want to be able to give sound answers to the people who will ask me why I worship as I do. Until I fulfill these requirements of study, I feel that I cannot worship in any church.

I must admit that I have pointed out more excuses than reasons why I do not go to church. However, I have tried to be objective in the evaluation of my previous experiences and in the attempt to give a suitable explanation for my actions. I

have been strongly critical of my parents' failure to help establish a habit of religious thought in my life, yet, I would like to
make it clear that I respect and love my parents deeply. If I do
not go to church, now, it is because I have not yet reached a
level of understanding which I feel is necessary to a sound and
stable religion.

Anticipating conflict in a mixed marriage, most students give more than passing thought to the idea of "converting" to the religion of their partner. But they fear that
the change may be caused, and not only influenced, by the
desire to please. As one senior expressed it, "The thing
that worries me most is I am afraid I won't choose the right
thing for the right reasons. I don't want to turn Catholic,
fooling myself that I believe it because I want to marry
Dan and decide ten years from now I have had enough.
Neither do I want to turn away from it merely because I
don't have the courage to believe and the courage to make
my marriage work." She decided to become a Catholic, but
only after "much soul searching and much praying to try
to find the answer." At times she felt "like I am completely tearing myself apart," to choose between love for
her parents' faith and the religion of the man she was
planning to marry.

Another girl with the same dilemma was not so sure.
She was also dating a Catholic but one who encouraged his
fiancée to make a compromise between the girl's Method-
ism and his Catholicism by joining the Episcopal Church.
Her main disagreement with the Catholic Church was
with the Church's authority, "the way it tells people to live
a certain way, especially in the matter of marriage and
raising children." She explains what she means:

If I can't afford children one after another, if my health
won't stand it, or if I need to complete an education first, then

I'll act accordingly. I don't believe birth control is a sin; I don't necessarily agree on artificial contraception, but I know that rhythm is too risky to chance. This is a matter which a husband and wife have to work out for themselves. Also, on the matter of natural difficulty at childbirth, I can't really believe that destroying the child for the mother's life is murder. The husband needs his wife more than he needs to raise that child alone. Even if the wife could never bear children again, there are millions of homeless children in the world that need her. Is this wrong to consider? Is it so selfish? You see, I do have conflict, and consequently, I think that a change to Anglicanism is better suited for me (and for Jack, too). Yet, I feel that theologically, I could be a good Catholic—if the Church would accept my departing views.

When discussing mixed marriages in class, students were extraordinarily alert because they rightly felt that for most of them this was the hardest decision they would be called upon to make. It was not only a choice between changing religious affiliation or making the best of an interfaith partnership. Sometimes it meant choosing between a person whom they intensely loved and fidelity to the deepest moral principles of their faith.

Interracial Marriage. Even where religious convictions are not at stake, prospective marriage can raise serious problems when social issues are involved. Interracial dating is fairly common at most large universities, and campus reactions to them differ, depending on the prejudice of the community and the way a young couple go about their courtship.

My own policy has been to tell students who came for advice that interracial marriages are not forbidden by the Church, that in some countries up to fifty per cent of the population are offspring of interracial unions, but that in the United States there are grave difficulties which must be pointed out. If, in spite of these obvious problems, they want to go through with it, I can only support their plans and hope their courage will sustain them through life.

A junior coed, who was dating a Negro, has strong feelings about the race problem and was convinced that marriage between the races was not to be hindered by a society reared on bias and misunderstanding. She also believed that a college campus was among the best places for interracial dating. Away from home and parental pressures, among adults, and with plenty of time to think, students are able to look at the matter objectively. Still it is not easy:

I am not saying that interracial dating is accepted on campus, but people can see and will sometimes admire others for standing behind and carrying out their own convictions. It takes a lot of hard times to be able to fight practically the entire society for something you believe in and know is right. It also takes a lot for the mixed couple. They have to know exactly the feeling of other people and be able to accept that this is just the way some people are. There has to be a great amount of feeling for each other, more than an ordinary couple would have. In fact, I know a girl who built an entire foundation and strengthened her convictions because she loved a Negro.

I have talked to many Negroes about interracial dating. There have been varied opinions about this subject, so I will first consider some of their opinions. Why do they want to date a white girl in the first place? One of the main reasons is to find out if there is any difference between the white and the Negro girl. To their amazement, there is found no real difference. A slight difference, however, would be that—in the opinion of several of the Negro students—the Negro girls, as a whole, are more emotional. Another reason would be the challenge as to whether they could date a white girl. There are additional reasons for mixed dating in the eyes of the Negro. Some Negroes have a deep-seated, hostile feeling for the whites for what they did to their race. One of the most effective ways to seek revenge is to date a white girl. Thus they feel that they have somehow gotten back at the white, because the white fellows resent this and the girl has limited her friends and prospective dates. The girl may do this in all innocence, trying to carry out the idea of equality, but is in this case being used.

Some Negroes feel that this type of dating brings them up socially in the world's eyes. At this point, I will interject a case with which you are familiar. Sandy and Bruce were quite open when they dated each other. All of both his and her friends were aware of this. Some of Bruce's friends saw this and felt that it *did* bring him up socially. So if Bruce can do it, they feel that they too should have such an opportunity. So now, more than ever, there is this big goal or achievement to date 'the white girl.' A situation such as this is very hard for the white girl to detect. 'Are they taking me out because of my color—or lack of it—or because of an actual interest in myself as an individual?'

I put this question to a Negro and his answer should be considered more of a personal than general opinion. He stated this is very hard to detect, even in the man himself, for he may not even realize why he's asking the girl out. One way in which you may be able to tell is if the person 'creeps.' By this, I mean when they go out where no one ever sees them. This limits their activity considerably for the purpose of remaining secret. This would seem to contradict a former statement, indicating the wish to show this girl off in public. There is, however, a very logical reason for 'creeping' and it is that if the Negro girls see them together, there is a chance these girls may not consider dating the man any more. It works both ways in the races.

Now ask the white person why he would date a Negro. One reason that would hold for both is to find out the difference.

When I first came to college, I had no intentions of dating Negroes. I was quite indifferent towards dating of this type and felt at that time that there was no real difference. Sandy considered them friends, but that was as far as it went. Last year, she even made the statement that if her boyfriend ever went out with a Negro, she would seriously consider that step as the end of their relationship.

I had never actually been close friends with any Negro until the beginning of last semester. The opportunity presented itself when I started working in our dormitory cafeteria. There were two Negroes working there and I got to know them rather well. One of them eventually asked me if he might call sometime. We talked on the telephone four or five times one week and then he began to question me about dating. He didn't push it, since I was a little hesitant. Because he was a lot of fun to be with, I knew I would have a good time with him. When we finally did go out, we went in secret. He wanted to come to the dorm to call on me, but this was very difficult at the time. I was dating him because I wanted to and, realizing society's feelings, I couldn't see getting everyone on campus upset when it was really no concern of theirs in the first place. I realize now that this is true to a certain extent, but if it is of no concern to society, then why not date in public? That is the big question. You don't want to be on exhibition, and yet, is it this fear that makes you think like this? In my case, it might have been a little of both.

If you have decided to 'creep,' which most do, there is a definite problem of where to go. If you have to go where you won't be seen, then an apartment is most probable. Records, dancing, and talking only last so long. No, I would say that an apartment is not conducive for dating purposes.

If you are one of the very few that have decided to date openly, there are a great many things that must be considered. It is natural that you are going to be the object of many stares and conversations. There will be a number of people at one time considered your friends who may not even speak to you after witnessing your actions. This may upset you considerably, but the true friends will understand even if they would not consider such dating. People's reactions generally are upsetting at first, but after a while it actually becomes funny. When you see people practically driving into a tree and bumping into others while they're staring, you can't help laughing. This is the best attitude to have, for if you keep laughing it is very difficult to show your hurt or anger. People that constantly see you together will soon realize that you're in 'a world of your own' and that nothing seems to bother you.

There is one consideration that must be taken into account concerning open dating. What will the university administration say and how much can they do? They can do a lot, in fact, too much! One girl was inquiring of a counselor what the administration could do and was told that if the housemother of the girl's dorm reports such dating she can be fired. Though this is supposedly true, no one has acknowledged it yet.

If a case is brought to the administration's attention, they will bring you into the office and give one of their 'naughty, shouldn't do' talks with solid convictions that you will never do this again. If they discover, to their utter amazement, that you did not heed their words, they will send letters home to your parents. The letter is quite informative, asking parents to tell their child that this is not the proper thing to do on a respectable campus.

Indeed, the administration can make it hard on the couple. A few years ago a girl was put under so much pressure by the administration while dating a Negro that she had to leave. As for myself, this is something I just can't make myself accept. The administration is supposed to look out for the betterment of the school and it certainly doesn't consider interracial dating any type of betterment. Though you are supposed to be adults when you go away to college, how can you act like an adult and express your adult ideas with adults (the administradition) cramping your freedom and rights? It is true, there are limits and you can carry some things to an extreme, but the more you curb the right to express and stand up for your ideas the sooner comes the time when you can look forward to a dead society, lacking initiative and any drive for achievement or success.

If the dating continues, the question of marriage will have to arise sooner or later. Just dating is one thing, often not thought of too seriously, but marriage is one important issue that must be discussed in great detail. The first big question that arises is the consideration for the children. Can the children lead a halfway normal life in this society of ours? With whom can they associate? Will they be accepted by either race? What will happen when they decide to marry? All of these questions can only be answered by actual experience or knowledge of the experience of others.

A male student of the Negro race willingly related the complications which arose in his family situation. His stepmother is white and thus his two stepsisters are of mixed parentage. Their caucasian appearance led to awkward situations when the three were together in public. They were often ridiculed. However, he remarked that because his family was close, as the children grew older they were able to discuss the reasons why people should act as they do. The two girls, thirteen and fourteen years of age, are well-adjusted in their brother's opinion, and unaffected by the now infrequent remarks. In this student's opinion, the children won't necessarily suffer *if* they experience love within the family. This is of great importance.

Of greatest importance is the strength of the religion in the family. It is almost a necessity that the couple be of the same religion in the family. Everything could be going wrong, but when you can sit down and pray together, everything has to work out all right. The statement that 'a family that prays together stays together' has a great deal of importance, especially within the mixed family.

It is very difficult for a child to understand why he is being treated the way he is. He can only see that people will not play with him or talk to him. Even when he gets older he will have trouble believing that this is really right and that the majority of people can't accept this. Here is where strong faith is a necessity. You can more readily accept this without knowing why, because with God there is an answer for everything.

There are a great many things to consider as far as the couple are concerned also. If they are determined to get married, they had better be living in the right state. There are *twenty-nine* states that outlaw Negro-Caucasian marriages. If they are able to obtain a license, they are not considered legally married and their children are considered illegitimate.

The couple should have full knowledge of what they would be facing with their marriage. Just dating in a particular area is not going to tell a person everything that can happen after the marriage. If you have the opportunity to talk to a mixed couple and find out the problems they had encountered, this will help to determine what will happen. The white person has to realize they will have to live in a Negro neighborhood and the conditions may not be as they would like them. Nonsensical as it may seem, white girls considering marriage to the Negro rarely concede to living in a Negro neighborhood. The problem of employment is a serious one. Neither the man nor the woman will be able to obtain the position they might have gotten in another situation. If the man's employer were to find belatedly out of the marital situation, he could refuse employment. One couple, in which both the man and his wife were teaching at separate schools, both lost their positions. A place to live, provided it were a Negro neighborhood, is not such a problem. If you were to live in any big city, such as New York or Chicago, you would find a great deal of mixed couples. In another country you would find an even better, more acceptable environment. In any other country the citizens are much more liberal and such a couple would not be considered outcast in society.

As for my personal views, I can not actually, at this time, say whether I will marry a Negro or not. I have thought a great deal about this and if I had no one else to consider except my mate, I would not hesitate. My parents are very broadminded and could accept the fact that I have chosen a Negro for husband, but the biggest consideration would be my parents' jobs. If it were known in the small town in which we live, it might hurt them a great deal. If I ever did decide to marry a Negro, it would only be because I loved him very much.

Catholics who are interested in dating Negroes suffer from a double liability. They have to endure the social pressures of the school community and, in most cases, risk the chances of an interfaith marriage. As one girl put it, "the main reason I would consider is the fact that so few Negroes are Catholic." Either problem is enough by itself, "but you are really walking on shaky ground when you try both at the same time." Paradoxically, though, interracial marriages are among the most stable in modern American culture.

EIGHT

DIVORCE

The Specter of Instability

WHEN students think of marriage, they also think of divorce. And the more serious they are about making their marriage succeed, the more anxious they become about a possible breakdown of their married life.

They have good reason to be worried. Classes in the social sciences inform them about the spiraling divorce rates in America, which has the highest marital instability of any major nation in history. All around them at the university are young people who came from broken homes. They soon learn at first hand about the trials that follow on legal separation and maybe for the first time in their lives it dawns on them what a massive problem the country faces in its breakdown of family life. They make friends with these people, date them, and begin thinking of marriage.

Suddenly they get concerned. What if their marriage should end up the way so many do, and there is something hereditary about marital insecurity. If the girl or boy they love came from a divorced home, is their chance of staying married reduced? If not, how guarantee the stability of their union against the stream of broken pledges almost everywhere they turn?

225

When I began writing this book, I seriously thought of using the idea of broken family life as a theme for *The Hungry Generation* because nothing, in my judgment, better characterizes the insecurity of our college population. Colleges have their share of children from divorced parents, and the close intimacy of campus life, coupled with the strong compassion of most undergraduates creates a unique situation that has largely escaped our social scientists. Young men and women whose parents were divorced differ immensely, and some rise above the normal pattern. But generally they suffered such traumatic injury to their personalities that the effect on their environment is inevitable. They crave attention and understanding to a degree uncommon in others; they fear and distrust even when all the evidence tells them to be confident; they need affection more than anyone else, and their sense of insecurity must be witnessed to be believed.

These attitudes are contagious. If nothing else, they evoke spontaneous sympathy among their fellow students and, when the prospect of marriage comes up, those who love them want desperately to break the chain of circumstances that produced such havoc in human lives.

As in the case of marriage, women are revealing about the evils of divorce when these are personal experiences. Men also write on the subject, but seldom go beyond statistics and theory. They hardly ever tell you what happened in their own family. As often as not, men take such a detached view of marital instability that they hardly consider it a problem. They find comfort in some obscure analyst's figures that in a particular county in New York State, ten times as many children were sent to the juvenile clinic from separated parents as from divorced parents. Therefore, concludes one college man, we have no reason to say that divorce has anything to do either with juvenile delinquency or with emotional disturbance in children stranded by the divorce courts! More cynically, a man concluded his study of family disintegration with the remark "divorce is here, it is a problem, so learn to live with it;" or again, "marriage is serious, but divorce is the escape hatch, so why worry about it?"

Women are never so callous. Their instincts are more sensitive and, when they are victims of a broken home, they suffer as a man seldom does. For I have enough testimonies of this kind to write another book. They speak for themselves, and every word is scorched with the pain of years of endurance.

A senior begins her witness with the word, "Failure!" The failure to realize that marriage is a sacrament of God intended to fuse two human souls into one in the nature of God: "This is the essence of divorce, and truly one of the saddest things that can happen to a family." Then she tells her story:

When I was thirteen and my brother eleven, my parents were divorced. I don't remember too much of it at the time, except my father coming in from Detroit one Friday night, and asking my brother if his friends, who were there, could come back later to play. The only words that I remember from that horribly revealing night were, "Sally and Tim, I've fallen in love with another woman." My heart was in my throat, but my eyes couldn't cry. I listened to everything he said, then went upstairs and said a prayer.

I couldn't believe this was happening to me. Our family, so close, so happy, now a meaningless shambles of persons who seemed oceans apart. Yet, it was true, and I had to accept the truth with a quiet finality.

When my dad was gone again, I must have asked my mother a thousand times, "Why?," not realizing, in my youth and naiveté, how hurt she must have been. Disbelievingly, this was now in our life, something that hurt terribly, but that was there and had to be lived with.

What probably really crushed mother was that the day

227

after the divorce went through, to permanently separate our Protestant family, my dad married. The impact of all of this never was terribly great on me until now, years later. I can partially realize the heartbreak my mother went through, seeing the man whom she loved and was loved by, leave to marry another women. It is almost unimaginable to sense the empty, futile feeling when the man in whom she had complete faith and trust, did that. The image and living proof of love she must have had could have been completely shattered. She could have become terribly emotionally upset. She could have taken this hurt out on her children. And all these things I'm sure she did in part, and that would be normal. But I say 'could have' because I speak of one whom I consider an extraordinarily strong and faithful person, and this is my mother.

Now, as I'm in college, and the first terrible blows of divorce are over, I'm only beginning to realize the awful consequences it's had. As my mom and I talk together, I can sense her sorrow over having "lost" and it is so tragic for me to have to watch her be mother, father, friend, and counselor to Tim and me. During our teen years we were alone, living with my mother, with only occasional visits from my father. He now lives and works in New York and although he couldn't be better about providing for Tim and me in terms of education and any financial needs, I've come to realize that without the love and emotion of the father's love right there in the home, all the money in the universe couldn't replace it.

Unfortunately, my father hasn't found this truth yet, and it hurts me. He is putting me completely through college and will do the same for Tim when he starts next year. He has provided a fine job for Tim for the past two summers working in New York. He is overly generous in terms of gifts. But all of this, I must say, does not add up to the time and loving care that's missing. For I have seen the most horrible and irrational of tempers, impatience, and inconsiderateness from him over certain arguments, in particular, money. I have had bitter, ugly fights with him about money, and it is all so useless. He is

228

convinced he's right, and will not listen to anyone else, and he must have the last word.

One of the marks of an educated man, I believe, is not only his applied knowledge, but also his integrity in accepting others' thoughts, being open-minded, responsive to others, and having an honest personality. And the odd part of it is, my father wasn't this way before the divorce. The change that has come over him since is so unbelievable to me. I can illustrate this by a serious incident that happened two summers ago. It was the summer that my brother, Tim, was in New York working, and I flew in to spend the last two weeks out of the four that he was there, with him, my dad and his wife.

Those two weeks were two of the most difficult in my whole life. I found myself putting on a social front not only for the people there, who were very different from those I'm used to here, but also for my dad. And I felt bad about it because why should I have to put up a front in front of my own father? I've figured out that it's because he has certain standards set for me to live up to and these are external standards. When I don't 'measure up' in terms of dress, grades, behavior, money-handling, and like circumstances, there's a big argument. To me, these seem like such trivial matters to make such a production of. However, I do not ignore these basic necessary codes of behavior.

When I was there, in New York, I saw such revealing things happen. From the very first night I arrived, his wife criticized something about me—my hair wasn't right for my face, this dress wasn't proper, I shouldn't iron creases in my brother's shirt sleeves, this, that, and the other thing. True, I'd appreciate little suggestions, but when it came to sheer criticism, my own sensitivity couldn't take it. It was probably jealousy in the 'family,' but it did hurt to be grinded at this way, day after day.

One night my father was speaking to my mother on the phone, discussing when we'd fly home, and they evidently got into an argument over it, and he was talking rather harshly to her. Although I shouldn't have done it, but I'm too sensitive, I said, "Don't yell at my mother!" and he got angry with me. I was then bawled out as a child for my immaturity, lack of self-control, and disrespect. I suppose this was true to a certain extent, but I could see where he had been disrespectful too. A terrible fight ensued, and left me in tears with really irrational comments flying. I was almost hysterical with nerves wrapped up with indecision staring me in the face—not knowing what to think of father's actions.

A large part of the whole thing was my fault because I know I should have contained myself, for I realize how sensitive I am. But I can't stand to see someone thinking he's doing the right thing when actually he's tearing at someone's emotions and leaving him, empty and thoughtless. This is not the approach to settlement, but at that time my dad and I hadn't yet found peaceful means. What this all resulted in was a thorough discussion about why the divorce had happened, and a kind of resolutionary talk on the immediacy of the situation and 'we may as well accept it.'

Needless to say, I was quite upset for a while after such an incident. It left me with a wondering, raw feeling. Exactly what was my dad telling me? I knew, for one thing, that he was trying to have me accept the facts as they were, for they couldn't be changed. And of course, I knew this too, but it's so difficult to play a passive role in the situation of family breakup. But, little by little, as time passed, and I had a talk with my minister, the air cleared, and my dad and I presently enjoy a healthy relationship. There is still a somewhat reserved attitude in me over certain matters with him, I feel I have to remain silent on unless I want to revive an argument. I don't like this lack of communication, but for my own peace of mind, I must accept it.

I am constantly being reassured that 'everything will be taken care of,' 'I will be glad to pay for your piano lessons next semester; just send me the bill' and so on. This is fine knowing that everything *will* be taken care of, and getting a check regular as clockwork, but when it becomes of prime importance, it loses its meaning for what it can accomplish. This external token must be given in love and not as a replacement for anything—inability to see us more often, or separated and perhaps somewhat more strained relations. I think that the reason for the overaccent on money affairs is that since my father *can't* see us that often, a substitute is necessary to prove he really still cares. Money is not a good substitute. As a matter of fact, there is no substitute for a father's love, devotion, and guidance. If, instead of writing a quick, 'Dear Sally, Here's your check for the next two weeks. I haven't heard from you for a while. Love, Daddy,' I could receive a newsy letter from him occasionally, one that wasn't accompanied by a check. I'm not saying that this doesn't ever happen. It does, but I sometimes feel whether I'm worth any more time than every other week when he sends the check.

I have also noticed that he is very formal in everything he does. Nothing about him is relaxed anymore. He wants Tim and me to strive for the highest possible goals, which, of course, we want for ourselves. But his ideas of 'high goals' are determined and idealistic, and what he wants us to achieve, I think, are his own ideals that, perhaps, he *didn't* live. This is what puts a strain on our relations, I think. He tells us he wants us to be original in our choice or aspirations, but when we are—and we're not way-out, non-conformists!—there's conflict. So, where is our free thinking and creativity? It is, contrary to what he thinks, being stifled.

I have painted quite a dim view of my father and I'm afraid I delved too much into personality. But I do feel that these truths must be realized, and this is the way it's been for us. I don't like to criticize anyone, much less my parent, for whom *pietas* is the highest form of respect I must show. However, divorce has brought on these changes, much as I hate to see them, and it is the truth with which I have to live.

My mother has been quite an example of faith during the divorce, and in the wake of such a tragedy. The loss of the love of the man in whom she trusted completely, before, left a woman empty, questioning her worth, doubtful, fearful, and quite alone. I can't begin to sense this feeling, for I haven't lost love. But she was left alone, knowing that her husband was marrying another woman. What can this do to a woman?

231

Nothing but tremendous sorrow and deep-felt emotional upsets. My own mother, I know, is a remarkable example of strength in the way she transcended herself out of the fear and horror of divorce, into the spiritual heights of life. And when she rose above the situation, she brought her children into these realms, also. I didn't realize this about her until only recently, but she and I have talked, rather freely, about her feelings on the divorce. She, of course, felt the brunt of the failure.

The tragedy of it cannot measurably be told in words. But my mother was left, to live alone and give all she could, including fatherly love, to her children. And I bless her forever for the wonderful outlook she has given Tim and me. I know her thought, her hurt; but I also know her strength. For she has prayed and had faith that she was yet young, and she had her life to live. She has turned her whole life toward a spiritual outlook; has not become fanatically religious, but has a practical religion, which is visible in her everyday involvements. She trusts people, and is not quick in judging others. Most of all, I feel, her virtue lies in what she has given Tim and me.

Statistics are against us as children of divorce. Our chances for stable marriages are supposed to be considerably less than children coming from a stable family. Our social and emotional relations with others are calculated to be more risky. But, in spite of these statistics and predictions, I feel very fortunate, and I know it's due to my mother's gift of love and concern for her children. She has given me such a positive outlook on love and marriage that I am looking forward to making my marriage a successful one. She has been perhaps the greatest influence in my life, and has given me inspiration for living, and in thus doing, has been fulfilling her own life with meaning.

My preceding purpose has not been to compare my parents, but to point out the different effects divorce has had on each of them, negative effects on my father, and for my mother, a realization that circumstance must be risen above, and love found in everything and everyone.

It is said that the worst effects of divorce are on the children. I have gone through, and Tim is experiencing his teen years without a father. We have the love and material concern for our welfare from my dad, but somehow, without his presence, physical and spiritual, we lack a part of identification. I think it's particularly important for a boy to identify with his father, else he can lose masculinity for want of this relationship. And for a girl, she too, must not thrive only on a mother's love, for she needs her father as a model for the love she will someday seek. This has, for the most part, been missing in our lives. But our mother has not overprotected us, so as to shelter us from the realities of human relations. We have both seen the good and bad sides of many different types of people, and through her guidance, have been taught to see them for what they are and respect them as themselves.

I must admit, I often feel so stifled in social relationships, and lack confidence many times. I worry about what others think of me, and try hard to be my natural self, pleasing, and not showing self-pity. Lack of identification with my father, I believe, caused me to be overly cautious perhaps in my relations with a certain boy. It was an adolescent love, but one from which I learned a lot; about him, myself. I matured a lot during four years. But I think I was somewhat afraid, and conflict arose in the problems every young couple faces. I wanted to be so careful in preserving that which is meant for marriage, for that time, and I desired nothing more than an understanding on this matter. But when it happened that I couldn't quite see his point of view, I had an awfully hard time expressing myself and, under the restraining circumstances maintain a good and healthy relationship. I still know I feel the same way on this matter, but I think I wouldn't have had such a difficult time, had I had my father's image in mind—something upon which to base my own feelings and attitudes toward the opposite sex.

In another respect I feel that Tim and I have lost a great deal by having to live, for the most part, separated from one parent. My father's encouragement for us is here, to be sure. We are fortunate that even in the divorced situation, his concern for us is shown, and our divorced family is not nearly as sad as some others I've seen and heard of. However, it hurts, if only in little things that we didn't have our dad there to enjoy with us, the little things that make up the biggest pleasures in life. My joy in music, which he shares, can only be shared a few times a year. My high school gay times and sad times could not be shared with, nor praised or sympathized with, for there was lack of communication and the distance was too great to have a real closeness.

It still hurts me to hear others talk about their families, what they do together, and even, 'Oh, my dad was so mad at me!' When I was going with the previously mentioned boy, I used to spent a lot of time at his home, and did many things with the whole family. And I still feel close to his father. I so enjoyed being with a family, who all loved each other and worked at maintaining unity in their family. For this is what I lack and I thrive on it when I'm made to feel such a part of a family as this. I cry often, wondering whether I'm being selfish, or whether my feelings are justified. For I know my mother has lost. She has lost what was probably her greatest source of inspiration for life—her husband.

But she has recovered, and discovered a greater life. I must do the same, and I know this is only possible with God's help. He has given my mother peace, and I often pray that I may be half the great person I think she is, and I have faith that this prayer will be answered. I want it to be answered for Tim and me, to give us direction for our lives without self-pity, but with genuine concern for others, and a real desire to live good lives, filled with genuine love. I also pray for our family as a whole. Though it be seperated, there may prevail a unity, a spiritual unity, that would ease our hearts, forgive us all and keep us as close together as possible.

Now that I've seen the effects of divorce on my own parents, and partially how it has restrained Tim and me, I want to be prudent and careful in choosing my life partner. I don't want to see my marriage patterned after that of my parents, but wish to learn a hard lesson, and make marriage the true and holy sacrament it is divinely intended to be. Only in this way can I hope for self-fulfillment and happiness in life, sharing my deepest being with that person who is to be my mirror for life unto death. For these reasons I believe that everyone about to enter the serious contract of marriage, ought to consider the Catholic viewpoint on marriage and divorce. If non-Catholic, they need not accept it, but it certainly gives a truer meaning to the most sacred of human relations. I take this concept in hopes that my marriage will be one of true love between two of us, blessed by God, the third Person in our marriage. I have seen all the hurt and sorrow from a marriage that wasn't this, and that is what I want to keep out of my own. God is the Author of all love, and to this end I want my own fulfilled.

Not all children of divorce are even this fortunate. In many cases, the father simply disowns his offspring or ignores them. In other cases, the mother crumbles under the strain or compounds the problem by remarrying a man whom either the children do not respect or who is unsympathetic with youngsters that are not his own.

An upperclassman begins her reflections with the statement, "I am the product of a broken home—broken by divorce. My parents are Catholic and lived together in marriage until I was almost seven years old. The two years following separation and eventual divorce were spent moving from one relative's home to another. Finally we were able to rent a house, and from this point on my life became pretty normal, as normal as it could be."

Her father remarried about two years after the divorce, but had no children by his second wife who befriended the legal orphans. They stayed with the mother and all went well until the father went on a drinking spree and the mother decided to remarry. The children dissuaded her from going through with the marriage and settled down to a precarious home life, with mother working at a bar and the father occasionally visiting his two daughters.

Writing after almost fifteen years of "divorced exist-ence," she reflects on the development of her mind and emotions since childhood. Looking back, she never felt any different from anyone else:

Having only one parent didn't appear to be abnormal. When parents or friends would ask me, 'Where is your fa-ther?', I could never understand why they would falter and apologize for having asked, once they found out my parents were divorced. Many of my friends were actually envious of me; I didn't have a drunken father around the house who always embarrassed me in front of my friends. They consid-ered me so lucky!

I was a better than average student in school but nothing I ever did was good enough to receive verbal praise from my mother. I now know that she was extremely proud of my sister and me and told everyone how good we were. I shall always remember her telling me 'anything you do will be twice as bad because I am a divorcée; and anything you do well will have to be better than just average in order to receive praise.'

One major effect produced by my fatherlessness was the strong attention I paid to the opposite sex. I began having boyfriends at a very early age (7th grade). I always needed a male companion to assure me of my worth. Because I always had to make my own decisions and wanted somebody else to do it for me, I wanted to be dominated and told what to do. I never participated much in high school because I was always too busy with my boyfriends. I could never understand how some girls could go a whole weekend without a date. This was a major catastrophe! Sometimes I wonder why I never com-pletely turned to these boys for the affection and love I lacked. It must have been my strong belief in my religion that kept me toeing the mark.

I was extremely selfish and self-centered. I wouldn't do anything that wasn't beneficial for me. The idea of sharing my things or talents with anyone else never even occurred to me.

I appeared to have a lot of self-confidence, but underneath I was terribly afraid of being rejected. I can remember not saying hello to some people when I saw them in school, for I feared they would not acknowledge me. I'm sure all of these feelings are the result of my home life. I was always very careful not to display my feelings or emotions, afraid I would make a fool of myself.

I don't regret the fact that my parents are divorced. I do, however, regret that I never had a father or a family life. Had my mother lacked the courage to leave my father, our lives would have been miserable and the toll much greater.

I always felt that my mother was a happy person and that nothing bothered her. However, all the years of loneliness and pain finally caught up with her. At the beginning of this year my mother began seeing a psychiatrist. She just couldn't seem to find any reason for living. At times my sister and I feared she would try to kill herself. The doctor seems to feel that most of her problems are the result of her unhappy childhood. Her parents were also divorced.

As soon as I was old enough to realize how lonely my mom really was, I began to pray that she would remarry. I know it is against the Church, but I can't accept the fact that someone should be miserable all of his life just because the Church says they cannot remarry. When someone you love very much is unhappy, it is very hard to understand why God has given you so much and them so little. I believe in God but I would not hestiate to put aside my religion for the happiness of my mother.

My mother is not the only member of the family seeing a psychiatrist. My sister, who is now twenty-six years old and the mother of two lovely children, recently began seeing a doctor. She had been suffering psychosomatic pains in the chest. The doctor told her she has been trying all her life to be accepted by her friends and family. I guess the effects on our family life were much greater on her because she was old enough to understand all that was going on, and had no one to turn to. At least I gained my acceptance from her and my friends. My only fear is that some day all of my background may catch up with me and I'll find myself on 'the couch.' Right now, though, I feel secure and happy with my life.

I'm engaged and will be married this summer. According to statistics my marriage doesn't stand too much of a chance. Not only am I a product of a broken home, but my fiancé is not Catholic. I imagine I'm just like everyone else entering a mixed marriage thinking it won't happen to me. I'm not so naive as to think all will be rosy and blissful. I realize that problems will arise concerning my religion, judging from past experiences and contacts with my fiancé but I'm sure they can be worked out. I would rather marry a non-Catholic than a Catholic who was only a Catholic on holidays.

Even though this makes it sound as if I hate my father, I know I don't. Yet I don't love him; I'm just trying to like him. I might add that he is trying very hard to gain my respect and love. I can't help feeling sorry for him because he has had so little love. I can also understand why he is the way he is. He was rejected by his stepfather and received little love from his mother, (because there were thirteen children in the family). He doesn't know how to give; he has always had to take in order to survive. I hope that some day my children will love and respect him to make up for the void in his life.

Still another girl's parents divorced before she reached the age of reason. She was about a year old at the time, and as far back as she can remember she always felt different and lonely. "It wasn't as if I never believed in God, I just never thought about it."

The only time she heard about God or the Church was in parochial school. But even that influence was minimized, because some of the children were unkind to her, she felt, because of her poor clothing and unkempt ways. For years she shuttled back and forth between her mother, who remarried, and her father who lived with her grandmother. As a young child she was asked by her father, with whom she preferred to live, to come with him. As she says,

"I really wanted to stay with him, but for some reason I couldn't." She could not bring herself to say she did not want to live with her mother.

This did not help matters because the mother was a distraught woman, who finally gave up the children to her first husband and died not long after. She says that when she found out that her mother had been beyond recovery, "I was almost happy she had died, because I don't think I would have been able to live with my father knowing that my mother needed help and wasn't getting it." From then on, life went on rather normally for her. She lived with her father and grandmother, until the latter died. A storm broke and it seemed that all her religious convictions were torn away:

I simply did not want to go to church. For the first time since anything had happened in my family, I blamed God. I felt He had let me down. I did not want any part of religion, or even life. I felt I had put my whole life in the hands of God and He just did not see me. I had prayed and studied, and I thought I truly adored God. I thought I possessed true faith and religion. Suddenly someone I truly loved was taken away, and I was again left alone to feel the hurt. I could turn to no one for relief.

At the time, I felt I was horrible for feeling that way, yet I could not dismiss the thoughts from my mind. I couldn't even receive Communion because I felt that I would be a hypocrite and commit a sacrilege to receive when I was feeling and thinking the way I did. I just couldn't understand why it had to happen again. It seemed that every time I had just gotten a good grip on life and was getting along pretty well, something had to happen which turned my world upside down. It always happened suddenly, with no warning. I wanted to run, run away from the hurt, the world, from God, and from everything that could ever make that horrible helpless feeling come again. I felt a complete void inside, and the only emotion I could feel was hate for everything in this world.

After I returned home from the funeral, I locked myself in my room and read my missal to try to find some reason to continue living; to try to find some answers as to what was happening, and why. One passage caught my eye: 'The Lord is near. Have no anxiety, but in every prayer and supplication let your petitions be known to God. And may the peace of God which surpasses all understanding guard your hearts and your minds in Christ Jesus, our Lord.' I read that passage over and over, and tried to make it real and true in my mind and heart.

It would be nice to say that suddenly I saw the light and became true to my religion again. But that isn't how it happened. I just made up my mind there was really nothing that would help me, and that even completely giving up my religion wouldn't do anything but hurt me. I knew that I would also be filled with guilt and that I really didn't want to give up my religion. As time went on, I gradually gave up the idea that God had forgotten me. I felt that things would happen the way they would no matter what. For a while I thought I had found the answer, by believing in God but remembering that no matter how hard I prayed it was up to God to take care of things. No amount of prayer or devotion was going to change this fact.

At this point in my life religion was just something you learned to live by. However, no matter how good or pious you were, life and death were ever present and just as uncertain. I knew that I should really talk to someone about my lax view of life and religion. So I went to one of the priests in my parish and tried to explain my confusion. But all I got was a lecture on how lucky I was to be better off than some of the other people in the world. I left feeling quite guilty about my having so little faith in God and so little charity. However, I was still as confused as when I went in to talk to him, and my religion was no nearer than before. Again I was at a stalemate with my world and religion.

Before finishing high school, she started getting sick after meals and gagged continually. She lost weight from not eating and exhaustion. When the doctor told her there was nothing physically wrong, "that didn't make me feel any better. I did, however, start putting more faith in my religion. For the first time in my life I started kneeling down to say my prayers at night. I felt that I wasn't all alone. For some reason I didn't feel completely lost."

Through this stage she developed her own religious faith. "I didn't believe in the things the priest talked about. I felt I had my own way of praying and believing, and no one else could understand it except God." Entering college with this individualist concept of God, she expected to find a whole new world, but "when I arrived, I was lost, not only in the literal sense but inside myself."

She started gagging and getting sick again, slept all the time and "just wanted to die. I turned to my religion but somehow I knew that wasn't the answer. How could I suddenly turn to God and expect him to make everything all right. I knew that I would have to help myself. However, I continued to pray and ask God for help."

This went on through freshman year, during which she muddled along with fears and doubts that continually plagued her. The turning point came the following summer, while she was alone traveling in the East:

I knew I was never going to find the answers to my questions and problems without help, and I also found out that my religion meant more to me than I would ever admit. I know this by the simple fact that, while I have had many problems in my life, there was always a way out.

It was like God knew when I couldn't stand the anxieties any longer; something would happen that would make everything better or at least so I could live without horrible fears. I could not miss Mass and I could not go to sleep without saying my prayers. Whenever the Catholic Church was brought up, I would never let any one belittle or abuse my religion.

I was also quite proud to be a Roman Catholic and let the

241

people whom I associated with know it. I feel I was also good as far as not committing mortal sins against God.

Returning to school meant a recurrence of the old problem of losing weight and getting sick. But this time she decided not to put the blame on anyone except herself. "I knew it was all in my head, but as to why or what I could do about it was beyond me." When she prayed, "I didn't just ask God to help me. I asked God to help me to help myself."

A graduate student suggested that she talk things over with a counselor at school, and for weeks she tossed the idea around in her head. Then came the final adjustment, after about six weeks of regular consultation.

One day I went in and my counselor told me we were going to start attacking my problems one by one and figure them out. We were going to start with my gagging and getting sick all the time. He said we were going to find the answer if it took us all day. We talked for about an hour and just like someone had thrown a ball and hit me in the stomach, I suddenly realized the answer. I needed and wanted to be sick because it was easier than facing the threats I saw in the world.

Here all the time I had been praying to God to take my getting sick away and I really didn't want him to. And in reality, if He had I would have been worse off than when I was sick. This also answers the reason why when I did get sick I never wanted to give up my religion or blamed the getting sick on God. And also when I was sick, why I just felt that everything was really all right except for my being sick; I got sick whenever a situation arose which I somehow perceived as threatening and I couldn't face it. So I would get sick because it was supposedly easier to face the sickness than the situation I was in. However, in reality, while I postponed my having to face reality by getting sick, eventually I always had to face it and thereby getting sick made it even harder for me in the long run.

That day I came out of the office feeling like a ten ton weight had been lifted from my mind and heart. I went to Church and thanked God for staying with me through all my years of little faith and religion and for helping me to help myself, which I never would have done alone. I knew I was on the road to becoming a complete and functioning human being, who would eventually be able to worship God with my whole self rather than only the part of me that could be torn away from my neurotic symptoms and my preoccupation with them.

I am now in the stage in my counseling where I am learning what is true reality and what I made up in my mind as reality, which, in effect, is all fantasy. Sometimes it is hard to accept and even continue to go to the counselor because at times it really hurts. However, I just keep praying that God will give me the strength to keep going.

The one big thing I have just learned is that the love I have always wanted and been searching for, especially in my religion and prayers, is the love I never received from my mother. I realize now that until I can accept and grasp the fact that I can never find that love, I will never be able to have a mature love which is needed to make a successful wife and mother. In all my relationships I have wanted a love which would guide me through the hardships of life.

I can see this in the way I reacted to two things in my life, my religion and the love I got from my grandmother. When I was with her I wanted to put my whole life in her hands and then everything would be all right. It wasn't. When she died, I put my life to religion. I gave my life to God and expected Him to make everything be all right. I wanted Him to be the mother I never had. I wanted Him to protect me from the world until I would be able to face it on my own. Yet this could not be. No one can take the place of my mother and no one can give me the love I was ever striving to receive from her. What seems hardest for me to accept is the fact that in actuality there was no reason for her not to love me except that I was me. However, I must keep remembering that she had many problems and probably just couldn't love me as a mother should.

I didn't realize this when I was younger and therefore blamed myself for her not loving me. Many things have now become clear to me, such as why, when I was living with my father and very happy, did I feel compelled to go home to my mother when I was really so unhappy there. The reason is that if I stayed with my father I would completely lose all chances of gaining my mother's love. It's a very lonely feeling to accept all this and in order for me to do it I will need God's love more than ever. However, I don't feel it's a neurotic need for I am honestly trying, on my own, to face life with it's loneliness and uncertainties. I need someone strong and all powerful to be with me on the lonely road of learning to live again and that someone or something is my religion and belief in an ever forgiving and merciful God.

I feel I am in the process of learning how to walk. At times I will make mistakes and fall down. It will hurt me, but eventually I will be able to stand up and walk by myself. In the process of my learning I will need a guiding hand, sometimes just to guide me and sometimes to soothe the hurt when I fall down. I realize that the hand I need is that of religion and a true faith in God. In a way I seem to be also learning my religion all over again, only this time in the right manner. Although I know it's going to be hard for me, with each step forward it's going to be easier than the last one. Also, knowing my religion is there to stand by with me I know I can become the woman God wants me to be.

Another story of another divorce victim gives a different insight, the terrible fear of marrying and repeating the mistakes of one's parents. Here the divorce came in two stages, first a temporary separation when the girl (an only child) was not yet in school, and a legal divorce with remarriage for both partners when she was in high school. "No divorce," she feels, "is a happy one, but theirs was exceptionally bitter. I believe that, at the time, neither of them wanted to separate. The final decision was arrived at because they both were too stubborn to give a little."

This senior's experiences through more than a dozen years of witnessing her parents drift apart are among the most tragic I have ever met in my years of counseling. The kindest treatment they deserve is a respectful silence. Our main concern is with the effect which the divorce had on the girl, and what her thinking is like on the eve of graduation and plans for marriage the summer after college.

For both parents she remains the only link with the past. They never discuss the details of their separation, though often they inquire of her how the other is doing. "Living this kind of life is hard for me, for I am not real close to either of my parents. Neither one, now that I am away at school, can claim me as their own. Both of them love me but the extent of that love is hindered in the remembrance of the kind of life they made for me and for themselves." One thing she knows with lucid certainty: her personality has been deeply scarred in the process:

I am haunted with the idea that I am the child of both my parents, mother and father. Although I do not know the true reasons for their divorce, I know it took both of them to break up our home. My fear is that I have inherited the bad traits of both and will not be able to make a successful marriage for myself. This is brought home to me each time I catch myself doing something or saying something that reminds me of either of them. I often stop what I am doing to realize that I'm doing the same thing mother or father does or did. Because I am aware of this kind of thing happening to me, I am unable to find my true self and consequently I lack confidence in myself.

I am unsure of myself. I do not know if what I do or say will invoke happiness or sadness, so I hesitate, usually until it is almost too late.

I hesitate because I do not want to do the things which will make me similar to mother or father. I do not want to appear stubborn, frivolous, opinionated or any of the other things someone might attribute to either of my parents.

My strongest motive for remaining indecisive stems from the fact that I believe I made the wrong decision once and am suffering for it now. That decision was the one to remain with my father after the divorce. I really believe that if I had gone away, to neither parent, I could have with the grace of God brought them back together. I will probably never know if this could have happened because of me, but I am forever blaming myself for my lack of courage in at least not trying. Now there are no outward actions which I can perform to bring my parents back together. I can pray for them and hope that my merciful God is theirs too, in the end.

Because I am indecisive I cannot wholeheartedly commit myself to agree to marry. I know my knowledge of marriage exceeds that of many a young bride, but my fear is great. I have only really seen the bad side, I can only imagine the good. When I do so I tend to idealize love. I want all the things attached to 'true love' including those details attributed to it by society. I seem unwilling to accept the fact that I have fallen in love without all the frills. I do not bounce around and sing, nor do I feel I would die if we ever broke up, nor do I feel that we have to be together every minute of the day. Because I do idealize love, I sometimes feel that I'm missing out when I don't feel these things. I particularly notice this when my friends are resounding from wall to wall with their echoes of love. I know that some of this is ridiculous, but I do not want to let go of it. Maybe this is my way of punishing myself for my parents' mistake, my way of not being to blame for something that might not work out in the end.

In addition to my lack of faith in myself I am also distrustful of others. Because two people whom I loved very much failed me, I am reluctant to place my faith in any one again. My mind has to be completely sure of the person before I can trust him. If it is uncertain my trust only extends as far as my certainty. Few people really are affected by this. Those that notice it the most are those closest to me. They cannot comprehend why our relationship is not always on the same even level. At times we are distant while at other times we are close. It is hard to explain but it does exist and is evidenced by the few people who can really claim to know me or what I am thinking.

One of the most unfortunate effects of my young experience concerns sex. Sex played a prominent role in my parents' separation. Its abuse was the cause of all the problems. Sometime before my parents agreed to end their marriage, something went wrong and more than likely it had to do with sex. The words that were tossed about concerning sex have led me to believe it was an evil thing. When I think about sex in their marriage I think it was probably used as the essence of their existence together. Neither of them seemed to feel it needed to be controlled inside as well as outside marriage.

I also think of sex as an animal passion, driving man on and on, so that he never gets his fill. He does not stop to consider anything or anyone except himself and his own desire. I find it difficult to imagine sex born of real love; it must be a wonderful thing. I see it only as a consuming fire, one I do not want to burn me. Unless I clear these notions I will not be able to have a successful marriage. No man would want a wife who would withdraw and cringe at his touch, or a wife who could not forget the idea that sex is wrong. It is too much to ask.

My parents' divorce has affected me in many ways, many of which I find inexpressible. My life would change immensely if it were possible to shut the door on the past. This cannot be done and I must bear the cross God has given me. If I suffer under its weight it is because I have chosen to accept God's will.

I have just tried to explain my reasons for hesitating to marry. It is hard to put into words the many embarrassing and confusing situations I have found myself in since their divorce. Little things are always happening to bring back memories better left forgotten. The most recent one occurred when my

247

mother was up here for mom's weekend. The first night she was here we were idly conversing with my friend and her mother. Slowly the conversation turned to talking about a sweater another girl had knit for her boy friend. Shortly after she gave him the sweater, they broke up. I thought that if she ever saw the sweater on the boy now, she would become upset, but mother told me that that was not her reaction when my father wore the sweater she had knit for him. She didn't mind if he wore it, why should she?

It is sad to say but even though both of my parents have remarried and established homes, I still believed that they loved each other. That small hope is gone now as I realize their love is.

Regardless of all that has happened to me, a little over a year ago I agreed to marry. I did not consent readily. In the last few months I have really known it is the thing for me to do and I am glad.

So much for the past. As she looks to the future, she sees in her fiancé the man whom God sent into her life to undo the evils she endured and profit from the lessons she had so painfully learned. Her marriage partner shares her own faith and in many ways complements her character, above all in giving her the self-confidence she desperately lacked when entering college. It is impossible to read of her hopes without sensing the power of faith that inspired them. By a strange coincidence, and without planning, the manuscript of what she wrote is being typed the very morning of her wedding:

It is odd how I have known Jerry for three years and yet feel that I do not really know him. I only know about him. Under certain circumstances I can predict his reactions, while under others I cannot tell what he is thinking. I fell in love with Jerry early during our dating, although I was not aware of its depth at the time. As I grew in knowledge concerning Jerry I found myself liking and agreeing with his personality and his being. I found I loved those things which I found only in him. I liked the way they agreed with or complemented mine, and I especially liked the way I could be myself when we were together. As time passed I found Jerry filling more and more of the needs I had. I found myself maturing, and growing, and liking it. But the greatest revelation was that I could love, and I did love, and that the center of my love was a man named Jerry.

Yes, it sounds too poetic but this is how it all looks to me. We are not entirely alike, but in the depths of our existence we are searching for the same thing, God. When we were first getting acquainted we would often talk about life and its various institutions, including marriage. We discovered that both of us were seeking a special person not just anyone to spend the rest of our lives with. Today I am always warmed by a conversation we had concerning marriage. I had asked the innocent question: "Why do you want to marry me?" Jerry carefully pondered the question and slowly said: "Because I think you can help me to get to heaven." If only I can be worthy of such confidence.

I was educated in a Catholic school while Jerry was schooled in a public school but attended Saturday religion classes for twelve years. I feel that even though our religious background is of different depths we seek similar goals and believe in similar means to them. This kind of sameness forms a solid foundation for our lives together. Because we are aware of each other's goals we can help one another to reach them.

When I was in high school the student body was too large for the accompanying church, so daily Mass was an option for us. I tried to attend Mass daily because I felt a certain security in being in church. I think that the graces received from this habit helped me to keep my faith throughout my parents' divorce.

My Catholic education has given me a deep devotion for the sacraments. When I first came to college I was lost among all the people. The thing I missed most was the church. There was no chapel in the basement of the building as there had been in high school. If I wanted to speak with God I had to find a half hour or more before I could feel the security of His presence. Although I do not often attend Mass during the week, I still believe it to be an important influence in my life. I hate to see the Sundays come when Jerry and I are unable to go to Communion together. When we attend church in this manner I am very sad because it is usually because we have failed to help each other remain strong in the face of temptation.

I like to think that I am helping Jerry in his faith. I know I am not his conscience but I try to suggest going to church or the sacraments often, especially confession. I think this helps Jerry because he has a tendency to put off doing things he knows he should do. For myself being out of God's friendship and in the state of sin, haunts me and makes me feel as if I have lost the dearest friend I have, which indeed does happen. It is this compulsion to remain in God's friendship which makes me impatient with Jerry when he doesn't go to confession when he knows he should.

When I really stop to consider all the things that Jerry has done for me, they far out measure that which I have done for him. When I am upset because of something, Jerry is there inserting his words of kindness and encouragement. He usually tells me to pray. His thoughtfulness helps me to remember that God is always at my side. Often when we write each other Jerry asks me for my prayers. I know that this is his way of reminding me not only to pray for him, but to be faithful in my own daily prayers which I am sometimes neglectful of.

The most significant thing that Jerry has done for me is to give me faith in myself and in others. Because he took the time to care and to help, I am not as crippled by my parents' divorce as I was when I first entered college. I can now really believe that what I have to say is important, that what I decide to do is important and that how I think and what I think is worth telling to others.

Love has changed me in many ways. Jerry has been the quiet strength who has brought me out of my shell. I told

Jerry about my home life when we first began to date. He had few comments about it and has since helped me to put it in its proper place. I still have a few things to straighten out, but now I have someone to help me, someone who can see my side and yet be apart enough to help me live with the cross I must bear.

All the things I mentioned as affecting me because of the divorce Jerry and I have talked over. He tries to understand and to help me understand. Sometimes we only confuse each other, but it is because of him that I can even really speak of it at all. Otherwise it would remain locked up inside of me.

Jerry realizes that I am not sure who I am. He tells me my fears are silly and have no concrete foundations. He has almost convinced me, but they are still somewhat real to me. However, instead of driving a wedge between us they are serving to bring us together. When I sense something is wrong I can easily recognize it and be spurred on to do the opposite, and correct it.

Jerry has made me feel I am an individual. He tries to let me make my own decisions and thereby develop self-confidence. Only the grace of God allowed me to know that I should say, 'Yes' to Jerry when he asked me to marry him. During our courtship I have prayed to know that we are doing the right thing. I have had no great revelations. A calm contentment has come to me and we have grown in assurance that our marriage is the will of God.

I do not mean to say that I do not suffer my share of pangs of doubt. I do. Yet somehow my doubts resolve themselves before I have a chance to do anything about them. Proof of this can be seen in my ability to write this paper. If I did not believe Jerry and I would marry and stay married, I could not write in this manner. It would be dishonest.

Perhaps my greatest doubts for us stem from the fact that I idealize love. Living in a dorm allows me to hear a lot and see a lot concerning love. Most of the things I encounter tell me I should be in some kind of seventh heaven; however, I know that this is not our kind of love. Deep in our hearts we are rejoicing and doing flips, but outwardly our appearance is only slightly changed. I hope I am not wrong when I say that this is the type of thing that draws us together. We both are too serious-minded to accept any type of flighty love. We know we love each other and do not care if other people are unable to read it in our faces or our actions.

As for being untrustful of others, this is a problem I must wrestle with myself. I trust Jerry, perhaps not to the degree I will in another year, but does any young bride have the depth of her emotions fixed when she marries? Trusting people is something that will come naturally as I gain in self-confidence, and as I grow in love.

The way I feel about sex makes things awkward for us. I do not understand it and am somewhat afraid of it. Jerry has helped me to see that sex is not as cruel and urgent as I once believed. I have confidence in him and know that he loves me and that our love-making will not become the focal point of our living together. I think we have the courage and ability to make this a truth for our marriage.

Jerry and his love have brought out many good things in me. They have aided me in developing a mature outlook on marriage and on life. My improvement is not finished, but I am ready now to help myself and am willing to accept the help of others. I pray that my marriage will not be greatly hindered by my past experience and that it will be the kind of marriage I have always wished my parents had. I also pray that my children will never have cause to suffer as I did.

One aspect of the divorce problem that few people consider, is the growing number of students in college who are married and legally separated. The national average shows that almost forty per cent of the men and sixty-five per cent of the women marry before the age of twenty-two. With teenage marriages notoriously unstable, colleges have their quota of "displaced persons" who are looking for a second chance.

The presence of even a handful of such eligibles on campus would influence the students' attitude towards marriage, but when they become personally involved, the results are predictable. Even though the stigma attached to being divorced has largely disappeared, it still raises some difficult questions for a young man who falls in love with a divorcée or, as in the following case, for a girl who was caught in the dilemma of giving up her faith or the man conscience told her she could not marry.

By the end of the summer I realized that I was in love with him. Then began a period of such complete confusion and mental, emotional, and spiritual turmoil that I have never known. I hope that I *never* have to go through anything like it again in my lifetime. For a whole semester I went along at complete odds with myself and the Catholic Church. When I was with him on the weekends, nothing else mattered. But Sunday nights through Fridays were living hell, to which those living around me will strongly attest.

I found myself hating the Catholic Church for not letting me have something which I knew was right. I didn't think about anything else all day long and when I should have been doing schoolwork at night, all I could do was cry myself to sleep. I have never felt more like a 'lost soul.' I'd ask myself over and over 'Why?' 'Why does it have to be this way?' God and I had many a long talk that semester and I realized that it couldn't go on like this or I'd end up in a padded cell for sure. During all this time, Clyde, my divorced friend, knew what I was going through and agreed that something had to be done. I thought of seeing you, but you were something of a 'Fountainhead' in my mind then, and who was I to trouble you with my little problem. Over semester break, Clyde and I went to see the pastor of my parish. He was most discouraging and upset me more than ever, because by this time Clyde and I were talking seriously of marriage.

Now a recurring thought in my mind was whether or not I would, or could, give up my religion to marry him. Here is where the real conflict came in: Clyde on one side, and my religion, family, and friends on the other. We broke up more than a few times during those past months and I began thinking real 'selfish thoughts.' How could I be so foolish as to let my petty emotions so cloud my reason that I would even consider forsaking twenty years of 'indoctrination' to marry this person? Could I disappoint God and my parents, not to mention myself, in this way? Was I so naive as to think that I held some special power to make our marriage successful and happy? I had these thoughts and many more. And after much serious thinking and weighing of the facts—I still believed that this was the person I wanted to marry—if the Catholic Church would allow it. I know now that I could never leave my religion. It is too much a part of me.

At the present time, we are applying for the 'Privilege of the Faith.' When I go home in June, we will sign the affadavit promising not to see each other during the procedure. Clyde is going into the service in June, so we have that in our favor. I am thankful for this interval because it will give us both time to think, to be away from each other. We both realize that the outcome of this will depend upon whether or not he can accept Catholicism. Not whether he *will*, but if he can in all honesty with himself and God. I still pray to God every night that I'm doing the right thing. But when I review the circumstances of his marriage and divorce, and think back over this past year, I find reassurance. I still can't honestly say to myself that this was 'in God's plan' for me. Nevertheless, God willing, I will marry him.

Not everyone has either the same faith or the same courage of his convictions. But even when the relationship with a divorced person does not end in marriage, it leaves a permanent effect on both parties. The single person is more convinced than ever that married people who make mistakes should not be forbidden to try again; and the divorced party finds himself accepted by a society from which he would have been ostracized two generations ago.

The prevalence of children of divorce in college, coupled with a growing number of divorced students, is slowly changing the campus mores on marital stability. Students with religious backgrounds suddenly discover that their churches are less intransigent on remarriage than was supposed. In panel discussions and dialogues, the idea emerges that Christ's condemnation of divorce is a hard saying. It is impossible, they feel, to follow the Christian ethic literally. No doubt the prohibition is normative for Christians generally, but there are too many cases where divorce should be allowed in order to avoid greater evil.

Consequently marital indissolubility comes to be ranked, with forgiveness of one's enemies, as something idyllic. It must not be considered a moral law binding on all people, and much less the basis of civil legislation.

What they see and experience is re-enforced by social theories in the classroom. Their textbooks tell them that divorce may be pronounced an evil, and attempts made to eliminate it; or it may be considered a form of social adjustment required in a given family-social system. The first view, it is said, lends little to an understanding of the basic problem as manifested in contemporary society. Approached from the other standpoint, divorce is looked upon as the end product, a device for mediating an unreconcilable conflict. It is a sad, but inevitable, answer to one of life's most difficult questions: "Must I put up with an impossible mate or may I remarry someone who is more compatible?"

The best witnesses to the tragedy of divorce are its first victims, the wives who were once loved by the men they married, but who lost in competition with other women.

One of the most poignant testimonies of this kind was given me by an undergraduate who returned to college after years of struggle to bring her children to maturity without a husband. Her story, as I know from personal observation, is even more tragic than its telling might show. It is a tribute to her faith and a warning, as she intends it, to those young people who are careless about whom they marry and cavalier about terminating a marriage that nature itself demands should be permanent:

My marriage, like thousands of others in America, went on the rocks. The reasons were many and the factors involved too complex to analyze. My point of view is not a defense mechanism. I am merely stating facts and commenting on events I could not control. My married life was threatened by my husband's egotism and irresponsibility. This is the best way I can put it. There was another woman involved, a woman divorced four times. The common triangle could not continue. Someone had to give in. A breakup seemed inevitable, given the circumstances. I tried my best at the time to save the marriage.

For two years my children were deprived of a mother. How could I give the time necessary to keep up a home and three growing children while I was spending so much time running to lawyers, the friend of the court's office, and preparing for trials? When I wasn't doing this I was too dragged down with grief and worry to prepare the nourishing meals growing children need. Much of the time our children had to shift for themselves. There simply wasn't time to care for a growing family and go through a divorce too. And now I had the whole burden of maintaining a home, paying the bills, and raising a family suddenly thrust upon me.

Our children were dragged out of school and into court to testify over and over again. What a terrible thing for children to have to testify against either parent when what they want so much is to have both parents. Yet my husband had stopped, many months before, the small payments for their support, on the grounds that he was not getting visiting rights with the children. They did not want to go with him when he was living with the woman who had chased him for six years and had caused the final breakup. So the judge said they

256

would have to come into court and tell why they would not go places with their father. On this and other occasions they were dragged into court. It does not take much to imagine how painful these ordeals were for our children. They had been taught from the very beginning to love their father, and they knew they needed not just one but both parents.

Left alone to support myself and the children, I had to find ways to earn money. I had to take in roomers and soon found out how humiliating it is to fill out applications, admitting being a divorced woman. And I would have to go through life with this stigma attached to my name.

I worked hard at various tasks and held numerous jobs and my children grew. To bring them up decently I had to make unbelievable sacrifices. Finally I found it necessary to go to school to study typing in order to get a job. Later, in order to keep my oldest daughter away from one of my husband's newly acquired step sons it was necessary to send her away to college. To do this I was forced to go to work in a plant. I paid my daughter's tuition for college while my former husband washed his hands completely of their support and yet tried to get credit for their success. And that was the man I married in a Christian wedding!

After the divorce our children had to find jobs and work all hours of the night. At the age of eleven they had to begin baby sitting. Since we now had to get along without a car, they had to walk to get home from work, school, which was two miles, and everywhere. Sometimes they had to get home late at night and walk along dark, lonely streets. They had never been spoiled or pampered with money but now too much was asked of them.

It is one thing to ask children to earn spending money and perhaps part of the money for clothing, but quite another thing to expect them to give up all their play time or social contacts with other children. It wasn't fair to take away their childhood so my husband could lavish his money on this divorced woman. He had money for Florida trips, to buy convertibles, pay for plane tickets, and stay in 'plush' hotels, but never enough to give our children a decent chance in life.

With God's help I won out partially in the end because my children are all college graduates, happily married and well adjusted and I am most happy as I hold their children in my arms, though the times I can see my grandchildren are far too seldom, owing to the distance between us. But in spite of our children's successes, there will always be a cloud over their lives as well as mine.

I have been in Reno, glamour spot and divorce capital, and have watched the divorce circus in operation. I sat in the courtroom and observed with sorrow how easily, in a few minutes, a divorce is granted. I stood at the bridge and watched while a giddy-looking divorcée, according to custom after a Reno divorce, tossed her wedding ring into the Truckee river, while her friends, behaving like morons, stood around and applauded.

Thus is the sacred value of marriage treated by a section of flippant America, the nation that wants to lead the world in everything. Afterwards, I visited the night clubs and gaped in horror as the gay, noisy parties went on celebrating the 'freedom' of the newly divorced persons. At one long table in a certain night club, the guests, like naughty children, when the parents are away, whooped and shrieked with delight because another divorce had just been granted, and the sacred vows of another marriage had just been torn to shreds.

A side often overlooked when divorce is discussed is the emotional life of the divorced woman. A woman used to a man's affection and care misses them when she is deprived of them and is often driven to instability, to say the least. The position the divorced woman holds in society puts her on the spot. What should she do? Can she accept attentions from other men? Can she stifle her emotional life completely?

What must the normal woman do, besides getting married again, if she is lucky enough to find another husband? For a woman who is used to her husband's affection, the sudden change is a shock to her system. For me it was no different. My desires did not end the moment the judge uttered the words 'Divorce granted.' I still longed for a man's arms around me; I still desired to dance when I heard music. Every night when I went to bed the emptiness there on the pillow beside me was unbearable.

No one knew what I suffered at times when I was left alone. I could confide in no one and trust nobody. Merely to know that he was there by my side was enough for my happiness which was now forever gone. Every night in the stillness of that empty room tears streamed down my face onto the pillow. The suffering one goes through during those lonely, tortured nights is indescribable. Life becomes a living hell. Is it any wonder that in spite of society's disapproval a woman weakens finally and accepts love and attention from other men? Who is to be blamed and who can condemn? In my case for two long years I suffered loneliness, thinking of nothing but my children and my husband. I found that when finally I accepted the attention and invitations and the affection of other men, it was a constant struggle of fighting them off, for they were not satisfied to let it end there.

Once or twice I even fell in love and wanted more than just affection. The turmoil that went on whirling in my mind and heart was too much to cope with and I had to seek the help of doctors for pains and complaints for which there was no apparent organic reason. Mind and conscience can drive a person to madness, and mental sufferings can be as acute as physical ones.

What is my life like today? With my children gone, I remain bewildered and confused, and my life is nothing but chaos. I am homeless. My furniture, paintings, and personal possessions are piled in other people's basements, and the things dear to me and to which we attach ourselves, are scattered all over town and I don't know where to look when I need something. I live in an attic room, deprived of all the charming things that make a home. From gracious living I have climbed down to eating in other people's kitchens or eating cold lunches from paper sacks. Gone is my well kept home that had books, paintings, tastefully arranged possessions; and the cozy, secure, atmosphere every woman needs and wants as the supreme goal in life. What have I left? Ashes from a once-glowing fire of love, affection, and happiness.

I still believe that perhaps ninety-nine out of a hundred divorces could be avoided. If judges, lawyers and people connected with the courts would do something, anything, to aid reconciliation instead of driving couples deeper into divorce, the separating couples might have a chance of getting back together. In our case, they drove the wedge between us even deeper. This is a time when people need help. Seldom are the couples able to patch up their difficulties alone; partly as a matter of pride neither one wants to take the first step.

Much of the fault of divorces lies in the hands of our judges and lawyers. The moment someone files for divorce or is involved in a separation and contemplating divorce, the case should be referred to a family court or family service center staffed with highly trained and intelligent people. A year before our divorce my husband came to me and said 'divorce is not a solution.' He did not want that divorce. I needed help right then, but there was never anyone to help, who was able or trained to give the help we needed, and I was dealing with more than just my husband; I was dealing for the most part with a woman divorced four times who didn't care whom she trampled on or hurt to get what she wanted.

Divorce is a social illness, a cancer that must be fought relentlessly as other diseases that torment mankind. A well adjusted family is the nucleus of a wholesome, sane society. A family without a husband is almost lost.

If my heartaches—mostly over my children's sufferings—can be of value to other people, perhaps the Lord did not make me suffer in vain. My greatest hope is to enlighten people on the divorce evil and help to eradicate it from our Christian society.

The value of this woman's reflections is mainly in the substance it gives to a mounting plea for more realism in teaching about marriage in the classroom.

Most commentators on marriage are blasé on the subject. Their philosophy begins with the premise that the only good of marriage is mutual satisfaction, so that when this good is not realized the breaking of marriages must be tolerated. Otherwise it forever condemns a certain number of couples to a life of misery together.

The prevalent philosophy, therefore, claims that those who have failed to find happiness in one marriage should be free to seek it again in another. What libertarianism ignores, however, is a basic fact of human nature: that where either party is free to pass judgment on how "happy" he is with his present partner, the odds are that a future partnership can always appear more satisfying. And when husband and wife are equally free to seek greater happiness elsewhere, chances are they will consult their own selfish, though mutually agreed, interests before those of the children. Their least concern is what effect this may have on the rest of the society.

With the increased enrollment of divorced persons in college, the dominant theory on "love" as the only foundation for marriage is sure to change. Instead of tagging monogamy as "old-fashioned" or claiming that "rigorous condemnation of divorce a few generations ago no longer exists," students are living too close to the chaos produced by family disintegration to avoid critical judgments of their own.

NINE

CHALLENGE AND CHANGE

Four Crucial Years

COLLEGE has an effect on the religious beliefs of students. They change in their acceptance or rejection of the faith of their parents, or at least they modify what they believed. This is inevitable, given the challenges they meet from the first day in shool. Everything around them suggests that old ways are to be questioned and new ones tried. The whole atmosphere of a university seems congenial to adjustment from childhood and adolescence to adulthood. This does not exclude a readjustment of faith.

The degree and nature of the change depends on many factors. Generally those with a strong religious faith before they enter college become stronger in creedal commitment through four years of exposure to academic and moral probation. But a deep faith is not to be equated with extensive religious education. Church-affiliated schooling is only a favorable precondition; it is by no means a guarantee that what a high school graduate has been taught for upwards of twelve years is also what he personally and intellectually believes.

There is enough of the sceptic in every believer to need only a powerful stimulus for the mind to waver in its early beliefs and, given the right combination of circumstances, even to turn against its former convictions. On the other hand, the same tendency to skepticism may serve as a catalyst for reassessment with the result that a weakly-believing freshman can become a strongly-committed senior. He has seen the moral shambles produced by disbelief and he wants none of it, and the harder his friends try to shake him the more convinced he becomes that only faith in God can save him from the groping subjectivism that characterizes most people who lack religious stability. In fact, he discovers that disbelief is often symptomatic of a more basic weakness of character, the inability to be sure of anything except one's own theories and opinions.

But not everyone makes this discovery. Some go to the opposite extreme and, though supported by years of specialized training, may lapse into some form of agnosticism which differs according to background and their impatience with Christian morality.

Just an Opinion. The freedom with which my students expressed themselves about matters religious was refreshing. If most of them were believing Christians, there were also those who had been Christian but decided against it and had no inhibitions about sharing their ideas with anyone willing to listen.

One man wrote under the cryptic title, *Just an Opinion,* and through ten pages of sustained logic proceeded to tell me what was wrong with Christianity or, more accurately, with those who still believed it:

Christianity, if it's good for anything, is good for making fools out of men, especially priests. I do, however, have sympathy for all who throw away their lives to the service of God. In most cases it wasn't their fault. Take any child and indoctrinate him with any religion you please until he is a man and he will, in most cases, be a firm believer in that religion.

There are those who are intelligent enough to put up a good argument on the authenticity of the Bible. After

all, didn't I sit through a semester of classes and invariably see my instructor come up with an answer for every sceptical question asked. Look at it this way. After almost two
thousand years of constant bickering, you should have a
patent answer for almost any question imaginable.

'You cannot combine a great mind with a humble religion.' That little sentence, thought up by some rationalizing Christian is supposed to be the answer to why
men like Paine, Washington, Jefferson, Adams, Franklin,
Madison, Hamilton, Jackson, Lincoln, Grant, Edison,
Einstein, and many other great minds were sceptical. Christians seem to have an answer for everything. Sudden deaths
are perpetually happening, and if they occur to persons whose
theology may be a trifle shady, they are divine judgments; if
a person drops dead in the pulpit, God called him to a better
life.

Anticipating objections, he says educated Christians
could reply to all his objections. However, "since it will
shed a little light on the origin of my beliefs," he proceeds
to bolster his position with arguments drawn partly from
reading but mainly from his own reflections. The first
argument reasons from the character of the people who are
featured in the Bible and reaching back to the earliest
patriarchs and prophets:

Jesus Christ's miracles and doctrines were rejected by
the only nation to which he preached. And when he was on
the cross and cried out 'My God, my God, why hast thou
forsaken me?', it makes me think that maybe Christ really
thought he was the son of God and suddenly found out he had
illusions of grandeur. Christ taught that 'Blessed are the
poor in spirit, for theirs is the kingdom of heaven.' It seems
to me you should be true in spirit and determined to resist wrong, then there would be a greater opportunity for
happiness.

Along the same line, Christ taught 'Unto him that

smiteth thee on the one cheek offer also the other.' I'm afraid there would be very little liberty if this was practiced. Another prize teaching was 'Blessed be ye poor, for yours is the kingdom of God . . . But woe unto you that are rich, for ye have received your consolation.' I'd sure hate even to imagine the condition of our world today if everyone believed this. And how about the time Jesus cursed the fig tree? The tree was created to bear fruit in the summer, but when Jesus found it without fruit in the spring, he cursed it so that it withered away. It seems to me that Christ was a little ignorant of the seasons, and showed he had a bad temper by destroying a profitable food-producing tree.

Now I'll give you my opinion of some of the characters in the Old Testament. Abraham was an insane, barbarian patriarch who married his sister, denied his wife, and seduced her handmaid; who drove one child into the desert to starve and made preparations to butcher the other.

Jacob was another patriarch, who won God's love by deceiving his father, cheating his uncle, robbing his brother, practicing bigamy with two of his cousins, and committing fornication with two of his cousins and two of his housemaids.

Moses murdered an Egyptian and hid his body in the sand; he exterminated whole nations to secure the spoils of war, he butchered in cold blood thousands of captive widows, and made orphans of thirty-two thousand innocent girls, and turned sixteen thousand of them over to slavery.

David was a traitor, he led enemy troops against his own countrymen; he was a thief, a robber and a liar; he tortured and slaughtered thousands of men, women, and children; and made them pass through burning brickkilns, carving them up with saws and axes, he abducted the wife of a faithful soldier and later had this faithful soldier put to death after desolating his home; he demanded with his dying breath the deaths of two aged men. They were a fine upstanding lot of men, the heroes of the Old Testament.

The next step is to examine the validity of the Judaeo-

Christian scriptures, which he finds less worthy of credence than the average secular literature of comparable antiquity. Among other items, he places the origin of the New Testament about the year two hundred and makes the Gospels out to be forgeries:

Now let's look at the origin of the 'infallible' Bible. Out of 250 Jewish-Christian writings, sixty-six have been arbitrarily declared canonical by Protestants. The rejected books are of the same general character as those now published together as 'The Holy Bible.' Circumstances, rather than merit determined selection.

For one hundred years the Christian Bible consisted of the sacred books of the Jews. The New Testament was not formed until the latter half of the second century, when Irenaeus selected twenty books from among forty or more gospels, nearly as many acts of apostles, a score of revelations, and a hundred epistles. Why were these particular books chosen? Why four gospels instead of one? Irenaeus: 'There are four quarters of the earth in which we live and four universal winds.' The Gospels were unknown to Peter, Paul, and the early Church Fathers. They were forged later.

The Bible did not assume anything like its present form until the fourth century. The Roman Catholic, Greek Catholic, and Protestant canons were not adopted until modern times. The Bible was recognized as a collection of independent writings. The Council of Trent (1563) determined the Roman Catholic canon, consisting of seventy-two books. The Greek Catholics at the Council of Jerusalem (1672) finally accepted Revelation. Their Bible contains several books not in the Roman canon. The Westminster Assembly (1647) approved the list of sixty-six books composing the Authorized Version, the one most used in America. Our Bible, therefore, is less than three hundred years old. Adoption was by majority vote.

The final test of Christianity is its uniqueness, but here

too it fails because, as certain comparative religionists teach, there are remarkable parallels to the history and teachings of the Christian religion. Why rest your case, he asks, on a faith that is not the most ancient or even distinctive, but has rivals and counterparts from several millenia before Christ:

The fable of a god or gods visiting the earth did not originate with Christianity. Historical facts have established that there were many cases of the miraculous birth of gods reported in history before the case of Jesus Christ. Many of these gods were born of virgin mothers and many like Christ were born on the twenty-fifth of December. Their advent into the world, like that of Jesus Christ, is in many cases claimed to have been foretold by 'inspired prophets.'

Stars also figured at the birth of several of them as in the case of Christ. Their lives, like his, were also threatened in infancy by the rulers of the country. Several of them, like him, gave early proof of divinity, and like him, retired from the world and fasted. Also like him, they declared 'My kingdom is not of this world!' Some of them preached a spiritual religion too, like his. And were 'anointed with oil,' like him. Many of them, like him, were 'Crucified for the sins of this world' and after three days' interment 'rose from the dead.' The same violent convulsions of nature at the crucifixion of several are reported. Many are reported as ascending back to heaven, like him.

They were nearly all called 'Saviors.' 'Son of God.' 'Messiah.' 'Redeemer.' 'Lord,' etc. Each one was the second member of the trinity of 'Father, Son and Holy Ghost.' The doctrine of 'Original Sin,' 'Fall of Man,' and 'The Atonement,' 'The Trinity,' 'The Word,' 'Forgiveness,' 'An Angry God,' and 'Future Endless Punishment' were part of the religion of each of these sin-atoning gods as found in several oriental bibles and 'Holy books' written by 'inspired and holy men' before the time of either Christ or Moses. All these doctrines, and many others were taught in various oriental heathen nations centuries before the birth of Christ.

For example, Chrishna, the Hindu redeemer, was cradled and educated among shepherds. A tyrant, at the time of his birth, ordered all the male children to be slain. He performed miracles, say the legends, and raised the dead. He washed the feet of the Brahmins, and was meek and lowly of spirit. He was born of a virgin; descended to hell, rose again, ascended to heaven, charged his disciples to teach his doctrines, and give them the gift of miracles. He did all this about one thousand years, before Christ. Of course we must realize that the people of those times had the intelligence to distinguish the false god from the true god, or at least that is the manner in which the Christians argue.

Christians might appeal to the survival of their faith for so many centuries as evidence of its being more than just a human construct. But their appeal is not convincing, as proved by the fact that survival was possible only through persecution and destruction of those who opposed the Christian way of life. Two cases are cited. "There are many more cases similar to these, but I'm sure Christians would push them aside saying, 'Yes, but that was during the years when the church was corrupt along with the governments.' I will not mention any more. What's the use? I can't fight those rationalized, patent answers."

Another excellent reason why we must have religion, so say the religious, is that without religion, life would not be safe for a minute; it is, they say, religion that makes people fear to commit crimes. Just reflect a little on this point. If we had no laws, courts, policemen, jails nor other penal institutions, what would happen despite all religion . . . But, they answer, without religion things would be even worse. My reply to such arguments is a polite request to consider the fifteenth and sixteenth centuries when religion was supreme and all-powerful. A good many people were burned alive, tortured to death, and bloody wars were fought, in the sacred name of religion. Crime and corruption were rampant, justice and morality were in complete absence. Does any sensible human being desire a return to such conditions?

The student finally comes to his own philosophy of life. He states frankly that what bothers him is not Christianity but religion, and, as Freud and Feuerbach explained long ago, all religion is projection of the self; it is the creation of a world of make-believe from the frustrated desires in a world of painful reality:

I'm not condemning Christianity, I'm condemning all religions. They are built on fear and survive on fear. As children are afraid to enter a dark room so are men afraid to die. What is it like to die? Consider how it was before you were born and I think you will have a good answer. Whenever man has been confronted with a mystery which he could not interpret by earthly principles, he has invoked the aid of the supernatural. Thunder was once said to be caused by the chariot of a god rolling across the firmament; the fiery thunderbolts were the god's weapons. When the angels opened the windows of heaven it rained. Insanity was the result of being possessed by devils. Witches made men wicked, and soured milk. Thousands of the mysteries of old were explained as the work of gods, devils, ghosts, witches, angels, spirits, or fairies; but in every instance when the mystery was finally understood, the supernatural explanation proved false; the true explanation has proved a natural one. I'm convinced that all the Biblical miracles will disappear with the progress of science.

If God wishes to be known, thanked and loved, why does he not show himself under his favorable features to all these intelligent beings by whom he wishes to be adored? Why not manifest himself to the earth in an unequivocal manner? This would be more convincing than these private revelations which seem to accuse God of showing partiality for some of his creatures. After all, since God is supposed to be all-powerful, he should have more convincing means by which to show himself to men. He should be able to convince the human mind in an instant of the things he wished to make known to it. And if God has spoken why isn't the universe convinced? If the knowledge of a God is so necessary, why is it not the most evident and the clearest?

I believe that of the Christians today, few are without some form of scepticism concerning their faith. But if they are told that they are wrong they will only resent the imputation and harden their hearts. If I were to generalize, I could say we are all incredibly heedless in the formation of our beliefs, but find ourselves filled with an illicit passion for them when any-one proposes to rob us of their companionship. It is obviously not the ideas themselves that are dear to us, but our self-esteem which is threatened. We are by nature stubbornly pledged to defend our own from attack, whether it be our person, family, or opinion.

Few of us take the pains to study the origin of our cher-ished convictions; indeed, we have a natural repugnance to do so. We like to continue to believe what we have been accustomed to accept as true; and the resentment aroused when doubt is cast upon any of our assumptions leads us to seek every manner of excuse for clinging to them. The result is that most of our so-called reasoning consists in finding argu-ments for going on believing as we already do.

We conceal the real reasons for our beliefs, he con-cludes. As we grow up, we simply adopt the ideas offered us in the environment in which we live. Then we come to college, and slowly "we find ourselves changing our minds without any resistance or heavy emotion." His hope is that Christians, "through a little rational thinking, will event-ually decide for themselves that religion is the world's greatest farce." It pretends to the possession of knowledge which it cannot prove.

A Critic of Catholicism. Another senior, who had twelve years of Catholic education before entering the university, begins her critique by quoting from an *Esquire* article she read shortly before, in which the author says that "In moments of stress, the youth of America turns to its idols." In her case, the idols were some of her college professors:

It's very simple. They were the first adults I ever knew that were alive. They introduced me to things that made me feel alive. And, on the whole, they were practicing Christians. Christian action! It was a new experience for me. I had been stifled in twelve years of Catholic education. I could just as well put *Catholic* in quotes, too. Catholic—talk about misleading labels, that's the epitome; those years were so narrow it infuriates me just to think about them. I came out so narrow that I barely existed. Twelve years without inspiration.

I wonder just what is the point of a Catholic education anyway. From what I've always heard, parochial education is supposed to be academically superior. I never got any of it, and nobody I know did, either. So then they say that after all, you get religious training, and that alone is worth it. From my experience, that leaves the system with nothing. The first concrete indication of my religious discontent was probably the reaction to the nuns. With only a few exceptions, my respect for them went no further than that which was enforced. It was the old story. They weren't human for me. I know now that they were. But I also think that it was their limited view of life. The careful acceptance of humanity, that is, the unacknowledgment of intolerance, of faults, and sins of people, taught by the nuns, backfired. This robbed the students of the ability of recognizing the nuns themselves as people.

That should be sufficient for this installment of diatribe against that segment of my education. Eventually I may reach a successful purgation and then I can forget about it. I think of Claudius and his struggle to pray. And I think of this paper as a prayer, however simple-minded and unsuccessful. Those twelve years are too vivid a pain to forget at present. The complaining always slips in whenever I'm talking about me. Maybe it seems that I'm avoiding the topic, "My Faith." That's just the point. The kind of faith I mean doesn't exist per se; rather, what I demand is that it be assimilated into the whole of life. Thus, to consider my faith is to consider my life. Which brings me back to the impact of my college professors. Stupendous, to say the least. Not that I immediately arose from the dead and became a political or social activist. Not at all. No miraculous, instantaneous transfiguration. Possibility of miracle hindered by my legacy of inhibition. *Inhibition,* usual cue for resumption of harangue for lacking college preparation. I'll nip it in the bud.

Two factors combined to develop her new outlook on life: the experience of seeing some of her best friends forced into marriage while knowing them to be essentially moral persons, and the relativism that she learned at college. She put the two elements together, arguing that if Catholicism, as she thought, condemns sexual weakness out of hand, it cannot be true:

What college gave me is a relative viewpoint toward life. "There are no absolutes except the absolute that there are no absolutes." It was difficult to adjust this to the scanty Catholic dogma I possessed. Not that I myself erupted. I didn't dive in and become a wild woman. Strange thing. But I find the theory invaluable in developing insights about people, the better to understand them. Hindsight hints to me that the situations of my high school friends were what sowed the seeds of my relativistic attitude. All I could figure out was that I knew them and liked them. My stupidity at the time allowed no outlet for the possibility of the coexistence of human worthiness and illicit pregnancy. A milestone I was forced to confront the stereotype lodged in my mind. Although the pressure was taken off somewhat, since our interests were diverging. They had their marriages. But turn the faucet on again. And full force. Enter my junior college years. Confrontation upon confrontation upon confrontation. It hit me again.

But I am so abominably slow. *Delayed Reaction* is my middle name. I am still wrestling over resolutions to things that happened years ago. But I have hope. Once, at a racial integration rally, I heard this motto: Be Interested, Be Informed, Be Involved. It 'grabbed' me I thought that more than just an integration motto, these three *I's* make an excellent motto for all of life. My exposure to *I* number three, involvement, has been severely limited. In the midst of the dynamic exertions of the faculty and the participation of contributing students, I accepted the role of sympathetic observer. 'Allow each person to proceed at his own pace,' they say in child psychology. I was surprised to learn that even my archery instructor applied this principle, for he understood my initial and recurrent misses and string burns. Any day now, I expect to reach the third plateau, involvement.

The missionary spirit of Catholicism slowly became repulsive, along with the absolutist doctrines of faith. She connected this spirit with the training she and her younger brothers and sisters received at home. Rewards and punishments seemed to be so ingrained in their discipline that, once separated from parental influence, she decided, gradually, to start living a life of her own:

I can't see how I can ever become a Catholic again. It seems that what is the essential of Catholicism is just the thing I can't understand or accept. This is, the missionary spirit of wanting to convert everyone else. When I think about it, I don't think I was ever a Catholic. I gave to the mission drives in school, but never with a thought about converting the people who were going to benefit. Rather, I thought of the collections in terms of the later transformation into milk, rice, plows, medicine, and whatever. If I connected religion with it at all it was in the sense that the people who were receiving these gifts ought to, out of common courtesy and respect, in turn please the donators and express their thanks by accepting the whole package, conversion along with the milk. The danger in this kind of a set up is the confusion of motives.

As soon as I write that, I also have to admit that mixed, complicated motivation is the personification of man. I could say I realize that, but I have a sort of idealism in mind that religion should have pure, clearly defined motivation. But after thinking a minute, I can't really say that either, because it demands that I accept the superiority, or even the existence, of simplistic motivation (which I don't.) It also demands that I contradict the idea that religion should be so closely integrated with all the other perspectives of life. I've seen that value can triumph despite mixed, perhaps depreciating, motivation. For instance, it disturbed me to no end that my mother insisted on my younger brothers' and sisters' reading library books for punishment. She even went to the extent of paying them for each one they read. Who knows? Maybe they'll turn out better than I did. But I feel that any curiosity for reading or enjoyment they may still develop will be in spite of this bit my mother imposes on them. Granted, the invaluable contribution is the acquaintance with books, but this is almost nullified by the high hurdle of disagreeable associations.

That's how it is with me and my religion. At least, because I've had so much Catholic exposure, the whole business keeps speeding crazily in and out of my brain. It still bothers me. But then, I've lost my faith, I guess. I don't really know. I failed 'the test,' as they say. I continued going to church during my two years of junior college because I was still living at home with my parents breathing down my neck. Somewhere along the line the child should have some leeway to breathe fresh air and develop lungs of his own.

While attending Mass, she felt increasingly uncomfortable over the inconsistency of external conformity and the lack of clear, internal belief. Each week she grew more fidgety and frustrated. All she could think of was that she was a hypocrite:

I also felt hypocritical and uncomfortable in theology class; although I took time occasionally to remind myself that this was a university course offered for credit. It was for exploring and learning. My religious status was irrelevant. This wasn't one of those milk-and-conversion package deals.

What intrigues me from my class notes is the statement that faith involves intellectual humility on the part of the believer. Intellectual humility is what I lack. What's more, I'm not an intellectual. Too bad. I've always thought the whole thing would be so easy if only I were. Unfortunately, I wonder if I'm not trying to play this role of intellectual anyway despite my incapability. That's inexcusable. It brands me as an uppity smart aleck. So I have been fighting to withstand the tendency to fall into the cliché trails that others I know have followed after confused confrontation with Catholicism. Most of the time this accomplishes nothing but wishy-washy inactivity.

She returns to the convert spirit of Catholicism and analyzes it to mean that if you know you have the truth you want to share this possession with anyone willing to listen. The smug self-satisfaction this implies is irritating, especially when it lacks the firm intellectual foundation.

I realize what the premise is that supports the conversion fever of Catholics. They believe theirs is the one and only true religion and that it is such a good thing that they wish to share it with as many as possible in the true spirit of brotherhood. Well, what happens when a cradle Catholic realizes that she isn't so sure whether or not Catholicism is the 'right' one? It's just that, the righteousness of some Catholics, that disturbs me. Not that I would expect to find every

275

member an ideal specimen, but still something in the atmosphere seems to breed this despicable righteousness.

I can't remember how it goes now, but in high school someone gave us a diagram of the Church's historical lineage and traced it back to Christ. Once we hit Christ, it was clear back in those days that that was that. And who could question once you arrived at Christ? Clouds have settled within my brain since, and I say so okay there's Christ. That proves that the Catholic Church was founded by Christ. And Christ is the Son of God. And Christ Himself is God. But there's still a gap between the statements that Christ founded the Catholic Church and that the Catholic Church is the only true church. I can't see the logic in inserting a *therefore* between them. The farthest I can go is to acknowledge that having Christ as founder undoubtedly results in some unique advantages. As much as I can figure it out, this means that I've lost the faith.

At this point, she speculates on just what must have happened for her to come to this pass. All sorts of possibilities came to mind, along with an interesting sidelight on the discernment of spirits, about which she had heard in class:

Was it just that I was getting lazier than ever, or that going to church and confession were more inconvenient than ever? It's difficult to sort out which came first. I wonder whether or not I started throwing all these doubts up before myself only *after* an acute attack of laziness and apathy.

For one thing, I tested myself using the 'discernment of spirits' diagram that I have in my theology notes. The one that measures good and evil persons against good and evil impulses. I assumed myself to be a good person. How explain the pangs of conscience, anxiety, and worry that meant I was receiving evil impulses. In church? If I assumed that the impulses in church were good, the chart labels me as an evil person. Either way, something was wrong. Come to think of it, when church-going has been reduced to inconvenience, what is its worth, anyway?

I would just sit there in a pew and be completely untouched. No communication. No stimulation. The artistic credo is 'Surprise me!' Not that I expect every priest to be an artist. But the sermons I've heard in Catholic churches are so dull so often that it makes a person wonder. The stuff of literature is people. Catholic action necessarily involves people. So where are the sparks of excitement?

Is it a mark of immaturity to seek authorization for one's own ideas? That's what I always do, chiefly, in books. Books were my only source of discovery before I started college. In college, I could talk to my professors. What comes into my mind right now is someone carrying out the above to its often stated conclusion. Why rely on just human authorization? Why not go right to the top, to divine authorization? Don't take his word for it; he's only human. Well, so am I. And so is Christ.

Now I've done it. And have probably done it many times before. Just what I especially intended to avoid. I've slipped into the traditional argument for this situation. It's a strange thing. I find myself doing this when I'm reading books these days. I resist identification with characters who are in predicaments that I recognize as similar to my own. The character has now upstaged me. When I get around to resolving it in my own life, I'll have to try something different because to use his method would be to copy. I wouldn't be being me. It's a stupid reaction, I must say. It ignores the universality of human emotions, but that's what I've been feeling lately.

By way of epilogue, she admits, "I don't have any answers. All I can do is keep going, hopefully not insanely." Then the demanding question: "What is Catholicism in the first place? What am I rebelling against? Considering my meager Catholic education, I can see readily that this may be the crux of my problem." After all the criticism and uncertainty, she admits that her rejection may not be of God or the faith she had so long professed. In common with so many intellectuals, she may have reacted "honestly against false religious imagery, which includes double standard morality, ethical hypocrisy, meaningless ritual, and separation of religion from life." She is willing to have some of these images smashed before making a rational choice between faith and unbelief, and being confronted with the reality of God.

Faith to a New Philosophy of Religion. Not many students can easily synthesize a lifetime development of their religious ideas, and still less to grapple with the underlying problems that beset an inquiring mind. They tend to get lost in detail and go off on tangents that give you only a clue to their real selves.

One student, enrolled in the General Curriculum, was an exception. He managed to cover so many facets of character that are typical of reflective college men that his short autobiography should be given in full:

Just as historians study the past to understand the present and project themselves into the future, so too must I examine my past to understand my present ambivalence concerning the nature of God.

I wasn't always in doubt about God. When I was much younger, my mother would often tell me about heaven, hell, and all those religious things that loving mothers try to instill in the minds of their little ones. During that time there was no doubt as to the certainty of what mom was telling me. I accepted everything. My belief was firm and steadfast. God was a mysterious, omnipresent, omnipotent, unearthly being. Heaven was the place where all good little boys go and hell where all the bad ones go. My faith was steadfast. I believed in God as I believed in Santa Claus, Easter Bunny, and Donald Duck. How could someone with such deep, abiding faith go wrong?

I guess almost all little boys are superstitious. They carry good luck charms, recite secret incantations to ward off evil ghosts, and even avoid stepping on cracks so as not to break their mother's back! The world of a growing boy is replete with superstition. Rare is the day that you encounter a small child that can discern the difference between Santa Claus and God. This infantile conception of God stems from improper and inadequate religious instruction in the home during the formative years of childhood. Parents are generally content with presenting a hastily improvised, often untrue, conception of Christ to their questioning young child. Although these conceptions are usually accepted and believed with firm childish conviction, the seed of potential doubt is sown in their young minds. Fortunately for the world, most of these highly impressionable young people follow a developmental process whereby they achieve a more responsible and mature conception of our conventional religious structure, though they do not always accept it.

Because of my parent's insistence I began attending Sunday school at six years of age. Still too young to understand or question, I halfheartedly attended classes every Sunday morning, alone. Mom would put me on the bus every Sunday and pick me up after Sunday school, yet she or dad never once attended with me. This puzzled me when I saw other parents walking with their children to and from church. Why were they so eager for me to attend, yet unwilling to attend themselves? More doubts were planted.

My early church experiences centered around a succession from one southern Baptist church to another. By the time I was twelve, I was irregularly attending church services as well as Sunday school at various Baptist churches in the neighborhood.

Although I was old enough, by this time, to think for myself, I rarely utilized the ability and was totally oblivious to the 'hard sell' approach or 'high pressure Christianity' methods

279

used by the Southern Baptist Church—methods I later came to resent and reject. Not until one of my Sunday school teachers attempted to impress upon me the sinfulness of watching television and movies did I grow discontented with that Church. My exodus from the Southern Baptist Church proved beneficial.

Whether it was from force of habit or religious dedication, I attended Sunday school at a new church the following Sunday. The people were friendly, but not like the 'Hallelujah, praise the Lord' variety I was familiar with from previous churches. As I was ushered into my Sunday school room by an elderly, grandmotherly type woman, I was introduced to my new Sunday school teacher, Tom White. This man impressed me from the beginning. He had a friendly smile, a firm handshake, a gentle manner, an air of authority, a build like a professional football player, and a well polished pair of chisel-toed shoes that I never expected a Sunday school teacher to wear! It was Tom White who exposed me to true religion. He opened my mind, challenged my religious complacency, and explained in adult-like, intelligent terms all those things that I had for so long accepted in childish faith. Possibly this was the turning point; that one period in time when my mind was opened wide enough for intelligent doubt to creep in and gain a small foothold.

Nevertheless, as long as Tom was around I believed, I accepted. I attended his Sunday school classes and sat next to him and his wife during church services. What a change this church was from the Southern Baptist churches I had attended earlier. Even though it was still Baptist, Northern, the people were of a different variety, the atmosphere was more relaxed, and the minister's sermons were on an intelligent, thought-provoking level. They were unlike the emotionally rampant sermons, seemingly filled with as many expressions of indirect hate as overt love, that I had grown used to previously.

It was at this time that I gained my first constructive, yet unfavorable, opinion of Catholicism. I had heard Catholics denounced before but no one ever took the time to explain why their religion was different from mine. I can remember hearing that they worshiped idols, that they could sin all they wanted to because they could have their sins forgiven every week, and most shocking of all, that Catholic orphanages were filled with illegitimate children produced by sex-starved priests and nuns! Fortunately, Tom dispelled all these irrational ideas. I came to consider him my expert on Vatican affairs, for he had been raised by Catholic parents and spent the majority of his life as a Catholic before converting to Protestantism because it proved more personally meaningful to him.

Because of a high degree of social and academic success in high school, and a seemingly unending religious faith and devotion, I entered my freshman year at Western with an abiding dedication to maintain my close personal contact with God. I was convinced that I would never fall victim to the immoral depravation that I had heard abounded on college campuses. My faith and religious dedication were not only to remain untainted but were to grow over the years, or so I thought. How I must have given the impression of a religious fanatic to my new-found college friends. Even my freshman themes in college writing class were heavily laden with expressions of my dedication to Christ.

> '. . . most young people today tend to overlook their obligations to God . . . we do not realize the necessity of living a good, clean, Christian life. In this world of today where we are in constant threat of complete annihilation; the day is rapidly approaching when it will be up to us to examine our pasts and decide if we will be fit to face the hereafter with all of its glories. We are smug and complacent with our 'devil may care' attitudes and unless changes are rapidly made we will see the day when the devil is the only one who does care . . .'

Finally it happened; exactly what I had predicted would never happen to me did happen. Quite undramatically and after periods of intensive reflection during the latter half of my freshman year, it occurred to me that my zealous devotion to God was based more on personal weakness than on religious strength. It had never occurred to me before that I was emotionally and psychologically weak. I had quite often heard the comment by antireligious people that religion was merely a crutch whereby weak people could prop themselves up when things got tough. I passed these comments off as agnostic rationalizations without really considering their plausibility. How sealed off my mind was. Certainly I can't take full credit for inspiring revelation that changed the course of my life. I would be committing an injustice if I didn't give recognition to the people and events surrounding me at the time that I became critical of religion.

The time was right; I was separated from the surroundings and people at home that made me feel obligated to attend church. I had attended chapel services on Sundays but I was quite unimpressed with the quality of the sermons. Constantly the same underlying theme prevailed, 'reject sin and remain in God's grace.' I was outright tired of rejecting sin and by this time God was merely an overt manifestation of man's inner needs. Call it pseudointellectual if you like, because I'll agree with you now. But at that time it had all the meaning in the world to me. I had clung to religion like a little child clings to his teddy bear. Mom had died when I was sixteen. I overcame my grief quite rapidly but I never overcame the need for love that she had provided. The comfort, the security, the happiness that comes from knowing you're wanted and loved by someone close should never be underestimated. Mom's death drove me deeper into my religious shell. The attention and care that Tom White and his wife gave me at that time perpetuated my psychological dependence on religion.

It was precisely the realization that I had been psychologically dependent upon religion because of inner needs which caused me to form what psychologists call a reaction formation against it. Up to now, I had been dependent upon religion; the realization of this dependence was repulsive to my ego, so I immediately began forming contrasting atti-

282

tudes. An excerpt from one of my final freshman themes will serve as an example of this reaction formation. In this theme I compared life to a circus and attempted to show the futility of religious conviction.

> Life is one big circus! The people, their societies, and the conventions of these societies are the sideshows and amusement rides which constitute this gigantic three-ring affair . . . No circus would be complete without its array of clowns who constantly engage in buffooneries while attempting to appease the clamoring crowds. The clowns in this circus are divided between two different types: happy ones and sad ones.

> You and I are the clowns! We are similar because we are both being laughed at by society. But perhaps you are of the happy, smiling variety who feels content with your life and environment. Contrarily, I am the opposite type who is not content with these things, but feels that there is much more to personal contentment than being stepped on by society, surrounded by conventionalism, or living a stereotyped life.

Much to the dismay of many people back home, my anti-Christian convictions ran the gamut from atheism to Unitarianism, with agnosticism, fatalism, and futilitarianism coming somewhere between the two poles. Throughout the period of my doubt and uncertainty, I took comfort in knowing that I didn't stand alone. Many around me were examining their faith and convictions also. Doubtlessly, the early years of college life are crucial years in the formation of Christian or non-Christian ideals. Whether a person continues in unswerving faith, forms extremely contrasting opinions, or flounders in a sea of doubt depends upon many factors. In my case, emotional instability led to doubt; reactions against instability led to temporary certainty of the nonexistence of God; and a newly acquired sense of dignity, pride, and personal worth or emotional stability led to an individual interpretation of the nature of God. A compromise was reached.

Now, perhaps I have constructed for the reader a picture of the psychoreligious chaos and turmoil that have permeated my mind since my early days of religious training. The questions now arise: What of your present convictions? What is your interpretation of the nature of God? Just exactly what do you believe?

After more than four years of honest uncertainty it isn't easy to formulate a new philosophy of religion. I say new philosophy because even today vestiges of my old doubt still persist. It would be much too easy to 'fall in line' and submit to the pressures confronting me to conform to orthodox Christian doctrines. I could accept, I could attempt belief, I could say 'these are my beliefs and I accept them wholeheartedly.' Would I be doing justice to myself and those who love me, or would I more be committing an irreconcilable act of sacrilege to those values that I hold sacred? What would be gained by making myself a religious hypocrite, what could be achieved by committing a shameful hoax against myself and those I love? Granted, God exists, I don't deny that anymore. What I can't accept is his form, his nature, and his portentous image conveyed to mankind. Destiny and God's power through nature determine our futures. The God that exists is the God that made trees, rivers, oceans, mountains, and earth; He is the God that can be seen influencing our lives daily through nature.

God is in nature as nature, and God is in us as ourselves. He is what we want him to be and is what we periodically need throughout our lives to sustain us till destiny and the temporary inabilities of science take our lives from this earth.

Beyond that my life rests upon natural values, natural morality, and a natural desire to live and enjoy life to its fullest. If my desires and earthly appetites need curbing, I'll remain content to rely upon a strong will and moral values grounded in society.

From Christianity to Bahai. Through my classes in comparative religion, I have met students whose religious affiliations shifted across the spectrum from dedicated faith to unbelief, or from agnosticism to a strong faith, or, more rarely, from an established form of Christianity to some type of non-Christian religion.

Although the latter phenomenon is less common, it is abnormally revealing when, as in this case, the change came only at the end of senior year. There had been a build-up through four years of silent tension between the religion of childhood and the demands of adjustment to so many conflicting religious claims.

This coed's background was in the Protestant Episcopal Church, mainly through the efforts of her grandparents and, as she got older, on her own. Her father seldom attended church and her mother, though she would have liked to, did not want to go alone:

The Episcopal Church has always meant a great deal to me and I, like most people who are brought up under the directives of one particular faith, felt that the beliefs we held were closer to the truth than any others, and that I could never be quite as happy in any other faith, whether close to my own or not. Until I came to college, I never questioned the teachings of the Episcopal Church and Christianity. I was never given any reason to question. I didn't really know enough about the beliefs and non-beliefs of the peoples of the world until I was introduced to them here. Then, like most college students, I went through a time when I did question and I did have doubts, because my beliefs were challenged. I found out that other people had very good reasons for believing as they did, too. But my faith seemed to renew itself and come back much stronger than before, stronger because I became concerned with protecting it from the abuses of others, stronger because I was made, so I thought, to think about and examine the validity of the teaching I had unquestioningly accepted all along.

In retrospect, however, I can see where my faith was weakened rather than strengthened. I still had doubts that lingered on, questions that remained unanswered, but I swept them under the carpet, so to speak, with the reasoning that in mat-

ters of faith there are many things that one is not supposed to
and cannot understand and must accept 'on faith alone.' So,
many times because I was on the defensive, I was defending
beliefs which in my heart, I wasn't really sure of myself.

After long reflection, she discovered that her basic
problem was the acceptance of Christ as Savior. Partly
stimulated by academic contact with other than Christian
cultures and partly by coming to know persons on campus
who questioned the unique role of the Redeemer, she
began to question the validity of her faith:

My greatest doubt, my only real doubt, concerns the nature of Jesus Christ. This is an understatement, of course, for
when one is supposedly a Christian and yet doubts Christ,
there isn't much left to doubt as far as Christianity is concerned, thus accounting for the use of the term 'doubt' in the
plural. I questioned the Christian beliefs that Jesus Christ was
'God the Son,' and was *alone* the Savior of all mankind. I
didn't question that such a very holy person lived, that He was
the bearer of God's word and will, and that the effects of His
life and death were far-reaching, beyond all comprehension,
but I found it difficult to conceive of Jesus being one and the
same as God, and more than this, I couldn't accept that He
was mankind's *only* Savior. I kept wondering, "But what
about the rest of the non-Christian world."

I have never been taught that their chances of going to
heaven weren't just as good as mine as a professed Christian,
but I had been taught that Jesus Christ was the one, true way.
I had learned that these other people would go to heaven if
they proved themselves worthy, because God wouldn't punish
them for what they didn't know. This was not a picture I had
painted of God. It made much more sense to me that He and
His one faith were present everywhere though slightly altered
in appearance. At the same time, however, it was taken for
granted I knew that I, as a professed Christian, believed in
Christ and all that his life and death represents to the Chris-

tian world, so outwardly I never admitted having such doubts. I put them aside, and didn't let them bother me too much at all. I still went to church on Sunday, took Holy Communion, repeated the service, and came out with a good feeling.

I must confess that I expected that I could wake up one morning believing in Him. I thought this was a belief that would come in all due time with small effort on my part, but it didn't happen that way. Until very recently (and again, this is material for another chapter, but I feel it needs to be said here, too), I never realized the crucial nature of these doubts. I never realized how my subconscious mind must have been constantly working on my questions, constantly causing me to search for answers without knowing I was searching for them.

During senior year she came to know some Bahais and her life was changed immediately. Bahaism is a Persian sect, founded in 1843, when a certain Bab ed-Din proclaimed himself successor to Moses, Christ, and Mohammed. When Bab was executed, his successor, Baha Ullah, took over and organized the present Bahaists. They believe in simple living, universal education, unity of all religions, world peace, and equality of men and women.

The girl's confession of faith is extensive. It shows the impact of strong feeling in shaping religious faith when, as in this instance, the feelings were a great sympathy for all mankind and a hope that everyone, not only Christians, had a good chance of salvation:

In a few short weeks I have 'inwardly' accepted the teachings of the Bahaist faith, and in doing so have, of course, denied not only my own church, but Christianity as well.

The suddenness of what appeared to me to be such a sudden and radical change, bewildered and frightened me at first. I couldn't understand how I was able so easily to overthrow, so easily to disregard everything that I had accepted, defended, and grown up with for twenty-one years on the basis of only a few short weeks of accidental reading. Just as difficult to understand was the fact that I felt so comfortable with this faith, so sure of the truth of its teachings, and so exalted in spirit, almost from the beginning of my study. Believe me, I looked for loopholes, I tried to find 'the catch,' I tried to find places where I did not and could not agree, but found none. All of my questions were given answers. All of my doubts were cleared away.

The question posed above has already been answered in part, as we have seen. My answer, which came to me not without some surprise, was that I *had not* accepted the essence of the Christian faith, or had done so only for the sake of appearances and with strong reservations. Thus the change was neither sudden nor radical. I did not feel as a stranger coming to a new way of believing or a new way of living. Rather I felt that the beliefs I had long held had been given form. I found my unvoiced beliefs justified, supported, and defended in a way that to me was not only wholly under-standable, but very right and beautiful. Thus, although my acquaintance with the teachings of the Bahaiist faith itself had been brief, I felt that in my heart I had shared their faith for a much longer time than a few short weeks, All that I had really done was to bring my doubts and questions to the sur-face, admit them, and realize that I could no longer cover them up or run away from them, because now I was faced with what would be the most serious decision of my life.

I know that my understanding of Bahaist teachings is far from complete and may be much in error, but as far as the extent of my knowledge about the faith is concerned at the present time, I am elated with what I have discovered.

I cannot possibly go into all the various aspects of the faith that have so impressed me, but there are two beliefs which form the core of the faith, and from which all other aspects stem. The first is the fundamental principle of the Bahaist teaching, the belief that 'the foundation of all religion is one.' The second which naturally follows and which is the central theme of the faith is the belief in 'the oneness of mankind.' It is upon these two beliefs that I shall center my discussion.

The main point of contradiction and conflict between

Bahaism and Christianity concerns the nature of Christ. The Bahais accept the founders of all the world's great religions as being "manifestations of God, possessed of the Holy Spirit and acting as intermediaries between God and mankind." They are not God, but they are the ones through whom God reveals Himself and His word.

I spent several hours discussing with her the implication of this change in religious position, pointing out the duty to follow one's conscience. She was willing to concede that the Christianity she was replacing with Bahaism had more to defend its claims than she gave it credit for.

What finally led her to this Persian cult was something she had looked for among Christians but did not find: "One of my biggest stumbling blocks in accepting the teachings of Christianity, is the inconsistency and hypocrisy which has all but taken its place." At first this was only a problem, but then it became an obstacle:

It's not that Christians don't believe that they should 're-ceive the spirit of faith into the world and that they should inspire and be inspired with a more ardent love for God and their fellow man,' but most of them don't follow the teachings of their faith. They don't live by their beliefs. They are more than likely to listen to a sermon on brotherly love and say, 'Wasn't that lovely,' and then burn a Negro church. Because of this, it had never really occurred to me that I could find all that I was looking for in Christianity, and much more. Yes, I think I could.

The last sentence betrays uncertainty. After criticizing Christians for being inconsistent, she credits the sectarians with something better. "The Bahai's believing in a new faith, live what they believe or at least try very hard to do so." What she had seen of these people locally, confirmed her favorable judgment.

"Naturally," she confessed, "I am still confused, but I do not feel afraid or guilty any more. I know that I must pray for guidance and search for the truth." Whatever the outcome, she is confident that her faith in the future will be "the core of my life" and no mere outer shell.

The Faith to Doubt. Experience has convinced me that obedience to authority is the crucial problem for young people who give up their Christian commitment. Their impatience runs deeper than repugnance to obey unwelcome church commandments or submit to difficult prohibitions. This is especially true of those who are otherwise responsible persons and whose intelligence is above average.

Everything around them conspires to question the propriety of obedience to anyone except one's own private judgment. Submission to authority is therefore identified with stunting the development of the human person, and unworthy of true, mature, and adult personalities.

These challenges are kaleidoscopic, but the one which touches most vitally on religious belief is the feeling that Catholics and Protestants are less than objective when they accept the teachings of the Church without empirical proof. The open mind is equated with the sceptical mind, and the closed mind is the one that believes. For years, through childhood and adolescence, a church-going Christian is never allowed to think for himself it is claimed. Doctrines like the Incarnation and the Eucharist are accepted on parental or ecclesiastical dictum, and seldom examined beyond the object of faith as to why a man should believe at all.

Students tell me that until coming to college they never felt free to look into a difficulty with the faith and would promptly dismiss it as a "bad thought," like an urge to obscenity. Rarely did their teachers in parochial or Sunday school discuss an objection or, when they did, easily dismissed it as shallow and unfounded. Equally seldom were they permitted, let alone encouraged, to voice their own problems; and to challenge the validity of a statement by the teacher was insubordination.

Things are different when they enter college. The whole curriculum is geared to questioning, and scepticism is cultivated as a fine art. Depending on who writes a textbook or teaches a course, every phase of secular knowledge puts religion to the test. The sciences may reveal that credulous people cherished beliefs that were false; history shows that religions have defended superstition, greed, hypocrisy, and the lust for power. Segregation and slavery, persecution and wars, class hatred and economic exploitation have at times enjoyed its generous support. It is no wonder that, unprepared for such critical analysis, students begin to think of religion as obscurantist if not positively deceitful. Christianity is included in the sweeping generalization that man's concern for truth will be served better by science than by faith.

Another more subtle factor enters the process: the everpresent doubt about the traditional sources of meaning for human existence. College people, no less than everyone else, know that life is a continual quest for meaning. "What should I do, what should I be, really to live my life at all?" I have talked with upperclassmen who frankly questioned if life has *any* meaning. Their anxiety was extreme and I have seen it verge on despair.

Until the past generation, the Christian religion was scrutinized indeed, but its premises were not widely called into doubt. This is no longer true, and the new era is reflected in sharp outline by the colleges. While exact figures are not available, I think the one-third of Americans, about seventy million, who never go to church are proportionately represented in schools of higher education. The effect they have on the campus is strong and very corroding. Their prominent trait is a continuing confidence in reason and trust, bordering on worship, of the critical mind. They set the pace for the challenge that every churchgoer is most frequently asked: How can you believe what you cannot scientifically prove?

The results are predictable and more profound than even books like *Honest to God* or *The Secular City* might indicate. A post-Christian generation of young people are graduating from college who no longer believe in any church and yet who consider themselves religious, moral, and decent, without worshipping *en masse* or joining an organized group. They feel that a person can get as close to the idea of God as any cleric or institution could bring him. They discover a new faith, in themselves, that men are responsible for what they do with their lives, without rituals or catechisms, or channels of grace to bring them to salvation.

TEN

QUEST

The Search for Meaning

THE FOLLOWING contribution was made by a student whose Odyssey from unbelief to faith was so revealing that I felt it should be given in full. I have called it a quest because it typifies so many who are searching for a meaning in life and hungry for the truth which modern agnosticism mercilessly denies them.

Nothing has been changed in this diary of a soul in conflict with itself. If the language and concepts are above average, they are explained by the writer's talents, among the best I have met in more than a dozen years of teaching.

I was personally involved in this quest because it was from contact in one of my classes that the author began to ask the right questions and had the courage to face instead of run away from life's problems. Before graduation from college there were uncounted hours struggling with God and many hours since in trying to reach some conclusion about the ultimates of human existence. Like-minded sceptics who admired this person's intelligence were baffled by the stubborn unwillingness to take a shrug for an answer.

Learning in grade school, junior high school, and high school, is mainly a process of acquiring indisputable facts:

Columbus discovered America in 1492, Aristotle taught the Golden Mean, *house* is a common noun. But learning in college goes beyond simple memorization to the more difficult stages of qualification and disputation of facts. Why do we call *house* a common noun? And when a student finds that he is expected to discriminate among facts, he discovers that in order to do so, he must commit himself to some point of view, hold some convictions, recognize some truths.

My search for a point of view began when I was a college freshman. I recorded the experiences of this search in a journal, which I continued throughout my four undergraduate years. The following paper, assembled from my memory and my journal, is a profile of my mental and spiritual search for commitment.

As a freshman then, I encountered the disputability of facts. My freshman history instructor pulled my basic assumptions, about religion in particular, out into the open, dissected them, and showed them in their most vulnerable light. My journal for that year is filled with questions about myself as an art major, about my relationship to my society, but most frequently, about my religion. The following entry was written during the second semester:

> I learned more about religion last semester than I had ever known. I have never been a very avid churchgoer, and when I did go, I seldom got much out of it. I had never thought enough about religion to have any opinions of my own and I knew next to nothing about the Bible. But with this new knowledge came doubts. We studied the growth of Christianity objectively and read books which were anything but stabilizers to faith. I now have a much different feeling for religion. I know that I believe in God, but I don't actually know if I believe in Jesus or not. It seems so funny. I think that I do, but then someone says something about Easter, for instance, and I find my mind filled with doubts. How do they know that what they are honoring was actually what they think it was? I feel this way at Christmas, too. It seems

strange that millions of people blindly accept this. Who can say that the Jews are wrong, or the Buddhists, or the Moslems? Sometimes I have the feeling that it might have been anyone whom millions would now worship. So many things, such as the shape of the cross, have been shown to have been changed. I wish I could settle these doubts in my mind.

In my history class we investigated the historical validity of Christianity; and that validity, when looked at through a certain school of thought, can be shown to be very questionable. I was soon and easily convinced that Christianity was not the truth. I developed this attitude toward Christ:

> I see a distinction between Jesus and Christ. It seems to me that Jesus was a person. Whether or not he was all many believe him to have been, is not for me to decide. But to me, Christ is the idea; a combination of all the teachings, laws, and beliefs that are believed to have come from Jesus. I see one as the man and the other as a more perfect symbol of what Christians believe the man taught.

My quarrel with religion was not with the theological aspects, as much as with the apparent consequences of religion, the tangibles such as church and religious prejudice:

> I wonder why religion, which is supposedly the sanctuary and conveyor of inner peace to people, has been the cause of many disputes and so much unhappiness and controversy. From what I have learned or understood, there is one truth. There is only one true meaning to life, the world, and only one truth which everyone should believe. Why have so many different interpretations arisen? If there is one God who created the whole world and is still controlling it, as I do believe, why has he allowed these conflicting opinions to thrive? It seems so stupid for people, all living in the same world which was

naturally created wholly by one God, to have such petty, conflicting ideas. I think these conflicting opinions and bigoted views are the cause of people becoming atheists.

Thus although I no longer believed that Jesus was God (if I ever really had), I did maintain my belief in God:

How can some people be so sure in their faith? It seems to me that only when you question are you more likely to arrive at the truth.

Also, if there were no superior being, why would men search all their lives to understand it? This searching proves to me that there must be something greater than man and incomprehensible to him. I don't see how man could ever fully understand God; because if he did, God would no longer possess the influence he does because of this incomprehensibility. Man's reason can make God more powerful, but not more equal.

Having never thought about the Bible or religion before, I was now preoccupied with placing this new area of thought in my mind.

As a college student, I had become a participant in the learning process. I was expected to test and examine new and old ideas. Early in the second semester I wrote, 'This year I have learned that I have been laboring under so many false assumptions. Today I learned that there was not one Renaissance. There were many different Renaissances that took place in many different localities. It makes me wonder why we've never heard these facts before.' And with the broadening of my general knowledge, came uncertainty in my proposed area of specialization, art:

It's hard to write anything tonight because I have had a rather upsetting day and I'm not sure why. It was just one of those days when I felt uncomfortable and insecure everywhere I went. I think one reason is that art classes can be very discouraging. I feel so inadequate and un-

296

satisfied with everything I try to do. I am only beginning to realize how much your state of mind contributes to your art. My art instructor said last semester that artists must suffer. Apparently this is true. But I'm not even sure I am capable of being an artist. And if I'm not, what am I suffering about? Perhaps this feeling of insecurity leads to greater creativity. There is so much patience and slow learning involved and no way for me to know if I really should be attempting it. Some say that you don't have to have any purpose, but I feel that I have to have something to aim at, and I'm not sure what it is.

A pattern of thinking began to develop along these lines which continues to today. I began to fear specialization. How could I learn all that I wanted to learn about English, for example, if I specialized in art? And relative to religion, how could I tie myself to one belief before I had thoroughly studied all of them? Later in the semester I used this analogy:

> I feel like a person sitting down to a huge table piled with exquisite food. There is so much that I don't know where to begin. Then suddenly someone tells me that some of it may be poisoned. He tells me only the meat is. Then someone else tells me only the vegetables, someone else only the desserts. Now I don't know whom to believe or what to try. What has been told me makes me hesitant to believe that any of it is good, but I am very hungry and I want to believe it's all safe. I can see that everyone will tell me something different so I can only find out if I try for myself. My problem is that I don't know which to try.

Learning how much I did not know made me hesitant.

I am continually learning new facts and new ideas— new to me—which change what I have previously believed or add to what I already know a little about. A week ago I believed Jackson Pollock to be creative. But my opinion has changed since then because I have learned more about him. It isn't fair to judge anything unless we know a great deal about it. I feel like a real dilettante, although I'm not sure I know enough even to qualify for that.

During the second semester I became committed to thinking for myself. And I thought a lot, speculated and theorized.

Are the mind and the soul one? I had never thought of this until one of my instructors mentioned it fleetingly the other day. The soul has always seemed to me to be a kind of abstract spirit which is somehow incorporated in your body and makes you more than merely matter. But I can see how the mind could be the soul. The more you learn and advance yourself the better developed your mind becomes, the better your soul becomes. But when you die, if there is to be life after death, the mind would have to be more than merely a brain, for the brain stops. Is the mind the accumulation of ideas and knowledge which a person collects while he lives, and is this what remains alive after he dies? Would our existence be as if we were in a dark room, thinking, conscious of no sensations at all? If only the mind survived would we be able to think for long without any sensations to add new thoughts to our mind? Or does your mind stop growing and do you spend eternity with your mind, your soul, developed only as fully as it was in life?

Tonight I held my foot in one position too long and it went to sleep. I had to move it to wake it. I think this is what happens to many people's minds. They never move their minds with new ideas or concepts. So many people go through life completely oblivious of the wonderful happenings around them. Their minds go to sleep, are dulled, and they are not aware. They get up, go to work, do a routine job, go home, watch television, and go to bed. I worked in a factory with a lot of people like that last summer. Their lives are horribly scheduled.

I have a theory. The way I explain it will sound

very self-centered but it can apply to anyone and this is the easiest way to express it. The day I was born, God created the world. On it he placed people of all ages: plants, animals, buildings, everything at various stages of growth. He created a history, libraries of books, and thousands of names and beliefs from ages past. He made it appear to me and to everyone else that the world had been revolving around the sun for eons.

I am a test. God is searching for the perfect person and the perfect world. There have undoubtedly been many worlds before me. They are all different and each one a failure. This world will end when I die. I would guess that another will follow because this does not seem like what God's idea of perfection would be. Perhaps He will take what He has observed as successful in each world and combine them to arrive eventually at a world that will not end after one lifetime. God created man, but how many times has He created man?

The summer between my freshman and sophomore years I spent in Europe as a member of a social studies seminar. We studied at Oxford University for four weeks, toured England and Scotland for two weeks, and the Continent for four. I did very little writing during the summer except lengthy letters home. I loved Europe and can relive even now practically every day by rereading those letters. My mind was not working with theories or concepts that summer; it was being saturated with new places, people, experiences, ways of living and thinking, which still play an active part in my thinking.

Returning to Western in the fall, I was much enriched by my summer but no less impatient to learn. As my freshman history class had taught me to question, my sophomore colloquium class spurred me to continue that questioning and to channel it toward a specific goal: selfhood, the shaping and recognition of my identity. We began the semester with the study of hero myths and their relationship to Hinduism and, to a lesser degree, Christianity. In the hero myths, the hero journeys along a long path toward the truth, finds the truth, and, if he wishes, returns to men to communicate it. I could see that I, although not a hero, stood somewhere on such a path. My task was to find out where I was and then move on, some-how, toward the truth. My colloquium instructor helped me to make my search a concrete action. He introduced me to Hin-duism, to Kierkegaard, and to existentialism.

In the second month of the first semester, this instructor asked us to write a statement of our religious beliefs, as he put it, our 'present state of confusion.' I kept that paper in my journal:

> My beliefs are continually changing. When I first began to question, I dropped nearly all my beliefs which I had held half-heartedly and for a while had nothing. But this is no good. A man who believes in nothing else finds it hard to believe in himself. So now I am searching ser-iously to find just what I can and do believe in. And I am searching with great hope that answers can be found. My hope is being strengthened, too, because I am evolving answers. It is a slow, but an exceedingly re-warding search.

> I read others' ideas and philosophies of religion and the meaning of life, not to make them my own, but to think about them. In considering others' ideas, I evolve my own. A person can agree with parts of another per-son's philosophy, but he must evolve his own if he wishes to truly find himself.

> I believe in a superior force, call it God, but I am not yet sure of the nature of this force. I can't believe in a personal God, one I can pray to, to fulfill all my wishes and show me my purpose in life, my self. I think man must find himself and when he does he will be closer to finding God, for God is in all of us.

> I think that perhaps I am a Christian, too. Not a church-going, God-fearing, trinity-believing Christian; but, one who looks to Christ as 'the supreme outsider,' one who searched and found his truth. I think everyone is

a 'son of God' inasmuch as everyone has God within him. If Christ symbolizes the search, which everyone who truly wishes to give his life meaning, must undertake, then I do believe in Christ and especially in what he symbolizes. This took me a long while to realize and it is something I still tend to question. Kierkegaard was right in saying: 'The same thing happens to Christianity, or to becoming a Christian, as to all radical cures, one puts it off as long as possible.' But every religion has its symbol of the search. I can be a Christian in the sense of believing in that symbol, but I could also probably be classified as a Moslem, Hindu, or anything else. The name is not important; the search is.

As far as church goes, it does me no good anymore. It pacified me when I did not question, but now I feel that it cannot provide the answer to finding myself. I must find my own truth. How can one doctrine be right for hundreds of people? Churches are fine, and very necessary, for those who do not or dare not search. But I feel they hide Christ's true message from the people. Christ was no conformist; neither were his disciples. If a person questions, searches and finds what he believes to be the truth, and if it is the truth his church preaches, then belonging to that church is right for him. But when people go without questioning, they are missing the point of being alive. I want to live each day as I feel I must. But I cannot be sure of what my purpose is until I have found myself. Presently this is my main purpose. Perhaps it will always be.

As a freshman, God had been very real and personal to me. But as a sophomore, I became a deist, of sorts, believing that God did not intervene in individual lives, but yet might in larger contexts. I stated once, for example, that God would not allow man to annihilate man. My concept of God is not carefully defined in my journal:

Chaos is man made. God, a supreme, unconceivable force, created the world and man. Then man was on his own. He has been given great powers and great freedom to make this a wonderful world. But he is very slow in doing this. When men finally realize, as some have, that they are what they make themselves, and could be so much more, then perhaps progress will grow in mankind, in man's inner self, as it has in his external life. In nature, God created; one sees beauty, peace, meaning; in much of man's world; man created; one sees chaos. It is up to man, alone.

My thoughts were not only preoccupied with the nature of God but also with man, as the existentialists saw him, and as I saw him in others and myself.

Man has always believed in something greater than himself. But could it be that this greater being is not outside of man but within him? History shows progress. History also shows that as man progresses he becomes more and more independent. There would be no point in man if he did not advance himself. Earlier people realized, perhaps without knowing it, what a profound creature man is. They made symbols and gods out of unusual people and events. Christ was a rare person. The people did not know how to save themselves and Christ appeared with an answer. But now men are growing less dependent upon supernatural fixed answers and realizing the necessity for searching, themselves.

To question the nature of God, to find a truth within oneself which will give meaning to existence, to the visual chaos surrounding the material world—this is what I must seek.

I held to Kierkegaard's conviction that man cannot be an essence until he has died and ended his existence which has determined his essence. And I used this conviction as an argument against Christianity. If man has no essence while in existence, how can he be made to conform to a dogmatic system of ethics based on the assumption that he has an essence? I was for no systems, least of all Christianity.

One danger involved in existentialist speculation is that the strong emphasis on the individual, on my finding me, can lead to breakdowns in social relationships. I often warned myself against selfish introversion:

> It is essential to be 'self—concerning' in thinking and, to a great extent, in action. But I've got to remember that I'm living with people. You can't ignore people always and act indifferently to them or you will lose contact with that part of reality. By talking, new ideas come. You just have to find the ones worth talking to.

My preoccupation with the search did not preclude my concern for the eventual goal of that search.

> There are many philosophies and ideas of truth, reality, God, the meaning of existence. Some I can't agree with, others strike me right. In time I hope I will have my own strong idea of the meaning of life, which I truly feel as right. But who can say, finally, what is right? It all ends up with what I as an individual can believe. Perhaps it will be wrong for others, but it will be my truth. Maybe we only experience the Truth, universal, when we die.
>
> Death is more difficult to understand than God. People experience God in a sense and try to explain it to others. But those who truly experience death, as it is actually, not as it seems, maybe cannot tell anyone living. But maybe God is ultimately the same, as far as realization.

A book which had a significant influence upon my search at that time was *Siddhartha* by Hermann Hesse, an eloquent and simple picture of the search for meaning in life, a search

both wonderful and tragic. *Siddhartha* not only showed me
how difficult the search is, it showed me that the search is not
futile. Siddhartha found meaning. Maybe I would, too. I soon
moved into a wholly deistic attitude toward God.

How can people believe in a controlling God? They
must have unquestioning faith. In two days 200 people
have been killed. Why? No war, no plague—just unnecessary, manmade carnage. Why don't people direct
more of their thought within and without to other people!
Only man can fix this mess. He has done much good, but
so much more is needed, crying to be.

My journal was primarily a vehicle for unloading my developing self-consciousness. Consequently, it lacks the data of
a diary. Introspection was not the only recreation during this
time. Normal college life and my own nature preclude such
isolation. I was having a good time too, and that was
important.

Speculation on God and Christianity continued.
When God lives as ruler
Man lives as slave
When God lives as creator
Man lives as man.
When God lives as man
Man lives as God.
This last line just came and I don't know if I believe it.
I think it would follow Kierkegaard's concept of Christ,
but his isn't mine. Man cannot actually live as God; he
can live with a mind of concepts which may bring him
nearer to God, or the Buddhist Nirvana. But just what is
God?
I think the thing about that last line (Man lives as
God) is that to me, God did not live as man, therefore
man does not live as God. Truth in contradiction?
Every so often while I'm thinking and questioning

religion, I get a mental image or feeling of the God, of my former pseudo beliefs, sitting in the heaven of my former pseudobeliefs, patiently watching and waiting for me to come back.

Interspersed with reflections on religion and selfhood are references to my social self, which, as mentioned earlier, was in danger of being neglected. I was impatient with people in general because I felt that they were too complacent: the masses going to drive-in churches with Reader's Digest condensed Bibles, gliding along glibly on the surface of life.

I am getting to the point again where I must get away from people for a while. I feel weighted down by people and their petty problems and ridiculous chatter. I have enough problems of my own. There are such deeper, more important problems to me that could be bothering these shallow complainers. If they'd but realize! Maybe it's better that they don't. They are only momentarily upset. I'm only momentarily not upset.

The factor that keeps me desirous of contact with people is that some of the people I'm around are very beneficial. They teach me, listen to me, cheer me, and keep me believing that man is basically good.

Take a person as he is. Accept him or reject him, but don't try to change him. If you don't you'll upset yourself by trying to do the impossible.

I rejected especially the masses' religion.

Don't attack the church. An attack is like a match trying to remain lighted under water. Sure, they're missing something. You know it. They don't; that's why they're missing it. They won't listen when you tell them that God intended Jesus and Buddha and all the rest to search and seek to find their own purpose and path of life within them, not to hear it spelled out to them page by page,

305

Sunday by Sunday. Don't attack the church. 'Forgive them, for they know not what they do.'

I felt that everyone should question and search for his own truth. And yet I was chastising myself constantly, for I felt that I was getting nowhere. I saw that convictions went unfollowed, the same questions went unanswered. I was impatient.

Who, what am I actually? I feel like different people different days. One day I feel very congenial and relaxed; the next I feel thwarted and annoyed by the whole world. I have felt so mean and annoyed that I scare myself. And now when I have no pressures of assignments upon me, why can't I do something worth while? Am I actually this lazy? Have I been fooling myself with hopes, plans of good works, fulfilling actions? Reading the first part of this I feel that I am digressing. Freedom is a hard thing to conceive. It is truly there for the asking. If one has the fortitude of character to grab it and then do something with it, he is living, he is an individual.

Why don't I act upon these ideas? Am I over practical? Or is it too easy to be practical and remain in the comfortable rut? My thoughts are redundant, my arguments repetitious. I think, I will not act that way anymore, and then I do. I resolve to be more an individual, more patient when I should be, more thinking, more acting, more 'adult.'

The tension between being myself and being part of a social whole did not decrease. College life breeds group living. A student is one among many—in his classes, in his dormitory, among his fellow students. The commitment to individuality is not an easy one to fulfill; the way to achieve that goal and still maintain sociability is a big problem.

I live in abstractions. They must become realities. The abstraction 'individual' must become more a part of me. The abstractions 'freedom,' 'thought' must be a part of my every action. I want to rise up and be myself. I feel that I've been groveling in the masses' temperament, petty angers and arguments, petty talk and thoughts. I will live in the mass—where else?—but I will be me. You don't have to be like everyone else. It must be possible not to be petty and still not let the inner revolt against pettiness upset your mind, thwart your thoughts; to be a peaceable rebel. I don't want to be hated; I can't expect to be understood, just accepted as I am—take it or leave it—and not care a hell of a lot which.

At times all this soul-searching grew tiring and I wanted to escape from my self and my world into a land of peacefulness. I had been thinking along these lines steadily, since nearly the beginning of the semester. The classes which I spent the most time on were fuel for the fire rather than diversions. But that brief period of complacency came. And then, ten days later, I experienced, perhaps mystically, a recognition of what was at that moment the basic truth. I was sitting in the dark one night, just staring at the light bulb outside of my window, when something came over me and made everything suddenly clear.

> There is one essence underlying the unity of all things, from man a living being in existence, to objectives which exist but not living beings. Man lives trying to relate himself to this unity, and to unite himself with the forms which surround him, he tries to find the unity in reality and feel his place in this one unity. Call it Essence, call it God.
>
> I see now what Siddhartha meant, how he could see the whole of life in the river. The underlying Oneness of all that was, is, and will be. Jaspers helped me to see it. The One which no man possesses but toward which all serious efforts gravitate. And this One cannot be fully comprehended because it is God.
>
> What a feeling! I can't fully see it, fully explain it, or

fully understand it, but there is a oneness, a meaning, a unity in all of all! I felt that I had surely arrived somewhere.

One of the big changes is that of perspective. Things, people that bother me are smaller; those which I enjoy are much larger.

The true test is to be able to enjoy everyday, no matter how.

Buber's God was not my God and I was thus forced to reexamine once more the nature of the God which I believed in:

I am afraid. Afraid to become dependent upon God. Afraid to acknowledge this necessity. But it is becoming clearer that I am. Everyone is. The God I have held is a part of God. But God must also be a Person, as Buber says, with whom one enters into the relationship of I-Thou. But seeing this, and acknowledging it, is the first but not the decisive step. It will come, not through thought but through being, an immersing of my whole self into the depths of that which I do not yet know, and will never understand. I have begun, but I have not fully become. Now I was definitely committed to people.

Relationships with others are what makes life, life; what gives a purpose to being alive. That there are people who matter to me a great deal and to whom I can see that I matter, is the affirmation, the ringing yes which obstructs any and all no's.

As the school year ended, I thought of the future. How would it be if man had no consciousness of the future? If his whole existence were based on the present moment, (grounded in the past,) would not the present be so much more meaningful? In thinking of the future, man is practical and still very presumptuous. Tomorrow is in reality so uncertain; each day might be the last. Yet man trudges on, worrying, fretting, hoping, and planning for the tomorrow he assumes will come. But if man had no realization of a future, would not the present, the moment, be much more emphatic, much more important and thus cause the future, (which comes in spite of it all,) to be better than if he had planned it?

During the summer between my sophomore and junior years, I lived at our cottage, reading for English honors in the fall and enjoying completely the beauty of summer. I wrote very little, but when I did, it was about nature:

'Great God, I'd rather be a pagan. . .' These months have been passed in an ever growing closeness to nature, to God. Each day is magnificent, different from the last, and beautiful in its own way. Nature cannot be anticipated.

The clouds were grey and white today. Crowded together above a slate gray lake; pillars of sunlight filtered through at intervals. A lone sea gull, coming from a cloud, flew by. The sky appeared done by the most exquisite baroque painters. It revealed peace and serenity, the promise of God that he is; that good, peace, hope, love, and life are. The sight was awesome. It was a gift, a sight of the glory of God.

This will be the escape island of my mind when I once again must return to the tumult of the world.

God, then, was a simple concept: the creator of the splendor which surrounded me. I did not pray, I felt His presence through my affinity to His creation, and I was grateful.

In September, I was back at Western and again embroiled in the affairs of society:

And now there is more talk of war. But it doesn't seem to bother many. We sit and talk of the future, as if it were assured. But it isn't. And at times we realize this and silence fills the gap of wonder. Could they be that stupid? Perhaps they could. Whenever I think of the lake, of the simple, untroubled life possible in nature, I wonder why man cannot live with this peace, lacking though it may be, in superficial enjoyment. To be able to live always aware of an internal truth, a feeling which continually makes everything meaningful and at least partially understood. There is a duality in everything. Could there have been a Christ who was solely good? Only faith can answer that. It's a wonderful thought. Perhaps someday I'll feel its truth. But to see, feel, that there is meaning in life, that reality is not purposeless, that is the first leap, the so important leap.

I did feel different and good. I had not reached the end of my search, for, although what I saw seemed clear and conclusive at the moment, it was only one firm step forward.

I continued as an art major, but remained unsure of my eventual purpose in life. If a student does not want to teach art, as I didn't, and does not have the talent and fortitude to be an artist, as I didn't, he begins to wonder just why he is an art major. That question added to my search.

During the second semester of my sophomore year, my colloquium instructor introduced me to the thought of Martin Buber. I had already experienced with my instructor and with others on rare occasions, communication of the sort that Buber teaches. Seeing that experience in his terms,—the I-Thou relationship—gave a new dimension to that part of my life. Communication, which I had already valued, came to be one of my central goals. I entered a quote from *Between Man and Man* in my journal which stands at the base of all that I believe today:

'What do we expect when we are in despair and yet go to a man? Surely a presence by means of which we are told that nevertheless there is meaning.'

The threat of war reminds man of his contingency, and causes him to fear that he might not be:

Man has gone far enough. I fear for what he may discover, or invent to further our jumbled chaotic existence. There are laws of nature. They are obvious and continuous. Man is violating these laws, and striving to prove he can improve upon God. He can't. He can only bring chaos. How far will they go?

As a junior, I was out of basic studies honors and beginning specialized study. English had finally won over art and I was a member of the English honors program. It was an intense, demanding class. Discussion was exhausting and probing. I loved it:

> It seems that only when I have much to do, do I strive to do well. Pressure breeds work. These past weeks I have felt an intense desire and ability to work. Last year when I began to study, I specialized in a certain field. My work led me down a path so that I might find answers to soul-searching questions. And it was interrupted by questioning, by depression, by soul—felt thoughts. Last summer brought me inner peace. Many of the questions have been replaced by convictions, which are, for the time being, strong enough to ward off lengthened wandering. How long it will last I cannot know. Who knows how long peace, life, happiness, and sorrow will last? But I feel a drive, a keyed-upness, and I find my mind going at intense white heat. The search is now channeled and has become an interest. A strong feeling of possible accomplishments is there. I feel more at home with myself, more confident, more independent. It's great to be alive.

I had settled the question of the nature of God for the time being. He watched but didn't touch. Even though I was now specializing, I continued to be unable to foresee a vocation for myself. It's a frightening feeling not to be able to see a future for oneself. Things become so comfortable that you're afraid to shake the glass ball for fear of the snowstorm. I did not feel ready to commit myself to a definite intellectual position.

An experience which had no immediate bearing on my

religious wanderings or my intellectual challenges, but which was one of the most unforgettable experiences I have ever had, occurred that October:

> I cannot actually describe how I felt tonight except by calling it a height of emotion, a filling of sensation until I felt as though I would burst. It came from the music of an Indian instrument, the shankar. The emotion called forth from that instrument was like none I have ever experienced from music before. These words don't express how I felt. Something in his presence and his music touched me. Such a deep immersion shows me that people can reach one another through a common ground; some agent must be at work, creating that common ground.

> This ground of communication is the reality which enables men to relate to one another in varying degrees of depth and meaning. When one feels that he has stepped out of that field of being, he feels estranged and frightened. I did it one day.

> Yesterday was hell. Yesterday for the first time, I seriously questioned my sanity. I felt the loss of a basic human trait: the ability to relate to other human beings, to communicate, and to respond. I felt estranged. I felt alone among people and even lost to myself. Yesterday I could not bear to be one among many. I could not bear to be one alone. I'm afraid I could not even bear to be. I'm not sure of what brought me out of it. Perhaps it was at dinner. I was in mental agony, trying to reason with this emotion—an impossible task—and felt that any minute I would just cease to be, would have to, for I could not stand this much longer. Then I saw our dietitian eating. She was so typical of so many people, a whole class, a majority, who exist equally as I, and with whom I must live, relate, share our world. It came to me. I must live with these people, with everybody. It was not an intellectual answer, but an emotional realization, and it fought an emotional anguish.

I don't think about insanity often. I did for a while that semester, because a friend of mine was on the verge of a nervous breakdown and I wondered about his disquiet and wished I could help. It seemed to me that insanity was a mental quest for freedom from reality. But what reality? I wrote:

> Who calls when your wrinkled wings
> Now dried and brittle
> No longer lift you, no longer
> Raise your reeling mind above reality?
> Will it ever be quiet?
> Yes, but do not hurry
> For quiet is forever.
> The soul seeks to soar
> Cries to escape and know peace.

What is the use of it? Words. Semblances of reality: crutches as we limp toward the unknown. Not by words, but by eyes, and ears, and fingers will we know reality. The cold wind is more real to me than ever the cold lines of books. Shut the soul in a vault of words and it too becomes but a semblance of reality.

In order to live sanely yet fully and sensitively aware, a person must have a firm grip on the reality of himself. If I cannot live with myself, with whom can I live?

> Restless, restless, restless
> Running blindly
> Where?
> O my God, how can you fight yourself!

I put myself on guard against insanity.

I was still deeply committed to the idea of true communication. College life is fast and fragmented, but it is also that way of life where the opportunity for true communication is most likely to be found. College students are learning and growing, and they test their developing selves on those around them. Communication does not happen with everyone, but it happens, and it is essential to education:

313

Tonight, again, that rare, beautiful, and all-necessary event, complete communication, occurred. Again two presences affirmed one another. What a welling up occurs inside, a choking feeling that 'I cannot speak' for the elation but knowing that you must speak, that you will, for this state exists and it demands its continuance. When complete communication takes place, life's meaning again becomes clear. Man lives for himself and other men and through these two entities affirms his existence.

Now it had become apparent that my life was going to be committed to learning:

I think now that there will never be a time when I will be able to sit down and say to myself 'I have nothing to do.' I hope I never consider myself finished. When I had talked to the visiting professor, he seemed to feel finished, unwilling or unwilled to open himself up to other people, to experience their minds. Some older people and some sterile inhuman intellectuals seem to feel that way: Self-contained entities, sufficient unto themselves. I think they're wrong. If man only experiences and probes himself, how narrow his human scope will be. Books can offer knowledge, but men can offer wisdom.

I felt older. My mind was branching out from its one way road toward self—definition and into consideration of broader aspects of being a person, such as my relationship to society as an institution:

I've felt a new era of maturity in myself in the past two weeks. I've been able to get along with people better, to communicate more meaningfully. It's a good feeling to begin to feel of more worth, of more value and concern to others. I've also encountered new problems which I'm not sure I comprehend. The strength of so-

314

ciety's intangible judgment becomes more apparent to me every day. Society wins by majority rule. But there must be exceptions. If there weren't there would never be any progress. The amorphous majority imposes an amorphous norm, which no one fits, but everyone tries to. Who is to say what is right and what is wrong in every case. There must be rules, else there would be general chaos, but they must be flexible for those who cannot and should not be bound.

A part of the social institution, a university psychologist, triggered a nervous breakdown in another friend of mine. His interference taught me a lesson:

> Another lesson from today: never try to give someone else answers to his searchings. You can perhaps lead him but if he doesn't find his own answer, he finds no answer. False props are easily displaced.

I was still testing my own developing cosmos and seeking to further define myself, my relationship to others and their worlds.

> Human relationships, the most wonderful and rewarding experiences in life, are also sources of the most tension and turmoil. The shades of my feelings for a person can run the gamut of the rainbow in a single day.
>
> One of my biggest problems is my difficulty in making value judgments, in deciding if something is more bad than good, or good than bad. There are two sides to everything and so many shades of meaning and 'truths' which are relative. I think there is only one Absolute.
>
> Reason, no matter how hard it tries in me, cannot overcome irrationality. It rears its defiant head, stirs a flame in the pit of my stomach, and demands recognition.

I was still wandering, touching truths here and there, but

yet unable to grasp anything. I was restless and impatient with myself:

> I want something, but I don't know what. Perhaps it's a new part of me. Perhaps it's another person with whom to share the wonderment of this mystery, life. Perhaps it's a beautiful fulfilling purpose. Perhaps it's all of these. I imagine there will always be something beyond, something more that wants knowing, seeing, experiencing, creating. I wonder if anyone is ever in a state of complete fulfillment and ready to die.

I was trying to understand what it means to be alive. Thus every experience was reflected in this mirror of questions. Death entered my life:

> Nearly a month. How time goes. Things have happened. I think I've learned a little bit more about life through death. My uncle died on Easter Sunday. There is no obvious justification for his death, and that fact must be faced. There are many things in life which cannot be satisfactorily justified—I mean tangibly, so that it really affects the fact he is dead. He is, and from all we know, would, be better off alive. Everyone would. Death is futile. Life must be meaningful. This is it.
>
> I entered another period of peace and experienced the reality of harmony.
>
> I think when things go right, whether in art, writing, feeling on an even keel, and getting along with people, especially people you want to get along with, you are acting in harmony with the underlying, or overlying scheme of things. And that is why certain people, thoughts, and acts are more right for me. They are more in my stream, flowing where I am in this river called life.

At the end of the semester, I had to decide upon a topic for my English honors research paper, for which reading is done over the summer and which is written the following fall semester as an independent study project. I chose to do a study of some aspect of the writings of Albert Camus, the contemporary French thinker linked to the existentialist school of thought. My reasons for choosing Camus are a good indication of my state of development at that time. I was attracted by his honesty, his dedication to man and human rights, his pagan affinity to his Algerian land, and his inability to come to terms with God.

I read Camus' essays and narratives during the summer. The development of his thought is expressed in his writing. Because of his changing point of view, he is a difficult and challenging man to define. I wrote more that summer. I was living at the lake again and was once more deeply tied to nature. Camus' early philosophy dealt with the Absurd, man's essential estrangement from his universe, a reality which has awesome consequences for the man who is aware of it. Living in the midst of nature's beauty, I found this philosophy of estrangement difficult to comprehend. Only once did I look at the large oak tree by our cottage and feel for a moment its overwhelming otherness.

> The days lately have been beautiful, extreme days in which nature seems to be in high key. The sky, a deep, penetrating blue with white, bumpy clouds moving gracefully across it; the lake a deeper blue, shiny and wrinkled by the force of the wind. I feel such peace here and such an affinity of mood to nature's beauty. I find it difficult to comprehend fully the idea of man's inability to relate to an alien universe. The estrangement of the philosophers is on another level. Nausea, a term used by Sartre, doesn't see the beauty of the tree's leaves.

The summer ended and I began my final year as an undergraduate. During the first semester I was preoccupied with writing my paper on Camus. I had decided to do a study of the themes of guilt and judgment in his three fictional narratives: *The Stranger, The Plague,* and *The Fall.* Evolving that paper into an intelligible entity was a frustrating and rewarding challenge. I often doubted that I would ever succeed.

My journal doesn't show much of this struggle with Camus. I was so immersed in his thought that in my journal I escaped that constant pressure for a time and wrote about other experiences which were also affecting my life. I had decided to become a college teacher. Consequently, I had also decided to go on to graduate school the following year and earn a Master of Arts degree in English. But when the pressure of my paper and all the other daily duties became overpowering, as they frequently did, I wondered if I really wanted what I thought I did. Did I want to perpetuate my busyness?

I am reading letters of James Agee to Father Flye. I can often see my own frustrations and despair in his searching life. There is never enough time. I must find my own answers. Friends are important. I desire to communicate. His talents and learning far surpass mine, but his words strike a very familiar note.

Agee's letters are making manifest to me several things which I have sought to ignore. Primarily, I am not doing as much or as well as I can do. My time is a shattered mirror in which I can reflect only snatches of myself and only at lucky times when I happen to be disposed at the correct angle to it. Living here in a dormitory I am in constant tension, and awaiting the next interruption. Also, when I do find the rare climate for total reflection, my time is not my own. I must do certain things, logically, if I am to keep up in school. My time has not been my own since I was a freshman. This, too, creates tension. Query: Do I need and desire one year for myself? If I had it, would I use it? Or do I need the tension to produce? If there were only some way to be alone when desired and with persons of my own choosing. Mental isolation not only causes relationship-friction, but the effort expended on creating inner aloneness detracts from the amount of effort available for creative and learning

efforts. I have not truly and wholly concentrated on anything all semester. Maybe even all my life. I am an intellectual dilettante, not learning over ten per cent of what
I read or hear.

I thought little about religion. My own search had reached
a point of arrest, although not completion:

> Saturday I walked into the sanctuary of the Congrega-
> tional church. I have always liked it empty. The big
> glass dome allows a soft beige light to filter in. It is a
> peaceful, silent room. I think it is impossible to shake
> off your past completely. I cannot help feeling a sense of
> being at home there, almost the same feeling as walking
> in the high school, but not quite. A big question in my
> existence is symbolized by that church. Not so much a
> question now as a finished phase which suggests an un-
> finished search. I am still a little bitter about its mater-
> ialism and un-Christian Christians. I demand Christ's
> Christianity of someone who calls himself Christian.

The outside influences on me that semester didn't lead my
thoughts into religion. Camus was, perhaps, an atheist. The
misery of mankind made him refuse to believe in God. Most of
my own friends also either denied God's existence or his active
effect on man's life. I believed in some kind of God, but he
was irrelevant to my daily existence. Camus made obvious to
me the injustice done to man by man. I have never been a
crusader, but my social conscience grew through his words. My
friends also increased my awareness of the reality of unhappiness and injustice:

> Painfully and surely I am becoming truly knowing of
> the reality of the unhappiness in life. There are lives
> where the sun will set and just never find the proper
> horizon for rising again. Sometimes people *are* trapped.
> But the amazing thing about humanity is its ability that
> some trapped people have to go on anyway, even though

as far as they can possibly see, the trap is locked and key-less. The blind man sings and wonders that he can hear.

The semester ended. I had finished the paper on Camus. It was uneven, but I had managed to communicate at least some of Camus' dedicated humanism.

The final semester will be the most difficult to write about because I am writing this in May, so it is still in progress. It has been a full and strenuous semester.

Early in the semester I again developed an inner restlessness. The two recurring question marks in my life, my future and religion, were again rearing their heads. My future hung in suspension. I had now to choose a school and find some money. These were two big enterprises. Religion was back in the picture because I was taking a course in Christian theology to increase my knowledge of Catholicism for literary purposes. I could not ignore either the claims of the Catholic faith or the priest who made those claims with such absolute conviction and commitment:

> I am really trying to understand the Catholic faith and the Catholic orientation to life. I think I understand free will, but the combination of that belief with all the rules and sins seems contradictory. I hope I don't often encounter the answer, 'That's one of the mysteries.' The priest is willing to answer, but I have never talked much about religion before to anyone so absolutely positive and filled with his belief. It's a different kind of communication. I wonder if it would, or will, or could ever become communication: or if we're at two opposite poles; and I know so much less about it than he. All I can say is, "'How?" I haven't yet.

> I must understand Catholicism. It is very difficult since I don't believe in it; for at the heart of Christianity are the mysteries, and faith in them gives a good foundation for comprehension of the fundamental beliefs which stem from them.

Is there a fundamental plan in God's mind? Isn't life something of a game like this?

In March I was asked to lead a group discussion on the theme of personal aloneness at a weekend retreat organized around the topic of aloneness. I wasn't sure how to approach the topic, so I thought it out in my journal:

There comes a moment in a person's life when he realizes what it means to be a self. He is unique, he depends upon himself for what he is, and, consequently, he is alone, essentially, absolutely, necessarily alone. What is this moment? This can only be a personal description.

I lose all of my masks and appendages, all social, religious, philosophical meanings for what I am fall away, and I am there, alone. What a feeling! Complete weightlessness. Where am I going? How will I get there? Why? What does it mean to be a human being? I must seek some form of meaning, something to relate to. I found a person who understood. I had begun my search for my self. Aloneness still exists. When you search for yourself, only you can find that self. It seems to me that a person of any religious faith could feel this way. I am given choices. What I choose becomes a part of determining my self. I will always be alone, for I will always be becoming, searching for, and developing my self.

What happens to aloneness in restricted freedom as in the case of an orthodox Christian or Jew? Is his God so present that he dispels awareness of, or belief in aloneness. Is this self linked up with God and consequently not becoming, but already become?

Is not the person who is aware of and working in the reality of his essential aloneness more capable of true togetherness? He is free because he has accepted the truth of contingency and insecurity.

This is an irrational experience of a great abyss. What it means 'to be' slaps you in the face. And you're slapped all by yourself. That's purposefully ambiguous. Is a Catholic ever slapped? What leads up to the slap? Christ slapped everyone.

In my religious search I continued to try to reconcile the Catholic claims to my own established convictions.

My attitude that anything is possible makes it harder to refute Christianity. I do believe though that what has gone before was not meant to be a mold but an impetus. Look what men did, and ask what you can do? In discussion the priest has the advantage. His answers can be found in libraries. Mine must be found in me.

That same month, I was awarded a fellowship which would enable me to go to any school for graduate study. Receiving the award was a wonderful experience. I felt as though I were emitting rays of pleasure for so many people were touched by my success. I received notification of having won when I returned from the retreat. My mind had been filled with ideas I had heard there, and after I calmed down, I attempted to record what I felt:

The retreat helped me to see, through the talk on Buddhism, my problem with the nature of God. I am fighting something which I already believe. I am seeking to create an object God, a being apart from even though also inside of myself, though he is inside me. I once experienced the knowledge of unity. That knowledge has kept me from being able to find a God in the Judaeo-Christian tradition. But perhaps in Siddhartha's and Taoism's One, or the Buddhism's Buddah Nature lies the road to my belief in the nature of God.

Many paths lead to the truth. Catholicism is one of them for some people. Who am I to judge?

I began to feel sympathetic toward Catholicism as I grew to understand it. In my new journal I wrote:

One of the very positive factors of Christianity is its causing man to aspire to be something greater than he is. He seeks to stretch upward, like a Gothic arch. The Christian God is a perfect man.

My efforts to come to a definite position relative to the claims of Catholicism made me more acutely aware of the difficulty I had in realizing my particular attitude toward any doctrine of belief:

> I have no real point of reference for my thoughts. My 'self' is becoming and thus grapples with almost all ideas independently. The process of thinking and placing an idea is like keeping a balloon in the air. No strings, but it's harder that way.

I grew more and more disposed to see the validity of the theology of the Catholic faith:

> This much of Catholicism I can accept, but I see it in theory. I cannot picture myself walking into a church, kneeling, crossing myself, and all the rest. The whole picture is hypocritical. The relation of man to God and man to man is good. It's perverted in general practice because men are human, but if I hold it in my mind, and maybe in my heart, I can seek to realize it. It's one way, I think. A valid one. But I cannot pray. And so I'm still only philosophizing. Am I destined to bounce around forever?

But the question remained in my mind: How can I know what I will be tomorrow? And how can I dare to accept a way of living today when it might become contrary to what I am tomorrow? I felt that my 'self' fluctuated radically and frequently:

> This is like being suspended. Not able to believe, not able to ignore the inner need to believe.
> Life is in constant change. How much in change am I? Is there something basic in me, essential, which does

not essentially change? Is man new every day? What is my nature relative to human nature? What in fact, is human nature? Good or bad?

But then, in the preparation of writing this paper, I reread my journals:

> I was amazed, at times excited, when reading over a journal I kept in my second semester freshman year to find that my discontent has established and maintained an obvious pattern. Guess I'm not as inconsistent as I thought.

I could no longer struggle with my questioning alone. I talked with the priest and he helped me to find something which I had lost, and always really wanted to regain.

> Tonight I can pray. I limp a little, like a healed leg newly removed from its cast. Peace is proof.

I was in touch with God again. But I was not and am not ready to commit myself to a definite doctrine of beliefs. Maybe I never will be.

> I feel a change within myself but I am not ready to conceptualize it. It has many constantly growing facets.
> I cannot accept the Catholic claim to the absolute truth because I am not sure and because of the consequences of that claim upon the mind.
> It seems to me that a full giving of oneself to Christ should be a wholly joyful turning.
> So many good things have been happening to me. Perhaps the 'winter of my discontent' has come to spring.
> I used to speak to God and it was easy. Now I can again speak to him but it is more difficult, shorter. I try to conceptualize God in human terms. It cannot be done. And my old questions still leer and lead my mind

astray. It takes time but I feel a new depth growing. I hope I never lose it.

I used to think that turning to God betrayed a weakness. Such a turning put me in God's hands and left responsibility for what I am to him. But nothing could be less true. Turning to God is a getting—in—touch with God. I have entered into a relationship with God; made that which was passive, active; and now through that relationship, I must seek to live as he has willed that I should. I have no less responsibility for my life. I have more, for now what I was, am, and will be, is, in my mind, not mere chance. And if I can relate in harmony, I can perhaps live my life as best I can, become the best I can become. My thinking has in part returned to the sense of the One. But now that One is an active, living One.

This summer I am going to India; next year to graduate school. I hope in time to become a good college teacher. The future is still excitingly unformed. I have faith now that I will follow my way in it.

PART THREE

An Epilogue

Most books are complete without an epilogue. They tell their story or describe the facts and then close, when the life or the lesson they had to tell is finished. I feel *The Hungry Generation* is different.

It raises too many questions, which are not answered but at most anticipated in the personal history introducing the students' account of themselves. It is also liable to be misunderstood, and things will be read into the book that were never intended. Moreover, I have no desire merely to inform people of what perhaps they already know a good deal, even if my experience has been rather unique. Fifteen years of involvement in religion and public education has been too revealing for me to be satisfied with talking about it. You do not enter human lives as intensely as I have done without wanting to communicate something of the hunger in which these lives are suffering; and if governments and parliaments are aroused by the physical starvation of millions in Southeastern Asia, I have a glimmering hope that my few words will alert at least one responsible educator or one political leader to afford millions in affluent America what their souls need to remain spiritually alive.

The United States is implicated in a devastating war

that may determine the future of man's history for centuries to come. We believe that what we have to offer the rest of the world is worth giving, and for others worth getting; then we are surprised when this offer is turned against us and our motives are twisted to mean the opposite of what we meant.

Will we never learn? No doubt a civilization is justified in seeking to buy survival by sharing its material prosperity with a restive world—like any other form of endangered life trying to save itself. But, as Whittaker Chambers pointed out, a civilization which supposes that what it chiefly has to offer mankind is more abundant bread—that civilization is already half-dead.

Sooner or later we are bound to learn, when we choke on a satiety of that bread by which alone men cannot live. In all probability, we shall know it long before. For it seems to be a law of life and history that societies in which the pursuit of abundance and comfort has displaced other pursuits in importance soon cease to be societies. They become prey. They fall to whatever power can rally the starving spirit of man, even though the rallying faith (like Marxism) is demonstrably worse than the soft complacency that would suffocate the spirit in abundance. The fall is more certain because a failure of spirit leads invariably by some inward influence to a failure of intelligence.

Failure of Spirit. It is this failure of spirit that so concerned me when back in 1952 I was invited by the Indianapolis superintendent of schools to work on a plan for teaching moral and spiritual values in the public high schools of the city. It was also this failure of spirit that urged me to leave a professional divinity school faculty to teach undergraduates at Western Michigan, and last year meant commuting up to four times a week by plane to teach a full schedule of classes in Illinois and Michigan.

I think I know my reading audience without seeing it.

One out of three who read these pages will smile in sympathy with a man who does not know the future belongs to the empiricist that measures reality by its size and speed and leaves religion to the poet and his dreams. For such as these I have nothing to say, though I feel the self-revelation of my students may give substance to my claim that what American education most needs is to educate, which is to prepare people for life and death, and not mainly to give them a job or teach them how to make money.

When I use the term, "Hungry Generation," I have in mind the appetite of young men and women who are hungry to know the meaning and purpose of life, to learn the need and value of sacrifice, and to find the beauty and inspiration of love—without which education is not worthy of the name.

They want to know the meaning and purpose of life. But this presupposes that life has a meaning and a goal, and that man, having a mind to think, can discover the truth and not spend his days groping in the dark and dying without ever knowing why he lived.

They are ready to have demands put on their generosity, and are willing to make any sacrifice—given a just cause. But their guides must show them by word and example that a philosophy of this-worldism is a lie. They are surrounded by the viewpoint that men have but one life to live and should make the most of it in terms of creative work and personal satisfaction; that human happiness is its own justification and requires no sanction or support from supernatural sources; that, in any case, the supernatural, conceived as a heavenly God or immortal heavens, does not exist; and that human beings, using their own intelligence and cooperating liberally with one another, can build an enduring citadel of peace and beauty on earth.

John Dewey charged that "men have never fully used the powers they possess to advance the good in life, because they have waited upon some power external to themselves and to nature to do the work they are responsible for doing." He thus gave Americans the formula for success, in earthly gain. But he also removed from a large segment of American thought the basis for generous self-surrender, by removing the ultimate ground for sacrifice and the cross (if need be unto death) which is the existence of a life beyond the present one and of a God beyond the Ego.

Young people today wish to find the beauty and inspiration of love. And what do they find? In the words of Eric Fromm, they discover that modern man is alienated from himself, from his fellow men, and from nature. He has been transferred into a commodity, experiences his life forces as an investment which must bring him the maximum profit obtainable under existing market conditions. Human relations have become essentially those of alienated automatons, each basing his security on staying close to the herd, and not being different in thought, feeling or action. While everybody tries to be as close as possible to the rest, everybody remains utterly alone, pervaded by the deep sense of insecurity, anxiety and guilt which always results when human separateness cannot be overcome.

As for love under these conditions, it corresponds to the social character of our age. Automatons cannot love. At most they can exchange their "personality packages" and hope for a fair bargain. They cannot give themselves to others with the altruism born of faith which sees in others an image of the divine. Where Judaeo-Christianity teaches that man's highest fulfillment consists in giving self to others, and finally to the Other whose very name is Love, latter-day Egoism preaches the very opposite. "You get only what you pay for, if you are alert," and "You give only what you have to, unless you are a fool," are in the atmosphere of modern society. True friendship and affection can no more subsist on these principles than a living being survive without air. Less in fact, because air might be artificially supplied, but there is no substitute for love.

There are pessimists who see in all this the beginning of the end. They hear defeatists like Harvey Cox saying it will do no good to cling to our religious and metaphysical versions of man, in the hope that one day religion and metaphysics will once again be back. They are abetted by novelists who make heroes of the dregs of humanity and playwrights who offer nothing better than Arthur Miller gave Willy Loman in *The Death of a Salesman*—a rubber hose to commit suicide and a widow who cries, "I don't understand it. Why did you ever do that? Why did you do it? I search and search and I search, and I can't understand."

The future is not so bleak and I have a great confidence that, given the vision and the will, at least one area of our culture—the crucial one of higher education—can be brought back to the sanity which this nation needs more than nuclear warheads to save it from its folly. But this will mean a drastic reassessment in college and university thinking of every type, private and tax-supported, secular and denominational.

No doubt my own experience has been mainly with a state university, and I feel that in tax-supported institutions the problem of the hungry generation has become a crisis, because it affects so many young people and is so closely tied in with political power subsidized by the resources of the State. Yet the need for self-analysis which this demands, concerns every form of higher education and not only schools that are called public because they are financed by the public funds.

Freedom in Higher Education. Before closing the book

I want to suggest that nothing will be done unless we face squarely the problem of freedom in higher education, by making a college degree practically indispensable but making the choice of a college (or curriculum) practically impossible.

Freedom in education is a byword in academic circles, and I subscribe wholeheartedly to the idea that a college should not be hindered by outside pressures in teaching what its faculty and administration believe is best for the students. State universities have achieved a remarkable immunity from such pressures, as a bare listing of court decisions clearly show.

As early as 1896, in a case that grew out of a legislative act directing the University of Michigan to establish a homeopathic medical college, the court spelled out the school's independence in unmistakable terms: "The board of regents (of the university) and the (state) legislature derive their power from the same supreme authority, namely, the constitution . . . They are separate and distinct constitutional bodies, with the power of the regents defined. By no rule of construction can it be held that either can encroach upon or exercise the powers conferred upon the other."

The effect of such decisions has been to give some state universities a constitutional status that is virtually a fourth government. Where this obtains, the public university holds co-ordinate legal status with the legislative, the executive and judiciary. Moreover, these constitutional corporations have had an influence far beyond their own campus. Their very existence has served to encourage legal insulation of the tax-supported university from the pressures of state politics—and state policy—throughout the United States.

Correlative with this immunity of the institution is the academic freedom that college teachers commonly, and rightly, enjoy to explore and communicate their ideas in lectures and publications.

It is a right claimed by the accredited educator, as teacher and investigator, to interpret his findings and to share his conclusions without being subjected to any interference, molestation, or penalization because these conclusions are unacceptable to some constituted authority within or beyond the institution. This is the core of the doctrine of academic freedom, prized above all others by members of the teaching community in higher education.

In order to safeguard this freedom, the faculty has developed a variety of supplementary protections. They desire no conditions of appointment or controls over promotion of educators designed or in substance so operated as to give preference, irrespective of professional qualification, to those whose views on any issue, social, economic, religious or political are more congenial to administrative or other authorities.

Behind this attitude lies the impulse of a scholar to search into the unknown and discover, if only a fraction, of the uncharted wisdom of the ages and the secrets hidden in nature. He knows the difficulties this represents and the obstacles to reaching the truth. He therefore resents what he calls the arrogance of authority that interferes with his task or presumes to dictate his premises or conclusions.

So much for the two cherished liberties of American higher education: freedom of the institution to pursue its academic aims, and freedom of the educator to think and speak out as the circumstances of his discipline may require. Both assume a degree of responsibility to the community and to good order, but the essence remains: knowledge has its own claims and the search for truth should not be hampered by vested interests, no matter how highly placed.

There is one more freedom, however, and it touches

on the heart of the problem—the option of a student (or his parents) to decide in which school and under what teachers he wants to pursue his education. I have already raised the issue in the preliminary history, and wish here only to place it into sharper focus. It is stated succinctly in the II Vatican Council's *Declaration on Education*:

Parents who have the primary and inalienable right and duty to educate their children must enjoy true liberty in their choice of schools. Consequently, the public power, which has the obligation to protect and defend the rights of citizens, must see to it, in its concern for distributive justice, that public subsidies are paid out in such a way that parents are truly free to choose according to their conscience the schools they want for their children.

In addition it is the task of the state to see to it that all citizens are able to come to a suitable share in culture and are properly prepared to exercise their civic duties and rights. Therefore the state must protect the right of students to an adequate education, check on the ability of teachers and the excellence of their training . . . But it must always keep in mind the principle of subsidiarity so that there is no kind of school monopoly, for this is opposed to the native rights of the human person, to the development and advancement of culture, to the peaceful association of citizens and to the pluralism that exists today in so many societies.

The Soviet school system is a current example of such monopoly under government control, where pluralism is not encouraged. Every subject in the curriculum conforms to the same basic pattern. The teaching of history is typical. As reported by the editor of *Voprosi Istorii*, writing in 1966, "Soviet historians proceed from the view that all human history is a single and natural historical process manifesting a consistent change of socio-economic formations: first the primitive society, then the slave-own-ing system, then the capitalist society, then the socialist system, completing with its last stage—in the U.S.S.R.—communism." Trukhanovsky adds the observation that the same principle is used in schools and colleges for the study of modern and recent history.

Given the philosophy of Soviet culture, we are not surprised at this monism. Then we turn to the United States.

American universities have a public purpose, whether in domestic or world affairs, founded on the traditions of American society and the heritage of other great universities in history. Their purpose is to advance human welfare through the enlargement and communication of knowledge in a spirit of free inquiry. At their best, universities free individual minds as they develop competence for the higher pursuits of life. They widen the horizons of the nation's judgment while supplying skills essential to the nation's tasks. As part of a larger community of scholarship, they also cooperate in an effort to enlarge man's understanding of the world and thereby promote the welfare of mankind.

In the pursuit of these ends, the university in the United States has become a distinctively American institution, closely identified with the growth and change of American society. Some of its counterparts in Europe embody Newman's idea of a university as a "place of teaching universal knowledge." In many countries the university as a center of learning further combines the functions of teaching and scholarship for the advancement of knowledge. The American university adds a third form of service to the society that nurtures it—training men and women in professional skills and trades, the physical and social sciences and, in general, for intelligent involvement in a democratic *politeia*.

Accordingly the university in America serves a broad community function that was long recognized. When the land-grant and state colleges were first organized, this societal purpose determined their foundation, and since then has figured prominently in federal, state, and municipal legislation favoring higher education for every qualified American.

But then arises the hard question of academic freedom; not the freedom to administer (for the institution), nor to teach (for the faculty), but to learn (for the student).

Equity is at stake unless young people have a chance to get the education they need and that society expects them to repay when they become productive citizens. Yet for a growing majority this education can be had only in institutions under the aegis of the state.

Freedom is at stake unless eligible high school graduates have a choice in the school they attend and (within the school) the curriculum they follow because, among other things, they are promised development in a preferred philosophy of life. Yet again for a growing number this is not a live option; they have no alternative economically except to go where (and as) the state has decreed to support their education.

I am too familiar with public education to call it godless. It is not. And I have too much esteem for its dedicated teachers and administrators to question their integrity or (of many) their religious convictions. My contention is that for a variety of reasons, historical and doctrinaire, public higher education increasingly favors a secularist outlook on life that I honestly respect but that I also know is not the "religion of preference" of many people of college age.

A recent National Education Association position statement correctly pointed out that public schools on every level cannot escape teaching religion. "Religion, in this sense," the N.E.A. explained, "is defined as that which is one's 'ultimate concern,' to use Paul Tillich's phrase, or, according to Eric Fromm, that which is one's 'life orientation.' The teaching of a religious attitude, from this standpoint, is inescapable in any school. There is no teacher, no school, which can escape the problem of life orientation, and culture must take account, either implicitly or explicitly, of those fundamental commitments which underlie every human action. This is precisely the domain of religion. Democracy, communism, and the various economic systems cannot be analyzed in their profoundest dimensions without getting into the questions of ultimate values. This is finally a religious question. Thus we teach religion in the schools, whether we would or not. It would be better if the teaching of ultimate commitments were done intelligently rather than blindly."

The burden of this book and its underlying theme is a recommendation that these ultimate commitments be taught intelligently, which means by responding to the human needs and respecting the inner freedom of the educand.

As highly as I regard the intelligence of educators in the humanist tradition and as warmly as I defend their right to teach their own philosophy, I consider it only one form of "life orientation." I hold that in a diversified society like America there is room for a dynamic pluralism of beliefs that is sustained by its forms of higher education.

Pluralism in Church-Related Colleges. I am not suggesting that a university, whether tax-supported or not, should reduce this pluralism to unity. For years I have urged church-related colleges to shed the image they still have in the popular mind of being sectarian because (ostensibly) they seek to advance the cause of their own religion with no relevance to the faith or unbelief of those outside the pale.

Two kinds of reductionism I consider intolerable anywhere: the agnosticism of a teacher who belittles the faith of his students on the grounds that no one knows the truth and that all religious belief is purely subjective or emotional, and the dogmatism of another who cannot see what is good and true in any religious system except his own.

But pluralism that respects the faith of others, that studies different religious systems, and that wrestles with alien modes of thought not only belongs in church-related colleges but, in the present age of dialogue, is an academic necessity.

On the broadest scale in American colleges is Christian pluralism, with over two hundred denominations stemming from the Protestant Reformation, besides the Roman Catholic Church, National Catholic bodies and Churches in the Eastern Orthodox tradition. Time and again students have told me one of the principal insights they gained at Western was knowledge and appreciation of Christian churches outside their own religious group.

For Christian educators responsive to the openness of the ecumenical movement, this should be a powerful incentive to teach and study Christianity across the whole gamut of its manifestations.

Christian higher education should be adjusted to the ecumenical times, above all by instilling in the churches' leaders a desire to share the knowledge of Christ with all Christians and not only with professed members of a particular denomination.

Equally urgent with Christian pluralism is the introduction of courses in world religion in Christian colleges and universities, which state universities have been teaching for years. Practically every tax-supported college in the country offers some form of study of the world's living religions. On the other hand, church-related institutions of higher learning have been slow to give an honored place in their curriculum to the religious beliefs of more than half the human race.

Fifty years ago it would have been naive to talk seriously about a dialogue between Christianity and the non-Christian religions of the world. A dialogue presumes a confrontation, where two people or two cultures meet in a common effort to understand the other's viewpoint and profit from a friendly exchange of ideas. But until the present century, about the only contact between Christians and others was on a limited missionary front in Africa and the Far East, and in the cosmopolitan fields of commerce and politics, where religion is the last, or at least not the first consideration.

Apart from many transient factors is the universal shrinking of the earth, with speedy means of communication that practically erase distance between nations. Ideas are never sterile and religious ideas are no exception. Christians are living in the atmosphere of a world that is mainly not Christian, whose principles and institutions are daily projected into their midst to produce an encounter that is as real and potentially transforming as the spirit of man, communicated from one mind to another and demanding a hearing.

On a lesser scale but also important is the daily meeting between Christian and Judaic cultures in all the major countries of the West, and particularly in America. To insure that the progress made in these relations be consolidated, a mutual and sympathetic knowledge of the other's religious position seems imperative, at the risk of ignoring the depth of conviction on both sides or of indulging in vague platitudes about the golden rule.

One more pluralism, and the most difficult, has to be included. Other religions than Christian are, after all, believers in some form of deity, and even Buddhism is basically theistic in spite of its reputation to the contrary.

341

But a university lives up to its stature when it faces systems of thought that are alien and antithetical to the professed beliefs of the students.

Let me insert a provisional paragraph. A Christian college has the right to determine its own philosophy of education and not be censured for insisting on academic freedom for the institution. If only individual freedom were defended, as against the institutional, no organized body in the country could long remain safe and we would soon see the end of any society that individuals decided was against their taste.

This is not to say, however, that no writer or system hostile to the established creed should be examined. The roster of names that comes to mind is endless, and the challenges they offer to Christian students are vital, with the vitality that secular schools claim to possess and that church-related institutions are said to lack. Freud and Jung in psychology; Nietzsche, Dewey and Whitehead in philosophy; Marx and Engels in political science; Coulton and Gibbon in history; Feuerbach, Renan and Harnack in religion; Altizer, Hamilton and Robinson in theology— are only samples of the exposure that any viable education ought to provide for mature men and women in college.

Until teachers are prepared to handle orthodoxy and heterodoxy, and are willing to trust themselves and the faith they profess to contradiction from the best intellectual critics of Christianity, they are open to invidious comparison with secular (especially state) university educators whose main boast is that they are free to examine what Christian institutions dare not touch for fear of offending the churches or endangering the commitment of their students.

The hallmark of an educated man these days is that his mind has not been confined to seeing only one religion, or one philosophy, or only what supports his own convictions. By this standard, church-related colleges are challenged by a prosperous tax-supported system of education to reassess their approach to secular and religious knowledge.

Pluralism in State Universities. Colleges and universities under state control have the same responsibility to their students. No more (rather less) than church-related schools are they called upon to reduce the pluralism reflected in their student body to a monistic unity.

But they are more tempted than church-affiliated institutions either to ignore the diversity or, by implication, dismiss it as something from which the more rational-minded person stands aloof.

This studied aloofness disturbs me. Students are not abstractions, no matter how anonymously the faculty or administration may treat them. They are human beings who have commitments when they come to college, and for most of them a belief in God as Catholics, Protestants or Jews. Granted that this belief is often simple and untutored; yet it represents a sacred trust that deserves respect and wants intellectual understanding.

A Jew may be uneducated in his religion and only minimally faithful to its practices. But he stands in the tradition of Moses and the prophets, and the heritage of Maimonides. Is he never once in the four years of college to be offered a single course that will give mental maturity to his faith, under a faculty member who is at once a Jewish scholar and believer?

A Protestant may have only a vague knowledge of the Bible, or what he remembers from Sunday school days. He is perhaps bewildered by the number of denominations, rivaling his own, that seems to challenge the validity of all Christianity. But he, too, has behind him centuries of Protestant thought and the genius of men like Luther and Calvin, and of contemporaries like Barth, Tillich and the Niebuhrs. Is it too much to expect the college that his parents support to give him a scientific appreciation of what he already, though dimly, believes?

Catholics enter college with perhaps more information about their Church, and about half of them have gone to parochial schools. But their knowledge of why they believe is often dismal and their rational grasp of anything beyond the elementary teachings of Catholicism is sometimes low. Yet they are in the same tradition as Augustine and Aquinas and, among moderns, Gilson, Maritain and Hans Küng. Are they never to have a class, under university auspices, to teach them what Catholicism—at its intellectual best—really means?

Anyone who has read the ten chapters of self-disclosure of my students at Western will agree that the religious background they bring to the university is part of their mental equipment and no more separable from their personality than the language they speak or the knowledge they have of American History. It is disastrous academically, and may be, psychologically, to treat them during the questing years of college as something which they are not.

More than anywhere else, in matters of faith a clear distinction should be made between belief as a component of the human person and the reflective understanding of belief that belongs to the critical mind. A young freshman may have a deep faith and yet be irritatingly unable to give a cogent explanation of what and why he believes. But his ineptitude is no more reason for denying that he really believes than ignorance of how to define patriotism is a sign of not loving one's country.

Religious profession, therefore, is not the same as religious literacy. Colleges are not asked to produce the commitment of faith; they are responsible to make intelligible the faith that already exists.

Moreover, their purpose should be not only to raise the religious literacy of the people they teach or help them understand religious pluralism in society and the world at large. "Colleges and universities," says the Association of American Colleges, "share with the church, the synagogue and the home responsibility for the moral and spiritual as well as the intellectual development of their students."

The sooner our institutions of higher learning, whether private or state-controlled, act on this conviction, the better for our nation, for education, and for the generation of youth whose hunger of spirit will upset American civilization unless it is given the only food that can satisfy the human mind.

A NOTE ON THE TYPE
IN WHICH THIS BOOK IS SET

This book is set in Baskerville, a Linotype face, created from the original types used by John Baskerville, the eighteenth-century typefounder and printer. This type has long been considered one of the finest book types ever developed. The letters are wide and open and have a businesslike approach. The finer hairlines give exquisite delicacy. The heavier strokes give color and strength. The relation of the two in combination gives a brilliant effect and makes for easy reading. The book was composed and printed by the Wickersham Printing Company of Lancaster, Pa., and bound by Moore and Company of Baltimore.

The typography and design are by Howard N. King.